Stanislavski and The Method for the 21st Century Actor

Stanislavski and The Method for the 21st Century Actor

A Practical Guide

David Barrouk

Translated by
Anna Popkin

methuen | drama
LONDON · NEW YORK · OXFORD · NEW DELHI · SYDNEY

METHUEN DRAMA
Bloomsbury Publishing Plc
50 Bedford Square, London, WC1B 3DP, UK
1385 Broadway, New York, NY 10018, USA
29 Earlsfort Terrace, Dublin 2, Ireland

BLOOMSBURY, METHUEN DRAMA and the Methuen Drama logo are
trademarks of Bloomsbury Publishing Plc

First published in Great Britain 2024

Copyright © David Barrouk, 2019

Translation copyright © Anna Popkin, 2024

David Barrouk has asserted his right under the Copyright, Designs and
Patents Act, 1988, to be identified as authors of this work.

Cover design: Ben Anslow
Cover image: Russian Actor, Director, and Producer,
Konstantin Stanislavski (© Corbis via Getty Images)

All rights reserved. No part of this publication may be reproduced or transmitted
in any form or by any means, electronic or mechanical, including photocopying,
recording, or any information storage or retrieval system, without prior
permission in writing from the publishers.

Bloomsbury Publishing Plc does not have any control over, or responsibility for, any
third-party websites referred to or in this book. All internet addresses given in this
book were correct at the time of going to press. The author and publisher regret
any inconvenience caused if addresses have changed or sites have ceased
to exist, but can accept no responsibility for any such changes.

A catalogue record for this book is available from the British Library.

ISBN: HB: 978-1-3504-0404-5
        PB: 978-1-3504-0403-8
        ePDF: 978-1-3504-0405-2
        eBook: 978-1-3504-0406-9

Typeset by Integra Software Services Pvt. Ltd.
Printed and bound in Great Britain

To find out more about our authors and books visit www.bloomsbury.com
and sign up for our newsletters.

To Noémie, who passed away at only five years old, with a smile. To Katharina, who was always so graceful, up until her last days. To Sylvia and her amazing energy.

To Stanislavski, his genius, and the monkey in the stroller. To Mona … You'll see why.

"I always tell the truth. Even when I lie."

*Tony Montana, in Scarface, written
by Oliver Stone and directed by Brian De Palma.*

Contents

ADVICE TO READERS	xiii

1 INTRODUCTION — 1
- The introduction to the introduction — 1
- The why and the how — 3
- Warnings … *Wait, what?* … Yeah, that's right, warnings! — 6
  - *Aspiration!* — 6
  - *A fascinating facet!* — 7
  - *For actors … and all those who choose to be actors of their lives!* — 7
  - *No taboos!* — 8
- Rumors — 9
  - *Rumor Number One* — 9
  - *Rumor Number Two* — 9
  - *Rumor Number Three* — 10
- Wait, one question — 11

2 BRIEF ACCOUNTING OF THE HISTORY OF THE METHOD — 13
- The origins of the Method — 13
- The future of the Method — 17

3 PLAY THE GAME — 19
- I have a question to ask you — 19
- The four barriers to break — 20
  - *Skepticism* — 20
  - *Pretending to be indifferent, or worse—being indifferent* — 21
  - *Being trivial* — 22
  - *An exclusively factual approach to life* — 24

4 THE W.W.W. QUESTIONS — 27
- The questions Where, When, and Why — 28
- Answering the questions — 29
  - *The question "Where?"* — 29
  - *The question "When?"* — 29
  - *The "objective"* — 30

The "motivations"	33
The "stakes"	34
The "obstacles"	34
The "actions"	35
The detailed answers to the W.W.W. questions	37
The detailed question "Where?"	37
The detailed question "When?"	39
The detailed "objective"	40
The detailed "motivations"	41
The detailed "stakes"	42
The detailed "obstacles"	42
The detailed "actions"	44
Creating a fictional W.W.W. situation	47
The W.W.W. protocol	49
Your turn!	52
The question "Where?" to embody	52
The question "When?" to embody	52
The "objective" to embody	52
The "motivations" to embody	53
The "stakes" to embody	53
The "obstacles" to embody	53
The "actions" to embody	53
The embodiment of the W.W.W. questions	55

5 EXPLORATION   59

To freak out or not to freak out?	61
Stage fright	61
Relaxation	64
Energization	70
Concentration	72
Listening	75
The moment to moment to moment	81
Tomorrow the day before I had will run after time	81
Real questions	82
Sources	84
Karl	86
The five steps in working on sources	94
The light bulb and the light switch	104
Internal and external sources	105
Intimacy vs. privacy	105
Sweat, blood, sex … and chocolate	107
Two sources of sources, one same approach	108
The imaginary in real life and the real life in the imaginary	109

	Imagination	116
	How do we develop our imagination?	116
	The magic if	121
	Living nightmares and dreams	123
	Imaginary facts	124
	Experience	130
	Sense memory	132
	Poetic sense memory	135
	Emotional memory	139
	Didn't hurt, nah nah nah nah nah!	144
	Tarzan	144
	Substitutions	153
	Reflex sources	158
	The first contact	161
	The wear and tear of certain sources	164
	The shower	170
6	**Aaaaaaaaaand ACTION(S)!!!**	**171**
	Physical actions	172
	Physical actions are partially what structure acting	172
	Our inner world echoes through them	172
	Physical actions help us believe even more in fictional situations	174
	Psychophysical actions	176
	In order to add variations, range and precision to your performances	184
	Because the characters that you play impose specific actions, but not the sources that will push you to do them	185
	To create characters	186
7	**HOW TO REHEARSE CREATE A SCENE**	**189**
	First reading, first impressions	191
	From a blank page to infusion	191
	Just in case the play or the script isn't good or doesn't resonate within you	191
	Giving life to what's in white on the page	193
	Breaking down a scene	200
	Active analysis and psychophysical structure	266
	In continuation: choices and execution	271
	Loosen up the structure	274
	Dialogue	275
	How to "learn" dialogue?	276
	Diction and projection	277
	Monologues	280
	Breathing life into the statue	284
	A word on tragedy	288
	A word on contemporary roles	289

8	PLAYING WITH YOUR INSTINCT	297
	Fifty percent machine, 50 percent animal	299
9	THE "GOOD" AND THE "BAD" EGO	301
10	TWO ESSENTIAL FLAWS	305
11	TO CONCLUDE	309
Index		310

Advice to Readers

Congratulations! You've just bought the wrong book! I'm kidding, but you really should buy the works of Constantin Stanislavski, the brilliant visionary of the late nineteenth early twentieth century, founder of what we call the Method and the author of *An Actor Prepares*, *Building a Character*, and *Creating a Role*. When you take the initials of these three books, it spells out the **ABCs** of Acting. And no wonder—you will find everything there is to know about the art of realistic acting. Well, nearly everything … Anyway, find those books and read them too.

So, whom is this book meant for? Allow me to specify that my goal was to make this book as accessible as possible for all actors, no matter the level that you're at. Whether you're a complete beginner as an actor, or you're an experienced actor just looking to perfect and sharpen your technique, there will surely be exercises and explanations adapted to your level.

But that's not all—this book, or any book about the Method, can be useful to movie and stage directors as well. You'll find that if you have a similar vocabulary or knowledge to the actors that you'll be directing, not only will the communication be clearer (and possibly more pleasant) but you'll achieve the result that you're looking for faster. Maybe more surprisingly, it can also be interesting for screenwriters and even authors to be familiar with the actors' process, as it is an amazing tool to create realistic characters.

Last but not least—this can be an interesting read, even if you're not an artist! Perhaps if you're passionate about movies or theater, and just want to know more about the history of acting? Also, since the acting process is entirely based on human emotions and the endless ways that we function, practicing certain exercises can help you better understand yourself. So I would actually recommend learning about the acting process for anyone who's simply interested in acquiring a deeper self-knowledge (you'll find out why soon).

This book is made up of two major approaches. The first one is explored in Chapters 1 through 3, as well as in Chapters 8 through 11, and the second one, in Chapters 4 through 7.

In Chapters 4 through 7, we'll broach the subject of acting in a very straight-forward, raw, hands-on way, with the help of tons of exercises. I'd say these chapters compose about 80 percent of this book.

Chapters 1 through 3, and Chapters 8 through 11, are obviously about acting too, but we'll touch on the subject from a more subjective point of view, so possibly more debatable. The history of the Method, ethics in art, and moral stance are among the subjects that are addressed in these chapters. That's already a lot to take in. Strong ethical positions are meant to be defended and expressed through art. Stanislavski often writes about this in his three books, as well as in many other of his written works, for example *My Life in Art*, to name just one. So, mostly during Chapters 1 through 3 and Chapters 8 through 11, it is without holding back that I give my points of view, which can be brutally honest and even controversial to some. It's not that I don't appreciate pastel tones, they do have their own charm, but there are certain games that I won't play, which mainly consist of passing off watered-down choices as subtlety and open-mindedness. I will not apologize for being passionate.

These two major approaches go hand in hand. While reading, you'll find that there is coherence in the progression of the exercises and the explanations that go along with them. It is vital to test them out, in order to get a complete picture. Take as much time as you need for each exercise, to do and redo them, to try out different techniques, and fully understand the connection between all of them.

If you choose to come back to this book, feel free to pick and choose certain exercises according to the needs you might have for a role in particular. Last but certainly not least, along with reading this book—or any other book about acting—I strongly recommend putting it all into practice regularly, whether you're by yourself or, preferably, in acting classes.

A true acting class is a place where you should feel *at home* and where you are allowed to make mistakes; thus, allowed to try again, to search, to deepen, to explore, ultimately to be able to make progress.

And here's what I believe to be a true acting coach: someone with true empathy and indulgence, who encourages freedom in your work and doesn't just give you their opinion. In other words, a true acting coach will always have a clear, precise, and concrete method that nonetheless does not become a "religion" and remains free and fun. A true acting coach is not some judgmental moron who just sits there only to rip apart and disrespect your work. They are supposed to be your ally—someone who is as invested as you are, and believes that if you've done a good job, they have also done a good job. And most importantly, this person must inspire you![1]

If you don't feel inspired by your acting coach, either your ears are clogged, or your coach has no business being a coach. Always question yourself and everything else while staying completely open-minded. However, that is obviously not the same as accepting anything that's thrown at you, without distinction or analysis. This also goes for being the actor who's so dazzled by the fantasy of success, that he or she will do anything to become a star—even if it hurts them.

I certainly hope you'll enjoy reading this book as much as I did writing it.

---

[1] For those who speak French, if you'd like to know more on that subject, you can read an interview that I gave, on a website dedicated to theater. You'll find it if you type "Un café avec David Barrouk"—A coffee date with David Barrouk.

1 Introduction

Man's maturity: to have regained the seriousness that he had as a child at play.
(Friedrich Nietzsche)

The introduction to the introduction (yes, I can be quite talkative!)

If, as I mentioned earlier, Stanislavski really has written everything there is to know about acting, why write a new and *billionth* book on the subject? For three reasons and here's the first one: ever since Stanislavski wrote his books, millions of theories have been thrown around about Method Acting, aka the System, and its principles. And a lot of them are absurd. I think it's necessary to separate the wheat from the chaff. Before we go into the other two reasons, let's first talk a bit about Method Acting.

It is basically the ABCs of realistic acting, which mainly serves actors, but also acting coaches, film and stage directors. It's a detail-oriented process of deciphering human behavior, in order to truly embody how we function, rather than merely *imitating* life. To be clear, there are different types of realistic acting. Even though we can definitely say that the acting in *Star Wars* is just as realistic as in any movie directed by John Cassavetes, or any play by Shakespeare; each time there are particular details that change the style of the acting. These details go along with the mood of the project, but each of these types of realism has this in common: the characters have coherent reactions according to their given circumstances. So in this case, realism should actually be referred to as *realisms*. As I said just before, acting is not about copying life, but *creating* it! That's the thrill of the Method, for actors and audiences alike. I often tell actors that I'm here to teach them *how to not act*. What I mean by that is to not pretend. No one needs classes to learn how to pretend, everyone already knows how to do that ... From a technical aspect, if right now, you were actually reading a play or a movie script and I were to give you only one indication on how to embody one of the roles, this is what I would tell you:

> *Don't act out what's written in black, act out what's written in white; and since there's nothing written, it's up to you to create it!*

The Method is basically a "tool box" which will help you fill out, color in, animate, and give life to what's "written" in white. It's basically reading between the lines. That's what breathes life into any role. And to create what's in between the lines, *that's* Method Acting. And *that's* the job of any actor who has any self-respect, who wants to give effective performances, and, also, wants to have fun! Ever since Constantin Stanislavski developed the main principles of Method Acting, these principles have been explored, revisited, deepened, sharpened and enriched by many great masters. Method Acting has been written about many times, attracting everything from the highest praise, to the harshest of criticism. Some have blindly turned it into a cult, others patronize it, just as blindly. One thing is for sure though: nobody is right or wrong here. The Method is neither unquestionable nor idiotic. It is merely a wide array of "tools," of options, made to serve actors, to help them decipher a role and let them create performances that are as inventive and inspired as possible—basically, what anyone would consider to be a great performance. It's not supposed to be a religion for actors, and it's certainly not meant to hurt them. The Method is not a dogma, it's more of an alphabet. In the same way that music theory is available to musicians, knowing by heart and using the Method is neither a guarantee for a harmonious song nor a cacophony. Music theory, just like the Method, is a map, not the finish line. And this map is made to help clarify the art at hand, in order to understand it better, and ultimately, to allow a more tangible approach. So, to sum up, the value of the Method depends ultimately on the person who's using it … in this case, you! That's why this book is filled with exercises that *you* can test out live, because:

> *It is not enough for actors to know the facts, they must turn it into experience.*

To explain my approach to the Method a little better, let's look at what Robert McKee wrote for screenwriters in *Story*,[1] in order to get them to adapt to actors:

> *A rule says, "You must do it this way." A principle says, "This works … and has through all remembered time." The difference is crucial. Your work needn't be modeled after the well-made play; rather, it must be well made within the principles that shape our art.*

Michael Beckett, coach at the Herbert Berghof Studio of New York, had a similar philosophy. Despite his practically surgical, detail-oriented way of working and undeniable expertise of the Method, Michael would jokingly say that we could forget everything that he had taught us and everything about the Method … *as long as we were having fun on stage!*

He was actually reminding us of the importance of enthusiasm and to never lose sight of the true notion of *playing* in the actor's work. These were two essential points, which were also often brought up by Stanislavski in his written works. What they were trying to say was that even though any true acting requires huge amounts of work and research, you should do it all while having fun and use the tools of the Method more as a "springboard" for your inspiration, rather than seeing them as rules written in stone to follow blindly, as a so-called "good student." Don't be a good student merely out of submission. However, don't be a bad student purely out of ignorance. Use the tools of the Method that you'll find in this book and elsewhere, but don't hesitate to distort, switch up and reinvent them. Transform *The* Method into *Your* Method! You can never be wrong. Because even if, as they say, to err is human, that's kind of impossible when you're having fun and as long as you have a playful approach to life.

---

[1] If you haven't already, I highly recommend reading the "bible" that is *Story*, by Robert McKee. Even though this brilliant book is destined for screenwriters, I truly find it to be a must-read for any actor who's sincerely invested in their art.

The why and the how

Ok, back to our question: "If Stanislavski really has written everything there is to know about acting, why write a new and *billionth* book on the subject?"

We've just elaborated on the first reason, now here are the two others:

— To clarify, review, recollect and try to broaden what has already been taught.

— Times change.

To clarify, review, recollect and try to broaden what has already been taught.

Nothing is lost, nothing is created, everything is transformed, said Antoine Lavoisier, a famous French chemist. This quote applies to all natural phenomena of course and it could also relate to the approaches of this book, as well as the origins of the work of Stanislavski. He was always inspired by human nature in particular, but also by nature in general. Now it's our turn to be inspired by Stanislavski and to decrypt the transformations and transformers (that's us) that continue to function and evolve. We're going to try to recover and glue back together the pieces of a vast technique, in order to get a bigger and clearer picture of the Method, all the while adding in the fine-tuning of the Method by Stanislavski's successors. I would also like to add to the fine-tuning of the Method, and to make this compilation of important tools accessible to actors: to get across its creative impact in a direct, fun, hands-on, and *desacralized way*.[2]

Last but not least, I would like to make my contribution to the acting structure conceptualized and mapped out by Stanislavski, based on my years of experience as an acting coach, mostly in New York and Paris with many different actors, in acting classes, on film sets and plays.

This book is the first one of a series. It will be followed by a book that focuses exclusively on the subject of creating characters, and how your self-discovery can serve them. The next volume will be an exercise book meant to put you to the test, perfect and broaden all of the knowledge and experience you'll have acquired from your investment in the two previous books. The fourth volume will be about the professional market, and focused on how you can become a working actor and be supported by your passion-turned-career. Lastly, there will be a monologue book made to help you challenge your knowledge and talent, practice your technique, without needing scene partners. So, you'll have no excuse to not sharpen your most essential tool: you. It will also give you endless possibilities of contemporary monologues, perfect for auditions and show-reels. In fact, it will be very complementary to the book on the professional market.

Times change.

Well, that's no scoop. Don't worry, we're not here to turn this into some kind of huge nostalgia session, which would be as useless as it would be shallow. Time is made for change. That's what's supposed to happen—times are supposed to change and change everything as we know it, for the best and for the worst. Forever.

---

[2]What I mean is that we shouldn't put the technique on an unreachable pedestal.

To me, Stanislavski's teachings are still just as passionate, stimulating and inspiring to this day. However, I've noticed, throughout the twenty-five years I've been coaching acting classes, that many actors don't feel the same enthusiasm while reading Stanislavski's books—to my surprise, actually. They find them a bit outdated. After a lot of discussions with many different generations of actors, I finally understood that this comes not so much from Stanislavski's actual teachings, but more from the form, the tone and the style of his work. That's another reason why I wrote this book, to modernize his teachings, without dumbing them down.

The actor's stance is no longer the same at all. Let's restate that: the actor's stance in relation to their art is no longer the same. First of all, during Stanislavski's time, being an actor automatically meant being a theater actor, on stage. Today, 90 percent of actors only want to act in movies. Besides a few technical differences, like voice projection and in some cases exaggeration of movement, the Method itself works fundamentally the same way. A good actor is a good actor, whether it's in a play or a movie.

> *This is how it happened: Peg and Bob had invited Jack and Roxanne over to their house to watch the TV, and on the big screen they saw Peg and Bob, Jack and Roxanne watching themselves watch themselves on progressively smaller TVs.*
>
> (Stephen Dobyns)

Here's one of the main reasons why actors no longer have the same relationship to their art: today's actors live in a world totally overpopulated with images of all types—movies, video clips, commercials, as well as the omnipresence of screens in our lives. Even though this overload of pictures can prepare actors for what it feels like to see themselves on screen, it also brings out a major inconvenience—actors no longer act as in real life, they copy what they see on screen. This only gets worse as we realize just how much we are all *tragically* influenced by all of these images that we constantly swallow and how our behavior is drastically affected. Who hasn't heard somebody say, during a defining moment in life "Wow! It's just like in a movie!" as if life could somehow be inspired by the fiction that it created—when in fact, it's the opposite.

For instance, gangsters nowadays "act like" the gangsters in the movies, cops "act like" the cops in the movies, etc. As if that, somehow, makes their status more legitimate and gives them permission to keep those personality traits. The real life version resembling the movie version might actually seem like a good idea, except that it's not: *it's up to the painting to look like the model, not up to the model to look like the painting!*

As one of my very talented coaches from the Herbert Berghof Studio, Uta Hagen, once said: "Anyone can be an actor on stage, but what we really want to see is a human being in imaginary situations." What she meant was that faking it is much less interesting than portraying real, human emotions. How can the situations seem real if they're being lived out by facsimiles of human beings?

As if all of that wasn't enough already, the work of the realistic actor is increasingly endangered by the influence of so-called reality TV shows and medias that we shockingly call "social." These things continue to wipe out the already blurry lines between fiction and reality. They put the audience in a kind of hypnosis. These works of fiction show human beings supposedly acting "realistically," even though they're being directed and set up in a completely fabricated situation. The snake bites its own tail, the tail bites the snake back.

Today's actors often get lost in a hall of mirrors, where they can hardly tell the difference between a reflection and the original, the original from the reflection ... It never ends.

However, not to worry! There is a solution to all of this: *to live! Purely and simply!* To dismiss the supposedly safer but superficial option of being a spectator of life and rejoice in the riskier but more exciting option of being human—in other words, a true actor ... not of fiction, but of life.

I'll always remember a class taught by Herbert Berghof,[3] when the "star" of our class had, once again, done a *magnificent* scene that blew us mere mortals out of the water. Sharp as he was, as usual, Herbert did something even more magnificent: he kicked the actor out of class! Sure, we were all secretly relieved that we would no longer see this acting monster run us into the ground each time. But actually, we really didn't get why Herbert made that decision. The "star" certainly didn't get it either ... and got all fired up. How could Herbert do this to *him*?! He, who was always driven by passion and showed diligence! He, who, without acting, found that life was not worth living!

"*That's* the problem!" Herbert said, in his thick Austrian accent. "You only live for *cinema*, you only *see movies*."

"So?" said the star outright, something we were all thinking but didn't dare say. "What's wrong with that? I didn't think passion for acting would be punishable in an acting class."

"It's not really that. It's just that your passion has stopped you from observing real life instead of life in the movies. *Live! God damn it!* Fall in love, cut your nails, touch a potato, get roaring drunk if you feel like it! But go out and live, then come back to my class when you're ready to act like you've lived, and not like what you've seen on TV."

We were all floored. We had just witnessed incredible coaching that only Herbert could pull off. Actually, it wasn't only directed at this particular student—it was directed at all of us. This actor's passion, like all artists who are truly dedicated to their art, was real and absolutely amazing. But he fell into a trap set by all passions: being passionate about his passion.

Any actor who falls into this trap inevitably starts copying life, being a copy of an actor, or even worse: he or she is no longer an actor embodying characters, but is playing an actor playing a character.

---

[3] The creator of the famous HB Studio in New York, where generations of actors have studied. He's a director, acting coach and actor himself and he was coached in one of the first classes opened at the Actors Studio, along with Marlon Brando and many others.

Warnings ... *Wait, what?* ... Yeah, that's right, warnings!

Before the twentieth century, being an actor was not exactly an appealing idea. There were practically no professional opportunities, so obviously no way of making money. You might have been ostracized by your family and loved ones.

Even if you were to become one of the rare people to actually make a living out of it, it was utterly impossible to become a star or famous around the world. Simply because that status, as well as the media platforms that go with it, didn't exist at that time. Not only that, but in many countries, actors suffered the worst outcome.

For instance, in France, actors were considered a disgrace and some even had their citizenship taken away. They were not allowed proper burials and were thrown into mass graves, with the beggars, convicts and other persona non grata.

The least we can say is, during those adventurous times, you had to be *extremely* motivated to become an actor against all odds.

Aspiration!

Anyway, history changed the course of things, and made things better for artists and actors ... for the best and for the worst. That also goes for the best and the worst of actors. Artistic professions have now become accepted and very accessible, which is major progress for our civilization. However, it is partly what is slowly destroying artistry itself. Of course, this progress allowed so many artists and actors to express themselves and to share their gift, their voice, their vision ... It also allowed the worst of it to spread. We are living through a period of our civilization that is extremely mercantile and losing the meaning of transcendence, which has helped and even encouraged beauty to be replaced by profit. Not that these two concepts can't work together, but we might as well recognize that the prefabricated "successes" boosted by charts and box offices will not share the possibility of posterity with true artistic masterpieces.

Now hold on a second! Let's not throw out the baby with the bathwater. My position concerning art here is just as transversal as it is selective. I take into account classical masterpieces, just as well as those produced by pop culture, culture in general and what we strangely like to call "counterculture." To name a few examples—William Shakespeare, Alfred de Musset, John Cassavetes, David Lynch, Kenneth Anger, Charlie Chaplin, Martin Scorsese, Bob Fosse, Milos Forman, Sofia Coppola, Federico Fellini, Gregg Araki, Dorothy Parker, John Cameron Mitchell, Charlie Kaufman, and many contemporary TV series including *Breaking Bad*, *The Office* and *Succession* deserve to be in this category. Rest assured—we're not here to systematically oppose entertainment and meaning.

Of course we grow up with a lot of confusion since a major part of our education consists of brainwashing us into thinking that success has to be worked for, hence that success rhymes with quality. Sometimes, it's true. Alas ... rarely. Nowadays, transcendence, which is one of the main functions of art, not to mention its purpose, is too often lost. A lot of artists have convinced themselves that their limits are choices. Therefore, they try to impose these limits onto others and cannot access the only true joy there is in art, and anywhere else, which is transcendence.

Now, let me clearly state that this is not a *Secret to Success* book meant for those who are only after the spotlight. Although, I truly don't have anything against the spotlight and can even find certain aspects of it appealing. As long as we can agree on its actual value—a superficiality to have fun with and not a god to bow down to.

This book is destined for passionate actors who are truly dedicated to their art, and ready to embody everything from light-hearted comedy to Greek tragedy. As long as it's uplifting, full of meaning and with excellence as the main goal.

If you achieve fame and success with the excellence mentioned earlier, the more the better. Everything I could ever hope for you is that you become an international superstar, *but of quality, thanks to art of quality!*

The Method can guarantee you constant perfecting of your art, if you work hard enough. Its tangible and fun tools will help you take on all the fascinating challenges you'll encounter among the many roles you embody throughout your career.

A fascinating facet!

We are here to make *great* art, as *great* actors, which is all about portraying the passions of the human being's soul. And those who want to make art out of it must, above all, try and understand the entirety of the Soul. Yes, with a big S, indeed! This is the most fascinating facet of this approach. On the one hand, fully understanding the soul of the human being, on the other hand, finding a way to transform it all into physical movement, embodying it, feeling it in our own skin.

To talk openly about the soul means exploring its darkness as well as its light: all of its greatest nobility, infinity and beauty, but also its deepest corners, nooks and crannies, its ugliness, flaws and insanity. What other way is there to profoundly understand roles of killers, saints, crazy but loving mothers, twins who hate each other, people who can be so close to ourselves, what other way is there to recognize their humanity? One of the beautiful aspects of the Method is that its process makes us ask ourselves the right questions about human nature, in order to portray any role with conviction. And without the stereotypes, the preconceptions—you must get off the beaten track of the politically correct. Anyway, simple and complex questions will be raised. The simpler questions help us find clarity, the complex ones enrich the process even more. When you find answers that complete each other, that's when striking performances happen. I think you get it by now, taboo is not welcome here. Banished. Finally, some air! And so much freedom!

You could even go as far as to say that acting has a rebellious streak. The reason I say this is that we are supposed to *tame* our emotions in order to live in society. We tend to establish a hierarchy among emotions and start to censor and format what we feel. This type of taming does not work in acting! Here, emotions are not categorized as good or bad, they all have the right to be. In other words, playing Jesus rather than playing Hitler won't necessarily make you a better actor. We are here to create and freely explore the soul, and *rejoice* in the rebellious pleasure we get from it. We are here to explore life in its entirety.

For actors ... and all those who choose to be actors of their lives!

The exploration in this book might interest another category of readers. Regardless of whether you're an actor or not, this book might be beneficial to those who are simply interested in the way their being functions. You will understand yourself better and bring out your unlimited potential, without having to go through the painstaking process of psychoanalysis.[4] Lee Strasberg, an emblematic figure of the Method (who coached Marlon Brando, James Dean and Marilyn Monroe, just to name a few) said that one day, the Method would be used in many other domains than acting. He was right.

For the past few decades, that's exactly what happened. However, keep in mind that we can only reap the benefits of the Method if its process is practiced with suppleness and of course, the fun it contains … But for this, you have to know how to read between the lines.

The Method is often used in play therapy and is very much connected with personal development, sophrology and neuro-linguistic programming (NLP). Without going into too much detail, the work done with visualization in sophrology is quite similar to many exercises of the Method. The connection between the Method and NLP is quite evident, as an actor who is preparing a scene is basically just doing neuro-linguistic programming. Being a coach of the Method, I've worked on and explored these practices a lot. I won't go on about all of the existing links between acting and these domains, but you'll find them all by yourself little by little. In terms of personal development, one of the major benefits of the Method comes from the unlimited self-expression it offers, without the presence of any crushing taboos and all the while taking in the sensitivities of everyone concerned.

Working on authorization is one of the main subjects that we'll focus on all through this book, for actors and everyone else. When I say "authorization," what I really mean is "self-authorization." This is only possible when you give yourself the right to make mistakes, a fundamental right which is much too neglected in every type of education and training. So, that also means that authority doesn't belong here, in any of the classes at the Method Acting Center[5] (the school I opened in Paris), or anywhere else for that matter. It's all about encouragement, it's never about coercion … It's about detaching ourselves from complexes and censorship, in order to dare to try and have fun.

No taboos!

A very special characteristic of the actor's work is the fact that an actor is the instrumentalist and the instrument at the same time. In other words, actors have nothing else to use other than themselves.

Some of the exercises in this book are related to our ways of living. It's not supposed to feel like an intrusion—you can adjust an exercise to what you're comfortable with. But we can't hold it against an acting coach to touch on every subject and every facet of life, even the most serious ones (without getting too personal of course). Just in the way that it's the duty of a sports coach to advise his trainees not to smoke.

But remember—any dignified acting coach *must and will* respect the private life of the actors that he coaches.

---

[4]To read more on the subject for those who speak French, check out *Le Livre Noir de la Psychanalyse*, which is a collective work supervised by Catherine Meyer. And for everyone, check out *The Holotropic Mind* by Stanislav Grof.

[5]A thought for the team at the Method Acting Center in Paris … And special thanks to Adeline, for her dedication, her thorough work, her great spirit and her humor.

Rumors

Decadence starts when one no longer dares to call nonsense by its name.

(Henry de Montherlant)

If I had to choose one word to convey the goal behind this book, it would be "Demystify." If I had to use one sentence, it would be "Demystify acting to make it more accessible and fun without taking away its magic." Having a method simply unlocks it for us.

There's another goal behind this book though: a big clean-up. All of the erroneous, unfounded and spurious beliefs that surround theatre, cinema and the acting profession need a good vacuum. The Method has been "tainted" by misunderstandings, prejudices and straight-up phonies, and unfortunately, we come across all of these quite often.

Rumor Number One

Let's start out by wringing the neck of one of the most idiotic clichés about acting there is, almost as idiotic as thinking that Earth is flat: "An actor must be like a child whose ability to believe is immediate and on hand."

Try out a small experiment. Play cowboys and Indians or even Star Wars with a kid. No, wait—play with a bunch of different kids. Some of them will instantly play along but you'll notice that others will be a little less enthusiastic, a little less inspired. Keep only the more inspired ones and give specific parts to each of them, specific costumes, give them stage directions and a script ... Now have fun watching the disaster that unfolds! Have any of you ever been to a school play and *truly* believed the story you were watching? What was at stake for the characters, the drama? The issue is not kids lacking spontaneity, the issue is that spontaneity cannot come from any kind of truth if it's being controlled by expectations. When children act, it's of course very cute, but it's cute precisely because we can see that they're pretending. They put their heart into it, but it's still pretending.

So, there is absolutely no point in asking an actor to play "like a child." However, there is something we can learn from kids: how most of them are so keen to "play the game." We should all be influenced by children, whose innocence—which is a big compliment in this case—and desire to have fun are truly inspiring.

Rumor Number Two

Here's another absurdity believed to be true about the Method that we must erase: "It can only work in cinema, it doesn't work for the theater." *Oh, please!* When Stanislavski started doing his research, cinema was just taking its first steps. Of course, the Method works perfectly with cinema, but it works the exact same way for the theater, simply because that's where the Method was born.

To better illustrate our approach to acting in the theater and cinema, we can make a comparison with architecture or jewelry. Even though these artistic domains are very different in many ways, they have a similar set of rules and aim for beauty. Great cathedrals, as well as complex jewels, search for beauty, all the while following precise blueprints, demanding meticulousness and filled with powerful symbolism. It's the exact same principle with acting, whether it be in cinema or in the theater.

Rumor Number Three

And one more for the road: "Acting isn't something you can learn." *Suuuuure* ... So why did actors such as Marlon Brando, Jack Nicholson, Meryl Streep or Bradley Cooper attend acting classes for years and from time to time, in the midst of their careers, hire schmucks that we like to call acting coaches?

The belief that this profession cannot be learnt is based on a simple sophism, which can be described like this: "Since actors don't have an instrument, there's nothing to work on." That brings us back to what we were saying earlier: the actor *is* his own instrument. Plus, only a tiny part of this instrument is visible in the form of the actor's body, the rest is hidden underneath—the actor's inner world. To top it all off, this instrument is constantly changing and evolving.

Actors face a considerable multifaceted challenge that can be resumed like this: actors have to play a temperamental instrument—themselves. And the keys are not only hidden, *but in constant movement*. Being as complex as it is, this subject is worth being studied and explored a little more. Basically, we're here to learn how to play.

Wait, one question ...

But really, why use the Method? To have fun! "Seriously," as good old Nietzsche said. If this answer doesn't seem obvious to you, maybe you haven't yet experienced the joys of the Method on stage. A performance that is inspired and truthful will most likely profoundly touch the audience; it's also meant to be just as thrilling and fun to live for actors themselves. You will have so much more fun if you act with your soul, as opposed to acting like an empty puppet. Any imitation, especially of life, will not have the same impact as life itself, on the audience and on the actors. With regard to realistic acting, there are really only two approaches: going with representation or going with experience. The approach of representation consists of representing situations, whereas our approach consists of creating situations in order to *truly* live them. *Truly, but all the while respecting these five safety rules at all times in acting!*

1. Do not hurt yourself or others, in any way.
2. Do not grope your scene partners (or yourself!).[6]
3. Do not ingest any alcohol or drugs that strongly alter your state of mind.
4. Never reveal your sources.
5. Always make sure you're having fun in your work.

We'll talk more about that last one in many other chapters about "Exploration." With our approach, there's an inherent gentleness with the Method and that's partly what makes it reliable and resilient. With a pseudo-method about representation, actors become circus animals, they demonstrate the outside aspects, without incorporating any kind of inner truth, without any real journey. With the Method, actors need to create sincere motivation that will help them truly live out fictional situations, in front of an audience or a camera. Here's a reminder I always give to the actors I coach:

Bad actors use their muscles. Good actors use their soul, which in turn, guides their muscles.

Just in case you were skeptical about what you were getting into, let me oh-so-casually drop a few names that came from the Method and might break the ice a little:

Constantin Stanislavski, Jack Nicholson, Benicio Del Toro, Leonardo DiCaprio, Gena Rowlands, John Cassavetes, Angelina Jolie, Ben Gazzara, Peter Falk, Seymour Cassel, Michael Chekhov, Marlon Brando, Angelica Huston, Jack Nicholson, James Dean, Mickey Rourke, Jessica Lange, Bradley Cooper, Robert De Niro, Hilary Swank, Al Pacino, Dennis Hopper, Matthew McConaughey, Woody Harrelson, Val Kilmer, Jack Nicholson, Meryl Streep, Robert Duvall, Dustin Hoffman, Daniel Day Lewis, Ray Liotta, James Gandolfini, Lorraine Bracco, Jack Nicholson, Naomi Watts, Nicolas Cage, Jennifer Jason Leigh, Montgomery Clift, Charlize Theron, Samuel L. Jackson, Robert Lewis, Katharina Sergava,

---

[6] By the way, the pathetic wave of so-called directors and authors that force actors (but mostly actresses) to actually have sex in sex scenes is just a perverted cover up for perverts who won't admit that they just want to make porn. At least they would have the decency to be honest about it. Please, let's ignore their poor excuses for movies.

Stella Adler, Herbert Berghof, Uta Hagen, William Hickey, Susan Sarandon, Glenn Close, Warren Beatty, Faye Dunaway, Gene Hackman, Eddie Murphy—yes indeed, Eddie Murphy—Maureen Stapleton, Ellen Burstyn, Martin Landau, Edward Norton, William Hurt, Jeremy Irons, Jack Nicholson, John Turturro, Jack Nicholson, John Malkovich, Billy Bob Thornton, John Lithgow, Gina Gershon, Sean Penn, Chris Penn, Forest Whitaker, Shelley Winters, Brad Dourif, Christopher Walken, Nicole Kidman, Peter Boyle, Paul Newman, Laurence Fishburne, David Caruso, Eric Roberts, Tom Cruise, Denis Franz, Steve McQueen, Frederic Forrest, Teri Garr, Jack Nicholson, Sam Rockwell, Burt Young, Marilyn Monroe, Brad Davis, Christian Bale, Elizabeth Shue, Karl Malden, Michael Douglas, John Savage, Paul Dano, Natalie Portman, Steve Buscemi, Ashley Judd, Jon Voight, Harvey Keitel, Philip Seymour Hoffman, Brad Pitt, Joe Pesci, Kevin Spacey, Ed Harris, Jack Nicholson, Denzel Washington, Jack Nicholson, Chris Cooper, not to mention the thousands of actors who are not as well known but whose performances are just as commendable as, for example, Jack Nicholson's (I'm a bit of a fan, in case it wasn't obvious?).

If you're still not convinced, stop reading, put this book away in your bathroom and use the pages as toilet paper. You won't regret it, its pages are very soft and resistant.

Just like the Method.

2 Brief Accounting of The History of The Method

The origins of the Method

All good actors are Method actors.

(Robert Lewis)

"*Woooah!!* Slow down there, Robert!" some might say. But behind that brutal statement, Lewis (who also happens to be one of the founders, along with Elia Kazan and Cheryl Crawford, of the legendary Actors Studio) is merely pointing out the undeniable fact that the Method is based on a profound, sensitive, and thorough study of life. Therefore, any good realistic actor, whether he realizes it or not and whether he likes it or not, *is* a Method actor.

Stanislavski said himself that there had already been many good actors around.[1] Part of his research had always been to study and learn from these pioneers, in order to create an equivalent of music theory for realistic acting. But above all, his studies were always focused on the deciphering of life, of the human being and its physical, psychological, and emotional functioning. His goal being to be able to truly *re*-live these functioning *broken down into precise moments* on stage. Stanislavski's genius actually lies in the fact that he technically didn't invent anything; he found ways to decrypt, study, and truly understand humanity.

Nowadays, it's totally normal to see actors act realistically. However, this wasn't at all the case during Stanislavski's time. Here and there, you would find a few mavericks who were exploring in that direction, especially in the Yiddish theater that inspired Stanislavski so much. But mostly, it was more common to be an empty ham rather than expressing inner truth. Most of the time, they would *over act* and *over do,* rather than act realistically. Overall, audiences were satisfied with this … But, one of the rare critics of this kind of pantomime was Stanislavski. And he would go on to revolutionize not only the acting game, but also the world of theater in general and this revolution would inevitably influence cinema later on—as well as our own points of view of humanity and of the world. Before we talk more about Stanislavski's legacy, let's get into a couple of subjects mentioned earlier:

1) Functioning of life *broken down into precise moments* on stage.
2) Realism and realistic acting.

These two notions complete each other. For Stanislavski, realistic acting is not about showing a reflection of life, but rather a reflection of the *essence* of life. Mostly for one good,

---

[1] One of Stanislavski's muses who always inspired him was Eleonora Duse, aka the Duse, as well as the actors from Yiddish theater. All of these actors were the groundbreaking pioneers of realistic acting.

simple reason—in the theater and in cinema, we don't have a whole life to tell the story of the character's life, we actually have a matter of minutes. So it is crucial to get to the point, to go straight to the heart of the subject. This also goes for TV series of quality—even though we follow the characters' stories for many hours, we only follow the essential parts of their stories and lives.

This whole matter is misunderstood by many pseudo actors, who like to claim that they're from the Method, as well as those who like to criticize it. According to the pseudo actors, the most important thing is how you do simple actions—realistically and "just like everybody else." This is false. So the critics think that the pseudo actors' anecdotal acting is the definition of the Method. These two misguided points of view are a result of one simple misconception—the confusion between realism and naturalism.

Realism is the essence of life, and the pieces of it that we choose to highlight are intense key moments of a journey, whereas naturalism is a mere copy of life that makes no distinction of anything in particular.

According to the story that we choose to tell, realism has us choose particular moments of reality that will piece together a specific point of view, of a specific storyline in someone's life. Reality becomes realism when we select bits and pieces to sculpt the meaning that we want. This applies to writing, directing, and acting. This is why great realistic actors are not only realistic, they are poetically realistic. Furthermore, all the while taking in that they're part of a whole, they're not simply there to perform and execute the ideas of the playwright, the screenwriter, and the director. The actors themselves become ideas. That's what Uta Hagen's book, *Respect for Acting*, is all about—the actor's creativity. It's the combination of the screenwriter's and the actor's creativity that makes the magic of great films. There are many examples that we could bring up, but let us pay tribute to one of the most striking demonstrations of this chemistry between screenwriter, director, and actor, when the three of them work together with common poetic realism … John Cassavetes and his favorite actors, Gena Rowlands, Ben Gazzara, Seymour Cassell, Peter Falk, and himself.

Let us also specify that realistic acting is not exclusively reserved to movies that are more "reality" influenced. Realistic acting is also used in movies that take place in alternate realities. For instance, many science-fiction movies are not necessarily "reality-based." But that doesn't mean that the characters' behavior, while placed in timeless or extraterrestrial places, becomes "extra-realistic" or unrealistic. Their behavior is still driven by human motivations and human logic. This also goes for many works of art that are, in a sense, out of touch with reality, such as certain masterpieces by masters like Federico Fellini or David Lynch. Thus, Stanislavski and a strong team of *realistic* stage directors and actors took over the world.

Let's put this all in context: cinema was just taking its first steps, TV and the internet hadn't even been conceived yet and audiences were pretty much used to dramatic theater actors whose acting was purposely exaggerated. Stanislavski and his peers came and transformed the acting game so drastically, that not only was the notion of acting changed forever, they also influenced so many other arts and even the way we define ourselves.

Here's one anecdote that says it all, when it comes to the culture shock that audiences experienced when first watching the performances at the Moscow Art Theater. At the premiere performance of one of the Shakespeare plays that Stanislavski directed, some of the members of the audience fainted during the murder scenes, while others cried out in revolt. They thought that the actors portraying the victims had actually been killed right in front of them. The braver audience members who managed to watch until the end, claimed to have seen a miracle when the "murdered" actors were suddenly "resuscitated" at the end of the play. Well, they had definitely just seen a miracle, but it wasn't a resurrection—it was the miracle of theater itself. They had not simply watched a show, they had truly lived through an experience that was out of the ordinary, and witnessed the actual creation of a true, alternate reality.

Their success was immediate and Stanislavski led the Moscow Art Theater on an international tour. Opinions began to be unanimous—the world was discovering something fundamentally new and the influence of Stanislavski's Method spread more and more. However, a lot depended on the cultural and religious history of each country they toured. The acceptance of the Method ranged from "How magnificent! But … let's leave it to those crazy Russians" to total admiration.

This was the case in the United States. Stanislavski and his troupe were the innovation that North America had been craving. They would help the United States to build a future that would be the size of the Americans' ambition and love for images—that future was realism. It's not that it wasn't already existent before the Moscow Art Theater's tour; however, it remained rare and was far from the worldwide reference that it was going to become.

Excited by such a warm welcome and wanting to leave their home country that was on the verge of the Bolshevik Revolution (allegedly Marxist), some of the members of the Moscow Art Theater moved definitively over to America. Richard Boleslawski, author of the fascinating book that is *First Six Lessons*, was one of them. He lays out, with charm and humor, the basics of the Method and its foundation, as well as the work of Michael Chekhov, one of the most prominent actors in Stanislavski's troupe. Chekhov is also the author of *To the Actor: On the Technique of Acting*, which is a continuation, but also a bifurcation from the original work of the Method. By the way, whether you completely or partially adhere to the work of *To the Actor*, this book is an absolute must: its fascinating exercises are perfect for learning how to create characters, which was always one of Chekhov's specialties as an actor.

Many other Russian actors and actresses, including my fabulous coach Katharina Sergava, soon followed suit and shared their knowledge with the United States. And from there, the Moscow Art Theater's little brother was born in the United States: it was called The Group Theater. It was composed of brilliant actors, amazing stage directors, outstanding playwrights, and fantastic set decorators. All of them being experts of the Method, The Group Theater would go on to win over the United States and then the world. Among its members were Harold Clurman, a visionary director; Stella Adler, an actress of high caliber; Lee Strasberg, a detail-oriented actor and director; Sanford Meisner, another quality actor; Elia Kazan, an expert actor then legendary film director; Clifford Oddets and Arthur Miller, revolutionary playwrights; and my dear, dear Robert Lewis. Overflowing with energy and talent, The Group Theater had the effect of a tidal wave on the world of the theater and soon the world of cinema. And in order to top off the impact that they had, a few of the members founded the Actors Studio later on—the temple of modern realistic acting, whose teachings inspired generations and generations of *mind-blowing* actors. One of them was Marlon Brando, whose magnetic performances and striking charisma reinvented, yet again, the acting game, along with American movies from that time period.

Even though all of the actors of The Group Theater agreed upon the main principles of the Method and used it as an important common ground for acting, they didn't feel the same way about a lot of aspects of the Method. Alas, this created divisions between them and one too many conflicts ... Eventually, The Group Theater broke up.

These divisions mostly stemmed from three different points of view on the Method—Stella Adler's, Lee Strasberg's, and Sanford Meisner's. To this day, these three conquistadors are (besides Stanislavski) definitely the most well-known and influential coaches of the Method.

According to Adler, the essential tools of the Method lie in our imagination.

According to Strasberg, the essential tools of the Method lie in sense memory and emotional memory. This approach is, without a doubt, the one that has affected people the most and made them either love or hate the Method, either way with passion.

According to Meisner, the essential tools of the Method lie in listening.

Each of their "essential" tools became their only tools over time. These three approaches to the Method are of course fascinating. However, I personally prefer Robert Lewis' approach, because:

According to Lewis, the essentials of the Method lie in its diversity of tools. His approach embraces all of the tools of the Method, *as a whole*. It consists of introducing these tools to actors and letting them experiment with them all, mixing and matching however they feel is right. As I said before, the Method must become *Your* Method.

The future of the Method

Well, that's you!

Just as well as the future of theater and movies. So ...

Time to play!

Every time you'll read this sentence, it means that there's an acting exercise to try out. Really try them out, do them (whether it be on the first or second read). Don't be a passive reader. Don't be satisfied with just knowing, *embody!* You're here to be an actor, not a spectator. That's why I consider them more like experiments than just exercises.

The indication *"CUT"* means that it's the end of the exercise.

Three times three dots "**... ... ...**" is a question that you need to answer; you can take as long as you need to think about it, embody it, try it out, explore it.

3 Play The Game

Be not afraid of the universe.

(Najagneq)

I have a question to ask you

Whichever method you choose to become an actor, to perfect your game, and to practice, there's a question that we never ask ourselves and yet that is absolutely essential before starting anything—"Are you ready to play the game? Truly?"

Maybe no one ever asks that question since we all assume that the person will blurt out, brightly and frankly: *"YEEESS!!!"*

Well, no. For one good, simple reason: "playing the game" is complex, as it consists of luring oneself in. Lying to ourselves and believing it! Truly and unquestionably. A lot of us, including me of course, already do that pretty well in everyday life. However, it's a whole other ballgame when the lie has been created by another—the author. And it's even harder when you have to experience the lie in a specific place and at a specific time (the shooting of a film or a theater performance).

This is one of the actor's biggest challenges—the lie isn't his to begin with and there are instructions that are imposed upon him on *how* to lie. And we're not just talking about little white lies that we let out instinctively during the huge improvisation that life is. Nope, the lie that we ask of the actor is (in a way) much more "twisted."

No need to worry—there's a very simple way to have fun with it: by turning the lie into an unquestionable reality. And that's where the Method comes in. But before you wholeheartedly join this adventure, you'll have to ask yourself the initial question:

Am I ready to play the game?

The four barriers to break

The question might seem simple enough, but really, it brings up a profound challenge that we must face. Our challenge is to push aside four barriers that have been embedded in us for so long.

1) Skepticism.

2) Pretending to be indifferent, or worse—*being* indifferent.

3) Being trivial.

4) An exclusively factual approach to life.

Sometimes, these barriers can come from moral stances or things that we grew up with. But even when these barriers are *personal*, let us remind ourselves that the only instrument that actors can use is their own *person*. Therefore, if you do not get rid of these burdens, it won't matter whether you use this book as a footrest or if you read it. Nothing will change. So, taking this first step is the only condition to experimenting with the tools of the Method.

Skepticism

Irony has only emergency use. Carried over time, it is the voice of the trapped who have come to enjoy their cage.

(Lewis Hyde)

This amazing quote applies to skepticism as well. Carried and repeated over time, it becomes the actor's worst enemy, if not the human being's. It injects venom that makes it impossible to even *believe in anything*, to be inspired, amazed, whatever … to "play the game." Non-actors can very well live a (miserable) life like that. However, actors who start out with no capacity whatsoever of believing (and who are not open to the idea) should change professions immediately. They will have no chance of giving a convincing performance. The tiniest thing will distract them from the fiction, bring them back to reality, and will destroy the illusion that they need to be able to believe their lies.

There's no definite way to fight off skepticism. But I do know one simple way to weaken it … Just ask yourself: "How is this repeated skepticism helping me? *Is* it helping me? Is it making me happy or is it stopping me from moving forward, from sharing and (most importantly) from creating?" Some people will hear a little voice resist and insist that their skepticism is a guardian angel protecting them, keeping them safe. To those people, I must tell you that this guardian angel is nothing but a prison … It comes disguised as our comfort zones— it doesn't protect us from anything, only censors us. Actors are made to think that their creativity is craziness and should be locked up. We should be able to express, freely and healthily, what we cannot usually express in society. After all, isn't that one of the luxuries of being an actor and one of the reasons we choose to become one?

However, putting aside your skepticism doesn't mean swallowing anything that's thrown at you, without any critical sense whatsoever. Critical sense is in fact essential to make choices that are daring, yet well thought out, in acting and in life. It's really just about being open, at least a little bit. We're going to try to make a crack in the walls of certainty that have been keeping us from seeing what they're blocking out. In order to play the game.

I don't necessarily encourage the exact opposite of skepticism, which is naivety, but rather curiosity. Skepticism can make you close-minded, whereas curiosity encourages action and opening up to the endless possibilities. Sometimes curiosity is a little risky, but in our case, *these risks are taken in a safe environment* and are inevitable for anyone who wants to create, live experiences and have fun.

Pretending to be indifferent, or worse—being indifferent

On my tenth birthday, my mother beckoned me. Since I was absolutely sure that it was to give me my birthday present, I ran to her. But I was a bit surprised and *very* disappointed to find out that this wasn't the reason she called me. She had a *very* serious look on her face. After a silence that seemed to last longer than the ten years I had lived, she told me that she had something of the utmost importance to tell me. I was imagining the worst, until ... "Don't ever marry an indifferent woman," she said. "*Never*, David, do you hear me?" I definitely heard her, I just didn't know what to make of it. "There's your present. Happy birthday, David," she finished. "Thank you," I said, with about as much enthusiasm as if I had gotten the death sentence and my executioner had opened my cell door for me.

At that time, I would've loved to get a comic book, but I realize today that those words were one of the most precious gifts that I had ever received. A spiritual gift, the wisest advice: to flee indifference as if it were the plague, flee anyone and anywhere that indifference could be found.

But what does this have to do with actors? An indifferent actor, just as any other human being, might as well be soulless. It's better to be tragic, to be enraged, or even bitter if you must, as long as you're not indifferent. Indifferent actors stay in one place, trapped with an empty vision of the world that stops any artistic creation.

At the exact opposite of indifference, there's the amazement. But be careful! We're not talking about the forced amazement that has become so widespread on social media, for example. It's all about cultivating inspiration wherever you can find it—meaning everywhere.

Time to play!

Let's do an experiment, right now, and ask ourselves this question: "What amazes me?" Truthfully, deeply. Allow yourself to visualize.

... ...

What comes to you? What comes to mind? Water, a tree, the miracle of life? What amazes you?

... ...

A baby, an old lady with young eyes? A bird, a plane, science? Being able to see, feel, touch? A loved one's hands? Walking on the moon? A painting? A poem? A song? An incredible performance given by an actor?

... ...

Search. Take your time. Always.

... ...

Put down this book. Either close your eyes, or wander around wherever you are without any other goal but to see, truly *see* the things that are around you. Go ahead, really do it. We'll meet up again afterwards.

... ...

—CUT—

So? What did you find? Personally, I chose a classic: I looked up at the sky. Incredible, infinite, majestic. How powerful its presence is, yet calm at the same time. The patience of a drop of water, passive and yet so alive. Its suppleness. The harmony, the fusion with the other drops of water that trickle into it. The speed of light. The electricity that's allowing me to type on my computer. Computers! Technology. The internet. Being able to communicate with someone on the other side of the world. Etc.

Often ask yourself what amazes you, for two major reasons concerning the acting profession. One, to sharpen your amazement potential—it works a little like a muscle, the more you train it, the stronger it gets. Two, to enrich your inner world with visuals and images that speak to you. This inner world is the source of any good performance and the visuals are the keys.

There really aren't that many indifferent actors, thank goodness. Unfortunately, many actors pretend to be indifferent—they like to *act* indifference. It seems to be in fashion. They think that if you seem indifferent, it means that you are above everybody else, that you are enigmatic, profound, deep, irreverent … *So cool*. Oh, please … I have a special disdain for these cynical, indifferent specimens, who think that their arid lives are standards that others should live up to.

There are a thousand other jobs that this type of attitude is perfect for. But not a creator. Not an actor, because, yes, with the Method, the actor is considered as a distinct creator. So, if you're *acting* indifference, if you're pretending to be indifferent or if you actually are, choose one of two things: stop that, right now, or stop being an actor. It's your choice, but you have to make it.

Still here? Fantastic! The complete opposite of acting indifference is enthusiasm. The etymological meaning of the word "enthusiasm" is "To be inspired by the gods." Whether you take it literally or as more of an allegory, it's a pretty good start!

Being trivial

I love acting. It is so much more real than life.

(Oscar Wilde)

As we saw in the previous chapter:

> In the theater and in cinema, we don't have a whole life to tell the story of the character's life, we actually have a matter of minutes.

In this case, the purely trivial doesn't have its place on stage or on screen. But be careful—this doesn't mean, unlike what so many acting coaches *love* to claim, that "You have to act as if *everything* is a question of life or death!" Aha! There's another misconception that we shall now throttle — of course, that an actor must find the intensity of a scene and what's at stake. Even in a comedy, he must understand the drama involved. But some scenes, or mostly some *parts* of scenes often simply do not contain intensity, high stakes, or drama.

Here's an example. After a long day at work, full of intensity, high stakes, and maybe even drama, Joe is doing his grocery shopping at the supermarket and is hesitating between a jar of strawberry jam or banana jam. Suddenly, a mass murderer barges in furiously, yells out a speech against society and starts shooting at people with his machine gun. Well, if Joe had already been hesitating between strawberry or banana jam as if it was "a question of life or death," what will he be able to act when it's time to fight for his life? This example might seem completely random, but these kinds of moments always happen at some point in plays and movies, and there are always actors (who, ironically, are almost always from the Method) who want to act out everything with pre-apocalyptic urgency. It's entirely to their credit, but it remains a big mistake. A role needs intensity, high stakes, and drama, but these aspects only become valuable when put in contrast with moments that are less serious.

But he who can do more can do less. In my opinion, an actor who is "theatrical" and inflamed about every little thing is far preferable to an actor who is trivial and remains insipid no matter what. Simply for these reasons:

1) There are many more intense moments than not when playing a role.

2) The trivial actor offers nothing, which means that you have to build everything from scratch.

3) It's rare to find a play or movie that actually has moments that are truly trivial.

Also, it'll be more or less easy to calm down an unruly actor who acts out everything intensely, than to have to energize an apathetic actor who makes everything trivial.

Let's review the example with Joe's jam. Even though Joe isn't dealing with a Cornelian dilemma[1] in the case of the jam flavors, it will be much more interesting for the actor (so, inevitably, the audience) if Joe does take this choice a little seriously. Maybe he's supposed to be on a diet but he's going to let himself go a little? Or maybe he likes strawberry but his wife prefers banana and their financial situation is forcing him to make a choice. Whatever the reason and whatever the action, don't make anything trivial. Always breathe some sort of importance into everything you do with a role, but keep the life-and-death questions for the life-and-death situations.

If the doors of perception were cleansed everything would appear to man as it is, Infinite.
(William Blake)

You get it by now, the exact opposite of being trivial is depth. "Depth" is often confused, quite unjustly, with "heaviness." That's because of overbearing actors who have not found anything truly profound inside of them (only because they haven't properly explored), but

---

[1] In case you didn't know, Corneille loved putting his characters in situations in which they had a choice to make that would send them into abysmal suffering. This suffering came from the fact that, no matter what choice they ended up making, it would inevitably lead them to their demise.

still pretend to be lost in their own depth. True profoundness comes from seeing the infinity of every little thing in their essence, as the brilliant William Blake said. Profoundness must be cultivated, but without any mannerisms interfering. The goal here isn't to dramatize or trivialize—it is to create, while playing.

And to truly see the depth of every little thing, one element is necessary: time. Exploring profoundness, the depth of ourselves, and everything around us demands attention, gentleness, curiosity, and time. Or rather the suspension of time, the possibility of removing ourselves from it. And no matter how hard it can be, it's up to you to make room for this precious time. Taking time is actually saving time.

An exclusively factual approach to life

Another obstacle that gets in the way of playing the game is having an exclusively factual approach to life, which, in some cases, can lead to skepticism.

You've probably noticed that I use a lot of words like "fiction," "a lie," "reality," "illusion," etc. The goal is to question these words, which have become locked up tight in an exclusively factual approach, and review their definition. Most of the time, this approach is necessary in everyday life—for example, when it comes to safety (fire burns you) and basic, indisputable facts (you can't eat a wall), etc. But, this approach is one of the worst hindrances to the actor's creativity. This doesn't mean that creativity must be completely devoid of the material dimension of life. But for creativity to be able to transcend this dimension, it must link up with the poetic dimension of the same life. So, just as much on stage as in real life, a wall is a wall and fire can indeed burn you. However, the definitions of "fiction," "a lie," "reality," "illusion," etc., are seen in a whole new light, when taking on the poetic dimension of life. Just like magic! As Blanche Dubois in *A Streetcar Named Desire* said so beautifully: "I don't tell the truth, I tell what ought to be truth."

And anyway, what *is* "reality," besides a supposedly objective vision that's actually subjective? The "truth" becomes merely a point of view. Is there only one type of "lying"? Whilst embracing all of these questions and the infinite horizons that they open up, the actor is no longer a "liar." Or, as we brought up earlier, actors turn the "lie" into such a believable and tangible "reality" that they end up bluffing themselves, then the audience. Here's what I often say to the know-it-alls who like to state that actors are merely liars:

> *Bad actors are bad liars,*
> *Good actors are good liars,*
> *Incredible actors are not liars,*
> *Since they believe in the reality of their fiction.*

This belief is short-lived and of course, ironically, self-aware. But it still remains a form of belief. For the least skeptical of us, including myself, we're dealing with the creation of another world, which is temporary, and yet coexists with ours.

So, there is one condition for any realistic actor to be able to embody any type of role whatsoever, convincingly. You must wholeheartedly believe in the story of the script or the play. And this belief is only possible if you take a poetic approach. Without this, we're stuck with the cold "reality" of what is exclusively factual …

Sure, the actor is not actually the prince of Denmark, but a waiter at a roadside diner. And yes, his name isn't Hamlet ... And it really seems to him like the actor who's playing the ghost of his father is wearing H&M tights ... All of this is making him merely recite his lines without any conviction and obey stage directions without motivation. And all of this makes him start to wonder if his mother was right—he really is a shitty actor.

Ugh!! But he always dreamed of embodying heroic or tragic destinies ... as long as it wasn't his own. He always dreamed of having multiple lives! Any life except this one ... Well, if he always dreamed of it, then that means that there is a poetic dimension inside of him. And if he's on stage tonight, that means that he truly believed in it for at least a second, an instant, a spark of eternity ... All he needs to do now is find that path again ...

Once again, I'm sure you get it by now: the exact opposite of an exclusively factual approach is a poetic approach. Many experts, from Albert Einstein, to Stanislav Grof and Stanislavski himself, have confirmed the existence of this approach and the need to be as close to it as possible, because:

> *On a cosmic scale—all of physics shows us that only fantasy has a chance of being the truth.*
> (Teilhard de Chardin)

So, figure something out—fall in love, believe in alternate worlds or in relativity, be a mystic, read masterpieces and/or simply open yourself up to the mysteries of life, to the unknown, to yourself! But don't be afraid to find the entrance to the poetic dimension inside of you.

Come on, don't be skeptical, it's right there. At arm's length, right inside of you ...

There you go, now we can get started!

4 The W.W.W. Questions

Let's get into the heart of the matter!

We're going to start with one of the most fundamental tools of the Method, which makes all of the others much more accessible: the questions Where? When? Why?

These questions are inherent in *every* situation, whether it's real or fictional. Every. Situation.

To make sure that you understand very clearly what this exercise is about, we'll start out by using two real situations as examples: you, reading this book, and me, writing it.

When we're finished exploring the questions of our respective situations, we'll do the same with a fictional situation. Then, I encourage you to act out that fiction while mostly relying on your imagination, so that you can feel its power.

The questions Where, When, and Why

You'll become familiar with a series of questions that are important to answer in any situation that you'll have to act out, whether it be one of Shakespeare's plots or out of an action movie. You will only be able to embody your character once you've answered the questions that follow.

> *Where am I?*
> *When is it happening?*
> *Why am I here: what is my objective?*
> *What's pushing me to want to accomplish my objective: what are my motivations?*
> *What are the stakes?*
> *What are the obstacles standing between me and my objective?*
> *What am I doing to beat my obstacles, in order to accomplish my objective?*

But remember, you're not here to merely answer these questions mentally and factually, you're here to embody your answers physically and psychologically. We'll go into more detail about how to do that in just a bit, as well as during the different chapters in "Exploration." The work that goes into embodying your answers is done progressively, slowly and organically. And translating your answers physically and psychologically brings us to this: *it is not enough for actors to know the facts, they must turn it into experience.*

So, in order to act out every situation, you'll have to first ask yourself the W.W.W. questions and then systematically embody your answers. We call the process of switching from the answer to the embodiment, "physicalization." If you're thinking that you've never seen that word before, don't worry, it's because it doesn't exist. I've allowed myself a neologism here and made up this word to describe the act of physicalizing, for an actor. (From time to time, you'll find other words in here that I've more or less invented.) That means to make your inner world physical, tangible, and visible. Without physicalization, even if it's very subtle (sometimes it's just a look in your eyes), the inner world will remain invisible. No matter how vibrant it might be, an inner world that is not physicalized remains a hidden treasure. And when it comes to realistic acting, this physicalization is produced *without miming or directly demonstrating anything* to the audience.

Unlike another popular misconception, the Method doesn't tell actors to "exclude" the spectators, but rather to include them while "ignoring" them. It's as if actors let the spectators be voyeurs. Actors don't make it their job to create a full-on contact with the audience—therefore, a more seductive relationship is created between the two. More seriously though, you might have noticed that we didn't bring up the emotional embodiment of your answers to the W.W.W. questions. It's not that we don't take it into account, we'll just talk about it a little later in the chapter "Exploration."

Answering the questions

Now, let's work on the W.W.W. questions concerning our own current situation.

First, we'll give brief answers, in order to truly understand the exercise. At the same time, we'll fully explore the usefulness and the function of each question.

Second, we'll give longer and much more detailed answers, this time in order to truly understand the influence they have on our acting.

Time to play!

The question "Where?"

Where am I?

Me: *on planet Earth. In France, the country where I was born and where I'm living at the moment. In Paris, the city where I grew up. Haussmann Boulevard. In a big office that belongs to some friends. In one of the rooms of this office.*

What about you?

... ...

Answer *all* the questions. Turn the *exercise* into *experience*, do it with every exercise that comes in this book—turn it all into experiences, don't let it be simple theory. Try to be pretty specific, but not too much, just yet. We'll cover more details with each of your answers a little later. Write them down.

... ...

Done? OK.

The usefulness and the function of the question "Where?"
Having this question be the first one of this exercise isn't just random. It's actually the first question we ask ourselves after having fainted or after waking up from a drunken blackout. More unconsciously, it's also the first question that we ask ourselves when we go somewhere that we're not familiar with. Or even when waking up every morning and just moving around. The question "Where?" is a vital point of reference that deeply influences our behavior, in real life and in our imaginary life while acting.

The question "When?"

When is it happening?

Me: *in 2021. Summertime. August 27th. A Wednesday. 12:55 am.*

What about you?

... ...

The usefulness and the function of the question "When?"
Just like the question "Where?", the question "When?" influences our basic behavior. So the time period, the season and the time of day or night must be defined and physicalized in your acting.

Here's an example: in general, are you the same when leaving your house in the morning and when coming back home in the evening, after a long day at work for instance? Nope! So that must be taken into account and physicalized. To do that, we'll use tools that we're going to discover (or rediscover) in "Exploration," that use the imagination or sense memory.

The "objective"

Why am I here: what is my objective?

Me: *I want to make progress in writing this book.*

What about you?

… … …

The usefulness and the function of the "objective."
Stanislavski insisted upon the crucial question, which is that of the objective. What do I want? What am I doing here, now? *If I don't have an objective, then I'm simply not supposed to be on stage.*

Every objective has to be in accordance with these four factors:

1) The given circumstances of the story.

2) Using the verb "to want."

3) It should speak to you.

4) The desire to change the situation that you're in.

The given circumstances of the story.

Within the situations that each of us are living here and now, our objectives are based on and dictated by something vaster: its coherence with our lives, or at the very least, a part of it. When you're working on a role, always make sure that the objective you set in each scene is based on the given circumstances of the story. And moreover, make sure that it stays coherent with, once again, a much vaster framework: the character's. All of his or her objectives must be geared towards what Stanislavski called the character's super-objective: what he or she is ultimately aiming for in the end.

For example, let's imagine that your objective is "I want to sharpen up my acting." This objective is part of a much vaster super-objective that could be, for example: "I want to have a passionate and interesting career."

Using the verb "to want."

The objective must derive from will, which can be more directly accessible than emotions. Therefore, it's best to avoid starting an objective with "I would like," "I desire," or "I wish to."

It should speak to you.

This third factor is fundamental. No matter how pertinent and coherent the chosen objective will be with the story, it will remain absolutely useless if it doesn't resonate with the actor. So, what do you do if, when working on a character, one or more of his/her objectives doesn't speak to you or just leaves you cold as ice? Try to redefine it and visualize it with more precision.

If it's still not working, you'll have to substitute it with another objective. Let's imagine that your character's objective is "I want to win the next presidential election" and that it has strictly no effect on you. Or worse, you find it totally pathetic, absurd, or maybe even nightmarish. You'll have a really hard time believing it and *truly* wanting it. Because this is really what it's all about—you have to find an objective that you *truly* want or would like to achieve. No need to panic. Whatever the objective of your character is, you can always substitute it with one that resembles it. This resemblance doesn't necessarily have to involve the object of your desire (in this case, being president), it can just involve willingness: "I want to win ..."

It can also involve the aspects that go with desiring this kind of victory—ambition, success, revenge, the ego, etc. Let's imagine that your character wants to achieve a certain victory that doesn't necessarily resonate with you: becoming president, the head of the mafia, a successful chef, or even winning a prize for the best sculpture made out of marshmallows. Among these suggestions, choose the objective that speaks to you the least. Now, ask yourself, here and now, "What would I really like to achieve? Which status? Which competition? Which type of role!" There you go, you just substituted an objective that doesn't interest you with an objective that interests you big-time. And the audience won't be able to tell the difference. They'll feel your desire to succeed, the power of the energy that you're putting into getting what you want, but they won't see within you and be able to tell that you're thinking about a particular role rather than a sculpture made out of marshmallows.

The desire to change the situation that you're in.

Every objective is born from a desire for change. Because if everything's fine and there's nothing about the situation that must change, then there is no action. If everything is fine and happy-go-lucky, there is simply no drama, which means there are no scenes to play. It's as simple as that.

It's no coincidence that one of the mottos of screenwriters is that "Happy people have no stories." Well, maybe we should've added the word "interesting." It's also no coincidence that at the end of every fairytale, we leave off with that god-forsaken "They all lived happily ever after," without bringing up what happens next. And you know why? Because witnessing happy people live their lives in peace and with ecstatic joy is the exact opposite of dramaturgy.

So, in order to better execute the desire for change that comes with an objective, you have two formulations that are possible. For example, "I want to make progress in writing this book," can also be written out like this: "I want to change the state of this book from that of a project to an achievement." The first formulation gives me a generalized overview of my objective, whereas the second one has me confront something specific that I need to accomplish. Therefore, my desire and need to spring into action is much stronger.

This second formulation—I want to change so and so from point A to point B—is especially helpful when you're working on a scene that has two or more people. Let us specify that in every scene with two or more people, each character has a desire for change that directly concerns the other characters. This desire for change doesn't necessarily lead to a confrontation or a negative intention towards the other characters. For instance, if your friend has a severe case of the blues, you'll want to change them from having the blues to having found happiness again.

Let's talk about the two possible formulations for the same objective again. Let's imagine that my objective is "I want Mona to become my girlfriend." A formulation that has many more propositions to offer and encourages action being taken would be: "I want to change Mona from being a distant friend to being my steady girlfriend." The actions that must be put into place are much clearer with the second formulation, because it describes Mona "*the way she is*," as well as "*what I would like her to be.*"

In a fictitious situation, this type of formulation—"what is" to "what should be"—is meant to help actors pay attention to the slightest gestures or intentions of the other characters, from whom they're expecting something. Tons of subtext is created, as actors truly experience the present moment and it makes the situation feel even more alive. This active listening is partially what makes a scene feel fresh, even after multiple performances at the theater or multiple takes on set.

Sure, some will try and remind us that there are moments in life when we don't have an objective. That's sometimes (but rarely) true in real life, but strictly impossible when it comes to dramaturgy. In dramaturgy, just like most of the time in real life, what do we do when we don't have an objective? We look for one! And finding one *becomes* our objective. In order to illustrate this, here are two examples, one is trivial, the other not so much.

Here's the trivial one. I forgot my cell phone in the kitchen and my objective is to go and get it. While heading over, I'm suddenly deep in thought about Mona—her smile, that mischievous look in her eyes ... and just like that, I forgot my objective. What happens then? I search for my objective. Most of the time, I stop in my tracks, just like you. Sometimes, I retrace my steps, hoping that some object or some movement will remind me of the reason why I was headed to the kitchen. *What the hell was it?* Not being able to remember what my objective was makes me search for it even more. Kitchen, kitchen, kitchen ... walk ... walking to the kitchen ... but why? To eat? No. I've been trying to diet, to be more attractive for ... Mona! Ahhh, Mona ... I should call her, maybe suggest ... *That was it! Call her, cell phone, kitchen!* Having finally found my objective, I drop the one of looking for it and pursue the one that is to go and get my phone.

In short, whenever anybody doesn't have an objective, they simply no longer move, since they no longer have any reason to move.

Anyway, here's the not so trivial example: Hamlet! This isn't anything new—Hamlet is tortured by doubt. He's so deep in his doubt that he sometimes doesn't know what his objective is anymore, neither the "why?" nor the "what for?" of this whole charade that is called humanity. Yet, there is not one moment when he just wanders aimlessly around his palace, all dressed up in his Danish tights, without knowing what to do ... he's looking for his objective! Ergo, he already has one: "I want to find my objective," which we can also formulate as "I want to change from a state of doubt and indecision to a state of assurance." The famous "To be or not to be" is the epitome of what I've been trying to get across: *there* is no such thing as a character who doesn't have an objective! Looking for one is precisely one of the most valid and fascinating objectives you can have.

Visualize the objective as a target that you have to aim for.

The "motivations"

What's pushing me to want to accomplish my objective: what are my motivations?

Me: *my desire to understand human beings. My passion for the Method. My desire to share this passion and make it more accessible and understandable. My love of cinema. Of art. My desire for it to be of better quality more often than it is at the moment, more transcendental, more awakening. Making my contribution to the edifice of the Method. My wish for actors to no longer have to hear any bullshit. Fun. Financial gain. Ego.*

What about you?

… … …

The usefulness and the function of the "motivations."

Motivations are what push us to want what we want. The motivations must speak to you, just like the objectives. And just like for the objectives, the Method offers an array of tools that can help you out if the character's motivations don't resonate with you. Among these tools are substitutions, which we talked about a little earlier. They're just as useful for the objective as they are for the motivations.

Motivations also generate floods of subtext, visualizations, and sources. That being said, the objective is the target to aim for, whereas the motivations are the sources of strength that are driving us to aim for it. Both are full of energy, but not necessarily the same type. Motivations are made up of energies that "push me to …," objectives are made up of energies that "pull me to …."

Our visualizations then jostle our spirits and influence the movement of our bodies.

Let us specify that motivations affect the type of energy we have when looking to accomplish our objectives: they influence our actions, what we do to get to our objective.

Let's imagine that the objective of a scene is "I want to kill Roger" and the motivation that's pushing me to want to kill him is "To avenge the murder of my daughter." This motivation will not only influence the choice of my actions, but the way I execute them. If you keep the same objective, "I want to kill Roger," but you change the motivation to "For pleasure," or "In order to spare him horrible pain," not only will this entail different actions, but they'll also be executed in a completely different way. If the same action is chosen for two different motivations, like slitting his throat for instance, the action will be executed completely differently according to the motivation that provoked it.

In the situation that you're experiencing right now, reading this book is probably either "out of passion" or "out of obligation." Either way, the action, "reading," stays the same. But according to the motivation, the way that you execute the action "to read" will change.

Visualize the motivations as the muscle that makes you point your bow and arrow towards the target, which is the objective.

The "stakes"

What are "the stakes?"

Me: *If I reach the objective that I've set for myself, I'll reap many different types of benefits from this project: personal, professional, ethical, financial ... I'll have reached the height of my ambition, of my aspirations ... I'll be very proud of myself, maybe I'll even be recognized by some people that I admire and respect. Method Acting Center, the school that I founded, might even profit from it too ... new opportunities will arise ...*

What about you?

... ...

The usefulness and the function of the "stakes."

Stakes are essential in dramaturgy; therefore, just as essential in acting. It clearly indicates "what is at stake," what it is that you'll potentially gain or lose in the situation that you're dealing with. The stakes are clearly what makes the difference between realism and naturalism. The higher the stakes, the stronger your motivation to reach your objective will be. *The stakes are part of what creates the energy of a situation,* but as we'll discover later on, they're not the only element that creates it.

Visualize the stakes as the reward *or* the punishment, according to your capacity to aim for your target, which is the objective.

The "obstacles"

What are the obstacles standing between me and my objective?

Me: *I'm a little tired tonight. I'm hungry. I have quite a few other things that I have to take care of. That stupid coffee machine. Mona.*

What about you?

... ...

The usefulness and the function of the "obstacles."

During a scene—and hey, maybe even in life—we must cherish our obstacles, because these are the challenges that will put the motivation we have to reach our objectives to the test. It's partially thanks to these challenges that we're able to know what we really want, what truly counts, and why.

Without obstacles, any situation remains trivial dramaturgically speaking, so it remains just as trivial in terms of acting.

It is the friction between the motivations, the stakes and the actions on one side; the obstacles on the other side, that brings the dramaturgy and the energy of a scene to life.

So, choose major obstacles as much as possible and always in accordance with the given circumstances of the scene. However, choosing an obstacle should never be at random. During a transition where all you have to do is cross the street, just cross the street, don't think to yourself that a nuclear warhead is about to crush you. Don't go towards one extreme or another; both will turn your acting bland. On the other hand, crossing the street can sometimes be a task of the utmost importance, with high stakes.

Visualize the obstacles as walls that stand between you and your target, which is the objective.

The "actions"

What am I doing to beat my obstacles in order to accomplish my objective?

Me: *Wandering around the coffee machine, on yet another observation round. Attempting negotiation with it. Splashing some water on my face. Looking for ideas that get me motivated. Seeing them come to life in a way that excites me. Re-energizing. Concentrating. Re-concentrating.*

What about you?

… … …

The usefulness and the function of the "actions."
These are the movements in dramaturgy, thus, that come with acting. Without actions, we remain in a world of mere ideas, where actors aren't needed because there is no embodiment.

There are two types of actions: physical actions and "psychophysical actions." We'll talk about these two types of actions later on; for now, we'll just say that when our objective is physical, we use physical actions. When our objective is psychological, we use psychophysical actions.

Let's say, when I want to have dinner—a physical objective—I *eat* a Pho soup and seventeen spring rolls. When I want to try to lose weight—a psychophysical objective—I *scold* myself for having eaten all of that.

Visualize the actions as the arrows that you use to aim at the target, which is the objective.

—CUT—

There you go! Are the questions "Where? When? Why?" that all situations are made up of a little clearer now?

Just to be sure, we'll sum it up in one sentence:

"Where? When? Why?" are a series of questions that you must ask yourself with every scene. The answers that you give will be the foundation of your embodiment.

At any moment, actors must always stay busy, stay occupied. That is the goal: *actors must keep busy with the situation that they're in, instead of being preoccupied with themselves and with the audience.*

This distraction can remain very strong, and pushes us to suppress any real emotions. And this is usually because our *very* strange education teaches us to censor our emotions, *especially* in front of others and most definitely in front of an audience.

To get over the stage fright that results from this, actors must learn to master two things that often go hand in hand:

1) Knowing how to use their nerves to their advantage or knowing how to relax.

2) Being truly and deeply occupied on stage. To be able to achieve this state of occupation, which then also becomes a state of deep concentration and actually helps to relax, they must answer the W.W.W. questions with as much detail as possible. The more detailed his answers are, the more actors will believe in what they're doing and, ergo, in themselves. In short:

Our bodies, our minds and our souls ask of us just one thing: TO TRIP OUT.
But under one condition: that we don't take them for idiots.

That is what we call the "self-bluff," so precious to the Method.

So choose details with passionate thoroughness, just like a lover who's arranging a bouquet, with the precision of a ninja and the patience of a mother.

The detailed answers to the W.W.W. questions

Let's get back into the game, this time adding as much detail as possible into each of our answers: you in your situation, me in mine. To do this, we'll break up our answers into parts. Some details will speak to you, others won't. Choose those that call to you and thus allow you to believe in the situation; these are part of the most important decisions that an actor must make. The author offers you the story, but not the belief that goes with it. It's your job to find it, partially through the details. If we're basing ourselves on real situations here, it's so that we can identify the material that they're made of. That way, in the chapters that follow, we'll be able to create a fictional situation from scratch and to wholeheartedly believe in them as if they were real.

Time to play!

The detailed question "Where?"

Where am I?

Me: *on planet Earth. In France, the country where I was born and where I'm living at the moment. In Paris, the city where I grew up.*

Yes, these are tiny details in the situation that I'm living right now, but the fact that I was born here and that I live here gives me a familiar feeling that I probably wouldn't have if I were in another country.

In my answer, I specify that I'm living here "at the moment," because having lived in other countries means that I can compare certain aspects. Again, this remains a detail, but I'm going to insist upon this one: in scenes where you're not in your country, you'll have to include the fact that there are a lot of things in your general environment that you're not used to in your acting.

For instance, in New York, the sound environment is very different from the one in Paris: the police sirens, the car sounds, the accents, etc. The smells are also different, the seasons, etc. All of these factors influence our behavior and if the given circumstances of the scene indicate that it's not your country or your city, you have to physicalize the influences. And they'll be even more pronounced if, for example, it's the first time that you've left your country or your city. You'll experience everything with a completely different type of excitement or apprehension than in a place that you already know. So, not being in your country has an influence on you, just as being in your country does. In both cases, you'll have to take that in and physicalize that factor.

What about you? Where are you?

… … …

Me: *Haussmann Boulevard.*

Like every street or boulevard, Haussmann Boulevard has its particularities. In this case, it's the tall Parisian buildings, of which a lot are office buildings. For instance, in the office where I'm working right now, I have a view of two other buildings, where there's no sign of life after 8:00 p.m. This aspect gives me a slight feeling of isolation, which is actually quite pleasant for writing. And yet, I'm right in the middle of the capital, which means traffic, voices in the streets, etc. This gives me a certain feeling of agitation, which combined with the feeling of isolation is creating a strange contradictory energy in me: that of being apart, kind of floating in the middle of the world.

Also, I'm not too far from the Saint-Lazare terminal, a big Parisian train station where travelers come and go. So there's also the energy of endless possibilities of escapades, that singular atmosphere that roams around train stations. Many people of many different nationalities can be heard in the streets, a lot of them are rushing, some of them are headed to new horizons, etc.

What about you? What neighborhood are you in? Which street? Or maybe which part of nature? How does this, that or the other thing influence your behavior?

... ...

Me: *in a big office that belongs to some friends.*

Some of the details we discussed have a bit of an effect on my behavior, some don't. This detail, however, completely affects my behavior.

Working in an office gets me concentrated in a very different way than when I'm working at home. I'll be less likely to get distracted by other actions: changing clothes, making a small or big snack, cleaning up, etc. And I won't be interrupted by a friend randomly coming to visit, or by the building caretaker who often stops by for one reason or another.

Anyway, the fact that I'm in an office that a couple of friends lent me completely alters my behavior. Even though I feel comfortable here, there are things that I wouldn't do and the things I do are tinted by this circumstance: I'm not at my place. Even the way I make coffee is full of tiny details that would clue someone in to realizing that I'm a "stranger" here, if someone were observing me. I'm not familiar with this coffee machine despite the countless times that Cyril and Isabelle (my friends who are lending me this office) have patiently explained it to me. Every time I want to make coffee, which happens quite often, this kind of stare off ensues with this coffee machine and myself. I've gotten used to its tricks, I try to approach it as gently as possible, talk to it sometimes, often insult it. Basically, I have a very specific relationship with this machine that adds so many layers to the situation. Add on the fact that since the coffee pods don't belong to me, I almost always feel slightly guilty. Same thing with the sugar, etc.

For those of you who still think that we're taking a long time with details that aren't majorly important, let me remind you that this is still an exercise. One of the main goals is for you to develop the habit, and of course the desire, of searching for the details that will allow you to fully believe in exciting situations in a play or a script.

What about you? Are you at your place or someone else's? Or elsewhere entirely? How does this affect your behavior?

... ...

Me: *in one of the rooms of this office.*

Ah ha! These offices might not belong to me, but this one room is starting to. I have my computer set up here, which I'm using to write at this exact moment, along with a few personal items, my mug, my pack of peanuts, my gum, etc. These little things give me a feeling of being at home and are here to comfort me after my arguments with the coffee machine.

What about you? In your bedroom? In the living-room? On the toilet? Not with my book, damn it!

… … …

The detailed question "When?"

When is it happening?

Me: *in 2021*

This detail might not always be that important, but in this case, this year was pretty hectic. Thus, when you're acting in a scene that takes place in a different time period, you must adapt to the given circumstances of that era.

What about you?

… … …

Me: *summertime. August 27th.*

The seasons have a very important effect on us. A lot of details entail a lot of changes in our behavior and environment. To me it's the temperature, what I'm wearing, the fact that I'm working with the window open, which means a different relation to the sounds coming from outside, the air, etc. The pleasure that I have when working while others are on vacation, the feeling of being apart, which is connected to an absurd feeling of pride in wanting to be different from the others.

The date, in this case, doesn't really have an effect on me. But it's still important to specify it, because in certain cases, other dates could affect my behavior. Let's imagine that it's a Sunday night or New Year's Eve. Working on those nights would have an impact on me, like a bit of pride mixed with an involuntary but inevitable feeling of sadness ….

What about you? What season? What day? What time?

… … …

Me: *a Wednesday.*

However, the day of the week has an effect on me. The beginning of the week always instills dynamism in me and, for the best and for the worst, a feeling of being connected to the frenzy of the world. At the end of the week, it's excitement: anticipating the weekend, feeling like a hard worker. Thursday, I feel strangely obscure. Wednesday reminds me of recess at school.

What about you? What day is it? What's your relation to each day of the week? Nothing in particular? That would surprise me.

... ...

Me: *12:55 am.*

Certain times of the day or night sometimes have a magical feeling to me, black or white magic ... as if there's a kind of higher force that escapes me, that has either targeted me or chosen me.

When it's close to 1am, for me, it means a different portion of the night is setting in, which means I now have to make a decision: whether I work late into the night and early morning or not. If I do, this will have consequences on my actions: rescheduling appointments the next day, risking (sometimes with pleasure) being offset with the rest of the world, etc.

What about you? How does this particular hour feel to you? In general, what's your favorite hour? It depends on the day? Just as it also depends on the time zone, whether it's summer or wintertime, the season, etc.

... ...

The detailed "objective"

Why am I here: what is my objective?

Me: *I want to make progress in writing this book.*

This objective is the reason that I'm here. That is my target. And it's the will to reach that target that's making me think, concentrate, type on my computer, etc. This willingness is creating the continuous flow of subtext in me: my thought process, my choices, my "real questions" (see the sub-chapter entitled "Real questions"), such as "Is what I'm writing clear enough?", "Have I chosen the right path?", "Will the readers take what I'm saying seriously?", "Will they really play the game by answering the questions?"

This willingness to reach my objective is also mainly, but not exclusively, what's influencing my choice of actions to execute. Which are, more or less consciously, to succeed.

What about you? What's your objective?

... ...

Have fun listening to your inner world, to truly experience what your objective is making you feel. Also check out what actions that it pushes you to execute. Truly listen to yourself.

... ...

Now, formulate your objective in the two ways that we brought up earlier. First, the wording that paints the overall picture: "I want ..." then the wording that specifies more clearly which change you desire: "I want to change so and so from ... to ...." Try to be as precise as possible and see how your choice of words impacts you.

Maybe right now you're thinking to yourself that there's nothing that you want to change, that you're just enjoying reading the book. If that's the case, great! But the fact alone that you're reading this book indicates, necessarily, a desire for change. This desire for change can be simple: "I want to change from not knowing what the book's about to knowing what it's about," or "I want to change from not knowing about the Method to discovering it and eventually mastering it."

That being said, even though reading this book involves a desire for change, it's not intense dramaturgically speaking. Well, unless …?

… … …

Unless there are high stakes involved, or you have pretty strong obstacles.

The detailed "motivations"

What's pushing me to want to accomplish my objective: what are my motivations?

Me: *my desire to understand human beings. My passion for the Method. My desire to share this passion and make it more accessible and understandable. My love of cinema. Of art. My desire for it to be of better quality more often than it is at the moment, more transcendental, more awakening. Making my contribution to the edifice of the Method. My wish for actors to no longer have to hear any bullshit. Fun. Financial gain. Ego.*

Obviously, I'm not connected to all of these motivations at once, all the time. But the one that I am connected to will clearly influence my thoughts, my work, my actions, and even the way I execute them. When I'm connected to "My passion for the Method," my inner world is flooded with actors' performances, whose work fascinates me: Jack Nicholson, Rosamund Pike, Marlon Brando, Anne Hathaway, Mickey Rourke, Naomi Watts, etc. And when I'm connected to "My desire to share this passion and make it more accessible and understandable," my inner world switches to other kinds of sources: the idiots who put down the Method without knowing anything about it, without even recognizing the undeniable fact that it brought to light ingenious actors. Also the lunatics who treat it like a religion.

Let us mention that each of our motivations is a well of details. When I'm connected to Jack Nicholson, I'm not thinking of him in a general way. I'm thinking of him precisely in certain movies, particular scenes, and particular moments of these scenes. My inner world naturally connects to the basketball scene in *One Flew Over the Cuckoo's Nest*, by the great Milos Forman. Or the toilet scene in the disturbing *About Schmidt*, by Alexander Payne.

These sources come naturally in the real situation that I'm living here and now, but the tough part is that it doesn't happen the same way in a fictional situation. The Method offers actors many possibilities of tools so that they can truly relate to a fictional situation, by connecting to imaginary or real details that will help them fully believe in the situation and trip out. That belief is what will make them think, act, and feel *as if* all of it was true. And it's that truthfulness that will strongly impact the audience and make them trip out too.

In the end, this is really what it's all about: tripping out and sending on a trip!

What about you? What are your motivations?

… … …

You see how many details they're made of? Single out the ones that impact you the most.

… … …

The detailed "Stakes"

What are the stakes?

Me: *if I reach the objective that I've set for myself, I'll reap many different types of benefits from this project: personal, professional, ethical, financial … I'll have reached the height of my ambition, of my aspirations … I'll be very proud of myself, maybe I'll even be recognized by some people that I admire and respect … Method Acting Center, the school that I founded, might even profit from it too, new opportunities will arise …*

Just like the motivations, the stakes are made up of sources that enrich my inner world. These sources are also composed of very specific details.

What about you? What's at stake for you? What do you have to lose or to gain, depending on whether you accomplish your objective or not?

… … …

Now, take a moment to connect to what you have to gain. Whatever it might be, observe how the sources coming to the surface are stuffed with details.

I'm imagining that some of you have the motivation to get roles. If that's the case, do your sources seem vague? I doubt that. Really observe them, look at the details, identify the ones that speak to you the most.

… … …

The detailed "obstacles"

What are the obstacles standing between me and my objective?

Me: *I'm a little tired tonight.*

It's annoying me and making me want to surpass myself.

Me: *I'm hungry.*

That's taking away my concentration … Pho soups and spring rolls are floating around my mind. There's nothing to eat here besides my peanuts and I'm kind of happy that I haven't even touched them: I've just beaten an obstacle.

Me: *I have quite a few other things that I have to take care of.*

That's also taking away my focus and is the reason that I'm occasionally losing sight of my objective. A bunch of subtext is flooding me: "Should I be taking care of such and such problem instead?"

Me: *that stupid coffee machine.*

Which is, like I've been explained to many times, supposed to be easy to use. This reminds me of how suspicious I always am when I read "easy open" on packages that apparently required the expertise of some guy who did prestigious studies in engineering. People are actually paid to invent these openings! What a weird job! Maybe they make easy open packaging that isn't actually that easy to open on purpose, as a kind of revenge for having to make other people's lives simpler? But no one forced them to choose that kind of job. Unless someone actually did? Maybe the guy's father was the pioneer of easy opens and made his son promise, on his deathbed, to keep the legacy of the easy opens alive? And maybe his son tried to tell him "But dad, I want to be an actor!" Then his mother said: "Can't you do anything to honor your father?" before bursting into tears. That scenario just made me think of Sylvia, my own mother, who always encouraged me to follow my passion. Which reminds me that I haven't seen her in a long time, but that I can feel her, wherever she might be. Sometimes quite vividly. Like right now for instance. I can see her. I'm thanking her. I love her deeply. Has she reincarnated somewhere? If she has, that means that right now, my mom is younger than me. Maybe I've already met her? Could it have been that little girl at the movies the other day, who kept looking at me as if she had something funny to share with me? What if my mother was actually a little boy now? You see, it's these kinds of distractions that pulls you away from your objective: that's an obstacle.

So, I finally get back to work, but another obstacle comes to mind and suddenly catapults me miles away from my computer …

Me: *Mona.*

Why didn't she answer the text I sent her the day before yesterday? Did she think it was too heavy? Should I text her again? No way, that would make it even worse! Or maybe I'm just paranoid … She could be thinking about me. She's so magical! Ok, that's enough David! Get back to work now (connection to the objective). Maybe she'll be intrigued by my book (the stakes) … but where is this deep attraction to her that I feel coming from? Her aura, distant and devoted at the same time, almost sardonic? The tasteful combination of aristocracy and street-savvy that emanates from her? Does she feel the same attraction to me? I know I didn't dream it all, we definitely shared something real the first time we met, as well as every time that we've met up since … Why did she specially want to show me the flame tattoo on the back of her neck? The way that she parted her jet-black hair to show me … The smell of fig perfume that waved over me at that exact moment …

Ugh, obstacles, obstacles, and more obstacles!!! But they're partially what influences my choice of actions: rereading my notes, re-concentrating. Hey, a cup of coffee could help me. *Ugh! That damn machine!* Re-obstacle.

When I say that it's mainly the friction between the motivations, the stakes and the actions on one side and the obstacles on the other side, that brings the energy of a scene to life, I hope you understand what I mean a little better now.

What about you? What are your obstacles?

... ...

Connect to one of your obstacles, all the while trying to accomplish your objective. Do you feel the battle that it sparks in your inner world? Do you feel the good or bad energy that it creates? Observe how you embody it, how you physicalize it. There will be an effect on your body or your facial expression, no matter how subtle it might be.

Disconnect from your obstacle and feel the inner differences (meaning your inner world) and the outer differences (meaning physicalization) that happen in you.

... ...

Just as a reminder, physicalization doesn't just happen out of nowhere, it's the inner world that provokes it. When physicalization is forced and created artificially, the acting becomes fake; actors become circus animals. They end up unnaturally imitating a result, whereas true actors will create the process that brings about the result organically.

The detailed "actions"

What am I doing to beat my obstacles in order to accomplish my objective?

Me: *wandering around the coffee machine, on yet another observation round. Attempting negotiation with it. Splashing some water on my face. Looking for ideas that get me motivated. Seeing them come to life in a way that excites me. Re-energizing. Concentrating. Re-concentrating.*

Concerning the physical actions, I splash some water on my face but I also do other things: sometimes I re-adjust the chair, light up a cigarette, chew gum, attempt to make myself some coffee, etc.

The physical actions form the skeleton of a scene.

Concerning the psychophysical actions, I wander around the coffee machine on an observation round, negotiate with it, look for ideas that get me motivated, energize, concentrate, re-concentrate, write, lose the thread, etc.

The psychophysical actions form the muscles of a scene.

What do you think—when I'm typing on my computer keyboard, is the action physical or psychophysical?

... ...

For those of you who want the answer right away, you can check out part VI entitled "*Aaaaaaaaaand ACTION(S)!!!*" As a matter a fact, you can all go check it out. Because even though actions are literally one of the two key elements of the Method (the other one being sources), they're often forgotten about or neglected.

... ...

It turns out that I'm going to be working late into the night, so that decision brings about other actions: sending a few texts to reschedule appointments for the next day, questioning myself on whether this decision is really a good idea or not, arguing with the coffee machine again, etc.

Among all of these actions, there are those triggered by my objective, my motivations and the stakes, and those triggered by my obstacles.

In the first category, we can find (amongst other actions) concentrating, looking for ideas that motivate me, bringing them to life on the page that you're now reading.

In the second category, we can find (amongst other actions) stretching, splashing water on my face (which are directly related to the obstacle of being tired), re-adjusting my chair, composing myself after thinking about Mona too much, etc.

What about you? What physical and psychophysical actions are you doing?

... ...

For instance, if you've had more than enough of this book, so you rip it apart and throw it in the garbage, is that a physical or psychophysical action?

... ...

Define the actions that are triggered by your objective, your motivations and the stakes, and those that are triggered by your obstacles.

... ...

– CUT –

When taking on a "fictional" situation, if you answer the W.W.W. questions with just as much precision as we've been doing, while taking the time to search for the details that speak to you and you're still not kept busy on stage ... Well, in that case, neither I nor the Method can help you and you should be seriously concerned about your mental well-being.

However, if you start to feel, even for just a short moment, busy with something other than the audience and yourself, then you're on the right track.

Now you just need to make those short moments last a little longer, little by little until the entire scene is an uninterrupted continuum of thoughts and actions that eventually bring emotions. That's what we call living moment to moment.

While we're on the subject, let's take the time to strangle yet another false idea (which might be the most harmful to actors) about acting in general and especially the Method: actors work directly on their emotions. *False! Incredibly false!!!*

Actors who have an actual work method very rarely work *directly* on their emotions. Emotions are a derived product, just like dialogue. But derived from what? From the honest belief that actors have in their objectives, their motivations, the stakes and their obstacles, if they have done detail-oriented work. In a nutshell: if actors truly believe that they must reach their objective, pushed by clear, specific motivations and with high stakes, and suddenly they're confronted by obstacles that might stop them from succeeding, emotions just come about naturally. Just like in real life!

Living moment to moment is as if actors were weaving a design in front of the audience. This design is born from actors' focus and their belief in what they're doing. Then, little by little, the audience too focuses on the fictional situation that's happening and their belief is stimulated.

While watching actors ask themselves all of these questions and embodying the answers on stage, the audience starts asking themselves a ton of questions too, about the fictional situation. Of course, they end up wanting the answers to these questions and that's why they end up paying close attention to what's happening on stage: they've identified with what's going on. They're not only watching a show now, they've found themselves on a spiritual journey along with the character.

That's mostly what I meant when I was talking about transcendence earlier. That's one of the things that makes our profession so noble.

Does all of this make sense to you? Ok, now let's try out the W.W.W. questions with a fictional situation.

Creating a fictional W.W.W. situation

Here's something that I often encourage actors that I coach to try out: we're going to make up a situation from scratch. It can include fictional elements, but shouldn't be that far from what you can relate to. It shouldn't involve a made-up character either. Also, don't reveal any private elements from your life, at least not as elements in the plot. Especially if you're planning to perform this in a class or in front of an audience. Some of you might be surprised that we're not just working with a plot that's already written. Here are four reasons why we're doing it this way:

1. To develop the actors' imagination.
2. To help them truly understand what a dramaturgical situation is.
3. To intentionally start from scratch, with no inhibiting preconceptions, which often trap us when approaching already existing works of art.
4. To help actors realize that their work doesn't lie with the words, the dialogue, but all the rest. Having to create a situation from scratch *that doesn't include any lines* is a radical way to understand that.

Yes, I know that you guys aren't here to be writers. Don't worry about trying to create a masterpiece that will forever change humanity. Even though that motivation might seem selfless, to my knowledge, it has never actually given birth to a masterpiece. And anyway, that's not the point of this exercise: you're here to be an actor.

Here are some basic examples of situations: cleaning your room, waiting for someone, getting ready to go out and eat a Pho soup and some spring rolls, etc. Despite the apparent simplicity of these situations, that doesn't mean that they should become anecdotal. To make sure that doesn't happen, you need to give these situations relatively high stakes.

If you've decided that you're getting ready to go out and eat a Pho soup and some spring rolls, don't get ready to go out and eat a Pho soup and some spring rolls "just like any other day." Unless the situation is already inherently faced with certain stakes. How could that be?

Start the exercise: really look for the answer. How can getting ready to go out and eat a Pho soup and some spring rolls have *stakes*?

... ...

Did you find the answer? Did you look for it? Truly look for it, and remember: *It is not enough for actors to know the facts; they must turn it into experience.* To be able to do that, really do the exercise.

... ...

Ok. Did you find something that works for you? Does it really speak to you? Does it make the *stakes higher*? Good then.

Personally, here's what I found: despite my irrepressible temptation to go eat a Pho soup and some spring rolls, the top model in me is harassing me to lose a few pounds ... More importantly, Mona works at the Vietnamese restaurant where I get my Pho soup. If I go there, she might see it as pressuring her to answer my text. Before creating your situation, make sure that you're respecting the following protocol ....

The W.W.W. protocol

Apart from the five safety rules that you must respect at all times in acting and that I'm purposely going to remind you of here:

1. Do not hurt yourself or others, in any way.
2. Do not grope yourself or others.
3. Do not ingest any alcohol or drugs that strongly alter your state of mind.
4. Never reveal your sources.
5. Always make sure you're having fun in your work.

… the W.W.W. questions that you're about to create have to follow these four conditions as well:

1. Being alone in the situation.
2. Not miming anything, doing real actions. Besides, obviously, everything that has to do with our safety rules: violence, sex, drug and alcohol use, as well as strong medication.
3. Not speaking *verbally*.
4. Work on the situation beforehand, alone, before performing it. It's not an improvisation, at least not in the way we usually mean it.

That last one often brings actors who are just discovering the W.W.W. questions to ask this: "What is there to work on, if I'm not allowed to talk or don't have any lines?"
Do you know the answer?

… … …

If you don't, let me remind you that you're not allowed to talk *verbally*.
Does that help you?

… … …

By the way, how can you talk in other ways besides verbally, if you can't even mime anything?
Do you know the answer?

… … …

That's one of the major points of the exercise: liberating actors from lines. Or at least to help them truly understand, with their heart and soul, that creating and embodying a situation doesn't consist of depending on words. Exactly like in real life! Because *acting, just like living, is not talking before anything else*.

So, by working on situations that have no words, actors are faced with their true mission: bringing an imaginary situation to life, on a physical, psychological, and emotional level. *Not on a verbal level!* Which is and must remain a derived product of physical, psychological, and emotional life.

Not one second of our lives goes by without those three aspects being present. Conversely, there are many moments in our lives when we don't talk. But whether the scene that you have to act out contains lines or not, your job is to create the subtext that we've been talking about. That's exactly what we mean when we say, *"Don't act out what's written in black, act out what's written in white; and since there's nothing written, it's up to you to create it!"* The subtext is first and foremost what gives life to moments, which then creates words. Even if sometimes that "first and foremost" and "then" are only spaced apart by a few milliseconds.

Here's an example: when you're cold, is it that feeling that makes you move and speak or is it saying "I'm cold"? Even if the words we say sometimes have an effect on us, they always come from an internal or external connection.

When you reunite with someone that you love, the person doesn't appear because you say "It's so great to see you old pal!" You said these words because you saw the person (external connection), which sparked what you feel for them (internal connection) which, only then, created the words "It's so great to see you old pal!"

Thus, the main goal of the Where–When–Why questions is to help actors understand, with their hearts and souls, the *fundamental* importance of subtext. We'll be exploring how to create it in this chapter and throughout this whole book. It's made up of the behavior, gestures, attitudes, beats, pauses, and actions that are derived from internal or external connections, which we call sources. These sources can come from your imagination as well as your personal experience. But how do we choose which ones to use?

... ...

Actors will choose their sources in accordance with the objective, the motivations, the stakes and the obstacles of the situation.

It's the combination of the actors' sources that creates the subtext. This subtext animates actors who physicalize it: this is the way that they give life to their character and to the situations that they're living through.

The subtext is then expressed and physicalized through the only interfaces between you and the audience or the camera, which are your body, your face, your eyes, your energy, and *only sometimes* but *always thereafter*, your voice.

Now, back to the question that actors often ask me when working on this exercise for the first time: "What is there to work on if I'm not allowed to talk, I don't have any lines and I can't even mime anything?"

Let me answer that by another question: If you had to play a character that was mute, like the main character in *Children of a Lesser God* by Mark Medoff, who goes through any number of situations, ranging from being madly in love to intense relationship crises, what would you work on?

... ...

You probably figured it out. But just to make sure that we're on the same wavelength, I'll just say that obviously you'd work on what we just talked about: the subtext.

Whether actually mute or not, you could say that *all* characters are mute in one way or another. Just like us, mutes always express themselves non-verbally. I'd advise you to keep that metaphor in mind whenever you're working on embodying a situation.

All characters, just like all human beings, are mostly "mute."

Your turn!

Time to play!

You'll have to fend for yourselves now!

Ok, fine, I'll do the exercise too, and I'll keep working with the Pho soup and Mona! But I'm counting on you: do your own W.W.W. exercise too. Seriously.

Write it down first. Then you'll embody it.

The question "Where?" to embody

Where am I?

Me: *at my place. In France. Paris. In the 2nd district. On a long boulevard. Montmartre Boulevard. First in the living-room, then in my bedroom.*

What about you?

… … …

The question "When?" to embody

When is it happening?

Me: *2021. The winter. February 20th. A Friday. 5:29 pm.*

What about you?

… … …

The "objective" to embody

Why am I here: what is my objective?

Me: *I want to get ready to go out and eat a Pho soup and some spring rolls.*

Which I'll also formulate like this: *I want to change from working on my book at my place, starving and being harassed by visions of flying spring rolls, to: being at a Vietnamese restaurant with a good Pho soup and some spring rolls.*

What about you?

… … …

Which you'll also formulate like this:

… … …

The "motivations" to embody

What's pushing me to want to accomplish my objective: what are my motivations?

Me: *starvation! Well … Ok, fine, gluttony more than anything. The fact that there's nothing in my fridge, which means grocery shopping and cooking, which would take a lot more time. Wanting to take a break, breathe a little … which almost always helps me to get back to work, with lots of fresh ideas.*

What about you?

… … …

The "stakes" to embody

What are the stakes?

Me: *saving time. The possibility of coming back with lots of new ideas. Pleasure. Re-energizing a little. Seeing Mona. The flame tattoo on the back of her neck. Smelling her fig perfume. Unless she sees me showing up as pressuring her.*

What about you?

… … …

The "obstacles" to embody

What are the obstacles standing between me and my objective?

Me: *the top model in me who's chanting his recipe for miracle weight-loss. The fact that they might burn incense at the restaurant, which would give me a massive headache since I'm allergic to incense and that would make it harder to get back to work. My doubts about the Mona situation, ever since she didn't answer my text. The fact that going to the restaurant where she works could destroy the "Mister Mysterioso technique" that I'm using, and would turn me into "Mister Heavyoso instead." The fact that I can't find my bad-ass hottie jacket, the one that she always compliments me on.*

What about you?

… … …

The "Actions" to embody

What am I doing to beat my obstacles in order to accomplish my objective?

Me: *(in terms of physical actions) Saving my changes. Turning off my computer. Getting a quick wash-up. Putting on a bit of perfume, just in case Mona's there, but not* too much, just in case Mona's there. Taking my keys, my wallet, my phone, just in case Mona answers my text from the day before yesterday. Leaving my place, locking the door. Etc.

What about you? In terms of physical actions:

... ...

Me: *(in terms of psychophysical actions)* Convincing myself to take a break. Deciding whether to go to the Vietnamese place or not. Negotiating with the top model. Ratifying my decision to go. Writing down some ideas that I had, so that I won't forget them. Trying to understand why my flash drive shuts down sometimes. Making a mental note to buy a new one. Checking myself out in the mirror at least fifty times. Boosting myself. Reminding myself of my "big moments" of seduction, of which no one was more surprised than me. Questioning my decision to go after all. Agreeing with the top model. Degrading myself. Re-boosting myself. Remembering that more than half of the other guys are assholes with women. Etc.

What about you? In terms of psychophysical actions:

... ...

– CUT –

So? Did you play the game? Did you really go into detail with the W.W.W. questions? Did you find details that spoke to you?

ALWAYS REMEMBER: *You're not here to merely answer the W.W.W. questions mentally, factually, and coldly, you're here to literally translate your answers physically and psychologically.* Soon, we'll talk about all of the tools that the Method has to offer to help you believe and truly embody the situation that you came up with.

But first, you need to try out …

The embodiment of the W.W.W. questions

Nature does not hurry, yet everything is accomplished.
(Lao Tzu)

Time to play!

Now you can explore your questions physically, concretely. See what works, mainly using your imagination and, why not, using a bit of your personal experiences. Use the detailed answers we did together when talking about our "here and now" situations as examples. And be inspired by life. Be inspired by you. Take baby steps. Go slow. Try to feel out the given circumstances of the situation. Go into more detail with your objective. Do you really relate to it? What about your motivations? Rewind a little. Do you see the stakes? Try and try again. Layer by layer. What about the obstacles? If you really give it your all to try and find the details, you'll be surprised to find that you're believing and naturally playing the game. Let's quote this acting mantra again: *Our bodies, our minds, and our souls ask of us just one thing: TO TRIP OUT. But under one condition—that we don't take them for idiots.* In other words: *that you don't take yourself for an idiot.* And inevitably: *that you don't take the audience for idiots.* Of course, some members of the audience might be, but don't run yourself into the ground with them. Raise them up.

Don't look for the emotion intentionally. Just be aware of the internal and external details and soon you'll be feeling, even if it's little by little, the magic of the "self-bluff," the "moment to moment" in acting.

Don't try to believe in every single facet of a situation in one go. It's basically impossible. Even the greatest painters don't create their masterpieces in just one brush. They dig deeper, they search, they pay attention to details, and little by little, the canvas comes to life. Gently. Naturally. Organically.

—CUT—

Don't be too much of a perfectionist while working on embodying the W.W.W. questions. If it's perfect, great! If it's not, that's great too. If it is, you'll be able to learn what works with you; if it isn't, you'll not only learn what works with you but also what doesn't work with you. Ask yourself lots of questions about what worked, but don't go into a whole university headachy analysis. Don't create a distance between you and yourself. Just ask yourself what worked and what didn't, while accepting as neutrally as possible the answers that you find. We'll be exploring all of it together throughout this book. But I have a feeling that some of you want to try out actual scenes. Act out something that you didn't write. Distance yourselves from your daily routine. Get into a role. Am I right? Well, I have a surprise for all of you … you're going to embody *my* W.W.W. situation!

Time to play!

Take baby steps. Go slow. In detail. Nope, that is neither rambling on nor a typo, that is a purposeful reminder and you'll find many others throughout this book. Go back to the answers that I gave in my W.W.W. questions and embody the scene physically. Don't worry yet about creating a character. Concentrate on living moment to moment, just like when you worked on your own questions; detail after detail, thought after thought, action after action. Let your imagination talk, it has a lot to say to you. But don't trap it inside your head. Embody what it's saying. Let it infuse. To be able to be sincerely preoccupied by the situation, turn my W.W.W. exercise into *your* W.W.W. exercise. For instance, if you can't relate to writing a book on acting or if this *mise en abyme* is too confusing, what should you do? Go ahead, actually look for the answer.

... ...

Obviously, it's not about changing the action, since the script has clearly indicated that the character (me) is typing on his computer in the beginning of the scene. You have to keep the same action and what it means to the character, but find an activity that speaks to you and is a match or an equivalent in importance. This way, you can embody the action with faith. It's actually simple: just ask yourself what *you* would be writing with as much passion. Would it be your diary, a poem, a flyer, your acceptance speech at the Oscars, a love letter? Then get on your computer and actually start typing.

Same thing for any other aspect of this scene, as well as any future scene that you'll act out. If the situation immediately sparks your imagination, work with that. If it doesn't, find matches or equivalents in you.

You're not that hungry? Imagine a different physical pleasure. You don't like Pho soup? Replace it by your favorite dish.

Now, look me in the eyes and tell me that you didn't think of someone when I was talking about Mona.

... ...

If you didn't, choose someone you're in love with, or who is at least very much in your thoughts. But actually choose someone! We'll need them, maybe in life, but most definitely in many of the exercises in this book.

... ...

So? Your "fantasized" loved one doesn't have a flame tattoo on the back of his/her neck? No problem. Find the detail about this person that moves you, drives you crazy.

... ...

Unless you just haven't met this person yet? Too bad ... but great! You can invent him/her from scratch! Oh, right! Don't forget your hottie jacket.

– CUT –

Don't be discouraged at all if you leave the situation (it'll happen often at first, then from time to time), if your belief cuts out a little. There's any number of tools from the Method that are here to help you. You're about to discover these tools in the next chapter. On two conditions:

1) That you keep playing the game.

2) That you accept to embark on an exceptional adventure—and I'm weighing my words here! The adventure that is exploring one of the most fascinating and vast galaxies of the universe: yourself.

5 Exploration

Know thyself ... But don't forget that you can change.
                                                    (Thales of Miletus ... and me!)

What a vast subject this can be! It becomes the curriculum of any actor who has any self-respect, as his/her only instrument is himself/herself.

What a vast subject! Because the subject that you have to know—thyself—is constantly changing. That's one of the main reasons why an actor, like any true artist really, must constantly be searching and learning.

What a vast subject! Because exploring yourself doesn't consist of remaining on the surface, it's about discovering all of the mysterious lands that you're made of, from the brightest to the darkest ones.

What vast subjects! That's why "Exploration" is the longest, but also the most important part of this book, because of the many tools that you're about to discover and rediscover with many different experiments, exercises, and games. Thus, "Know thyself" becomes the actor's nourishment and fuel.

So, in order to nourish the embodiment of your Where–When–Why questions, as well as the many other scenes that you'll act out, we're finally going to explore all of these tools from the Method. We're going to learn how they can help you through the many challenges that these subjects offer.

He who stops, is mistaken.
(Louis Pauwels[1])

That quote perfectly sums up the attitude that you need to have when going into exploration. Exploration is about knowing yourself as much as possible, in order to be able to better "use" yourself. But the challenge is in the fact that the actors' instrument is constantly mutating. And this comes with yet another challenge: the actors' art is unique in the sense that actors are the instrumentalist, the instrument, and sometimes, with the help of their life experiences and maybe their coaches, the creators of the instrument. All at the same time. Pianists play the piano, painters play with colors and paintbrushes, actors play with themselves, all the while constantly *building and re-building themselves*.

Take a second to imagine if a pianist was the pianist, the piano and the manufacturer of the piano all at the same time. Not only would he seem crazy for attempting this weird

---

[1] Oh, Louis! What a master he was, a gifted writer, an awakened journalist, a pioneer in so many ways ... A visionary of the press, free, too much for some. He was the creator of a few of the most incredible newspapers in the world—*Planet, Plexus, It's a Question of* ... An iconoclastic mystic, a poet. One of the greatest and noblest men of the twentieth century. A beautiful, true soul. Unmatched. An example.

triple-faceted adventure (which is often what actors go through), he'd also have to discover and build the instrument's framework, as well as its keys, strings, pedals. He'd have to make sure that every minor detail was in place so that his piano would be in perfect condition, well tuned, efficient, and ready to perform …

And all the while discovering the ins and outs of his piano, the pianist would also have to learn how to play it. This would be made even more difficult by the fact that the piano wasn't even done being built yet and the musician was already being asked to play it.

And to top it all off, imagine that the piano had a life of its own and was constantly changing. What if the piano itself created new strings, got rid of others, invented new keys, added white ones, black ones, etc. Just imagine if the piano was in constant metamorphosis.

I warned you—it's a vast subject! That's why … *Actors who aim to master their art must be armed with the patience of a sphinx, a fiery passion, and a solid method. Rock-solid.*

Here's another allegory that relates a little more to actors but that's just as paradoxical as the piano comparison: being the marionette that's letting it loose on stage and being the puppeteer at the same time, who's perfectly controlling the marionette in order for it to be able to let loose. The tools needed to master the two ends of this paradox are to help identify and operate the actors' physical, psychological, and emotional levers. Some of the tools and exercises are very hands-on and directly related to acting, like the W.W.W. questions that we worked on. Others are more like satellites, orbiting around acting: the connection to acting will seem less obvious. To better understand their purpose, I'd compare them to the push-ups that a basketball player does during practices. Of course, we never see the player do any during a match, but the push-ups strengthen his muscles, reinforce his endurance, and so ultimately help him to perform better. An athlete doing push-ups is just like an actor working, for instance, on listening; both are needed satellite experiments/exercises.

Whether it's hands-on or satellite, some tools and exercises will speak to you more than others. Try them all though, without prejudice, many different times before definitively choosing those that work best for you.

To freak out or not to freak out?
Stage fright

Let us thank our enemies, for they are the ones who sharpen us.

In order to delve right into the major subject of stage fright, which is the actor's public enemy number 1, let's start with a ridiculously easy exercise. Once again, I'm counting on you! Really do it!

Time to play!

Choose a simple physical action that you're completely used to doing: making yourself coffee, pasta, or a twelve-cheese omelet, getting dressed or undressed, taking a shower, going to the bathroom, etc.

But BE CAREFUL! Keep this instruction in mind throughout the entire exercise: JUST BE NATURAL!!!

... ...

—CUT—

So? How was it? Were you able to do the action while being natural? *Really, truly natural?* If that's really the case, I tip my hat to you. Without any sarcasm whatsoever. However, if it didn't feel at all natural to you, that means you're all right! Really. Because the instruction "Be natural" is by far the worst thing you can say to an actor, or to anyone for that matter. For one very simple reason: having to keep in mind that you must be natural, is absolutely anti-natural! It's the absolute definition of the absence of natural.

"*Just be natural, for fuck's sake!*" Isn't that what we usually say to ourselves when we're in social situations that make us uncomfortable? From what I've seen, yes. Does it work? From what I've seen, no. Not at all. It actually has the complete opposite effect!

Drilling "Be natural!" into your head is actually one of the tools that I advise actors to use when they have to play the part of someone who's painfully shy. And it almost always works. You could even say that:

The essence of painfully shy people is being focused on their behavior.
The essence of great actors is being focused on everything except their behavior!

Time to play!

You probably won't be able to put this next exercise into practice right away, unless you're reading this book in the middle of a meeting organized by the horrible P.A.N.D.E.M.I.C.—the Pro Annihilation and Nuclear Destruction of the Ever-persistent Method Induced Characters group. But the next time that you're in a really awkward social situation, say to yourself "Be natural" over and over again. "Look, take that bottle over there and pour yourself a glass *super* naturally," "Flirt with that girl or guy, but naturally" and last but not least, the repulsive "Smile at him/her naturally." Keep those catchphrases in your head like a broken record and watch the situation get progressively worse.

—CUT—

In my humble opinion, there's only one other instruction given to actors that's as stupid as "Be natural," and that's "Be yourself." What generally ensues is a pathetic imitation of the image that we'd like people to think that we have of ourselves. Yeah, reread that sentence if you have to, it does actually mean something. Very surprisingly, "Be natural" and "Be yourself" seem to be the two fetish phrases that most agents, casting directors, directors and so-called acting coaches love yelling at actors. Is it a trap that they set up deliberately or total lack of knowledge about acting? Yelling at an actor *"Look, it's not that hard, we're just asking you to be natural!"* is as if you were yelling at a tightrope walker, who's trying to find his balance on a thin rope that's about 2,000 meters above concrete *"Look, it's not that hard, we're just asking you to walk, one foot in front of the other! Capiche?"* Yeah, well, hoping that at least 75 percent of these "professionals of the profession" (as Jean-Luc Godard used to say, to make fun of them) have a little bit of smarts, a lot of compassion and endless patience is like hoping that a stuffed tomato could be a Boeing 747.

Also, even though playing is truly an instinct—babies and animals are solid proof of that—playing has also ironically become "unnatural." As I said while we were working on the W.W.W exercise: Our *very* strange education teaches us, at best, to censor our emotions. At worst, to not feel them at all, *especially* not in front of others and most definitely not in front of an audience. Then I said to get over this suppression and the stage fright that results from it, actors must learn to master two things that often go hand in hand. Knowing how to use your nerves to your advantage or knowing how to relax; being truly and deeply occupied on stage. You could think that "knowing how to use your nerves" is impossible and even counterproductive, because nerves are precisely the actor's sworn enemy. False. For two reasons:

1) A lot of scenes include a character that's nervous himself/herself, or has some sort of stage fright.

2) Stage fright contains a phenomenal, fabulous energy, which is a gift for any actor who knows how to use it.

A lot of scenes include a character that's nervous himself/herself, or has some sort of stage fright.

So sometimes, you can use your own stage fright, which becomes that of the character. As we said earlier, drama is only possible if the characters actually have problems to solve. They can't remain inactive, even in an ethereal world. Plus, they're often faced with high stakes. They live through internal and external conflict that puts pressure on them and makes them nervous, even if they try not to show it sometimes. With a case like this, try not to fight off your stage fright—include it in the scene instead. Let me think of a completely random example, like … Mona! In the W.W.W. exercise that you had to embody, the possibility of seeing Mona at the restaurant made the character feel vulnerable. So why not distort your stage fright to be able to use it in the scene?

I think one of the worst acting performances that I painfully had to watch was that of a pretty well-known actor, who was playing the part of a very nervous and anxious character very badly. The character's nerves were understandable, considering that he had to save the world. Everything could've gone splendidly if this idiot hadn't killed himself trying to overact the character's nerves, in order to make us believe that he, himself wasn't nervous.

Just like trying to imitate a nutjob doesn't mean that you aren't one, trying to imitate being nervous doesn't mean that the audience can't see the actual nerves that you're trying to hide. So, if you're nervous and your character is too, use your own nerves rather than trying to imitate his or hers.

Stage fright contains a phenomenal, fabulous energy, which is a gift for any actor who knows how to use it.

We are truly capable of turning our stage fright into a strength. This is one of the many facets of the Method that I call the Aikido technique. For those who don't know, Aikido is a unique martial art, unique because it's not strictly about fighting your adversaries. It's about using your adversaries' own strength and muscle against themselves. Imagine for one second if some fierce colossal giant had a bone to pick with you and intended to crush you into dust … Trying to fight him off frontally would be hopeless. However, trying to fight him off from a different point of view, "obliquely," might help you win. Right at the moment that he's about to punch you in the face, if you're able to let yourself be guided by his strength, he'll most likely make himself fall over and will end up breaking his own teeth on the pavement. That's what I call the Aikido technique: using your weakness as a strength.

Well, more often than not, that's the attitude to have when facing stage fright. Don't try to fight it off frontally because that never works, and because the energy it offers is of great value. That energy is absolute pure adrenaline. It can serve in any number of scenes. It's up to actors to guide their stage fright towards the path that they need. To succeed, they'll have to kind of subject their stage fright to their inner world, which is orchestrated by their sources, which in turn are orchestrated by themselves. Some might counter that by saying that the very essence of stage fright is that it stops us from keeping our inner world under control, that it completely takes us over and weakens the smallest attempt at anything. Well, that's sometimes true and that's why the next chapter is about relaxation.

In a lot of cases, the sources of our inner world can completely influence our stage fright in our favor. But you can get to that only under one condition: having very, very, VERY strong sources. That's one of the things we'll talk about later in the sub-chapters "Sources" and "Reflex sources."

Now, I'm going to let you in on a huge, make that *ENORMOUS*, secret: stage fright is not a virus. You can't catch it, it's man-made. Saying "I have stage fright" is technically nonsensical. I have strep throat, but I *make* stage fright. From scratch. Mentally.

While going to the Vietnamese place, the closer I knew I was getting to Mona, the more the stress built up. The euphoria that I would've been feeling knowing I was going to see her soon was totally annihilated by her non-answer to my text from the day before yesterday. The fact that I was wearing my handsome hunk jacket was not making any difference whatsoever …. I just felt like the scratch paper version of myself. The top model's incessant venom didn't help at all: "Hottie, yeah right … piggy is more like it! Hey, Porky, did it ever cross your mind that maybe that's the reason Mona never texted you back?" He's right, it did, in fact, cross my mind. But there was no way that I was going to let him know that and told him "Shut up Brad!" The idea of not being able to just ask Mona why she didn't answer my text, like a well-tamed little boy, is giving me spoon-fed societal bullshit nausea and acid-suck-up reflux. Or maybe the answer's already there: maybe that was just her way of telling me to shut up or worse, maybe she has decided to ignore me forever! "Be natural!" I said to myself, "Be yourself, man!" ... which of course only multiplied my anxiety times ten ... and all of that for nothing, as I soon found out. "Not here! Holiday!" Min-Mân, the old Vietnamese guy told me. "Girl not here! Tomorrow here."

Anyway, I tried to save face by asking Min-Mân "What about Pho soup, here or not here?" "Here David, always here!" he said, while getting behind the counter and expertly cutting up meat with his kitchen sabers. "Pho not like women! Pho always here!" I had become a nervous wreck for nothing. Yet another experience that has proven to me that, more than half of the time, it's our mind that fabricates our stress and ergo, it fabricates stage fright.

Time to play!

Try out this experiment the next time you're feeling nervous about something. Stop for a second and connect yourself to a powerful source that makes you feel good. An idea, something or someone that/who affects you in a very strong and very positive way. Two things can and will happen, depending on the source you've chosen: either your nerves will calm down, maybe even disappear entirely; or the energy of your nerves will let itself be guided by the source.

Instead of seeing stage fright and stress as ferocious beasts or undefeated colossal giants, instead of allowing them to have diabolical superpowers, try regularly to transform your anxiety into curiosity: to be able to unlock and discover the energy it contains.

I've already had to coach actors in the "indifferent/I've already done it all" category, whose main problem was that they didn't have enough or any stage fright. They weren't necessarily bad actors. But their acting game remained weak and lacked that tremor of passion, if not life.

Even though Lee Strasberg was obsessed with relaxation for actors and was known for his endless meditation sessions, he often said "If you have stage fright, that means everything's ok, the machine is running well." Because, as we've been saying, our education has turned showing and living our emotions in front of other people feel so unnatural, that it's become stressful. Don't turn stage fright into your enemy, when it can be your most precious ally.

Ok, now that we've made peace with stage fright, let's try to learn how to live without it too. We'll need to for the scenes that absolutely cannot include it (of which there actually really aren't that many).

Relaxation

Nothing is more stressful for an actor than to be stressed out when he needs to be feeling the opposite. Telling him to relax just makes the situation worse ... unless you have actual relaxation tools to help him out with. That's one of the many things that the Method offers, but that's very much thanks to Buddha—meditation, yoga, and many other relaxation techniques are the foundation of the relaxation exercises that we put into practice. So if you're already familiar with those kinds of practices, you can skip this chapter. If you're not, let's get right into it. Here's a reminder of the four barriers that you need to break to be able to play the game:

1) Skepticism.

2) Pretending to be indifferent, or worse—*being* indifferent.

3) Being trivial.

4) An exclusively materialistic approach to life.

No worries, I'm not over here sitting in a lotus position and expecting you to worship some higher force. No, I'm not here to convert you to anything other than the Method. But after having tried them out, I have to say that many yoga and meditation exercises can help with a much deeper relaxation than most skeptics would realize. Also, to the nuts that are tougher to crack, let me remind you that meditation isn't only praised by mystics. To this day, it's used in sophrology, personal development, NLP, and many other types of practices. Even NASA has done profound and thorough research on these subjects, to see if these practices could be useful on long-term expeditions in space. Conditions where fear of the unknown or simply the stress of having to live with many others in a confined space could have very tragic consequences.

Still not convinced? Give up relaxation then and only play CEOs with high anxiety, bloodthirsty MMA fighters or junkies going through withdrawal.

So! Now that we've freed ourselves of the four vicious weights, let's explore two relaxation exercises. The first question that you need to ask yourself is "How do I feel?" Don't start judging your state of being, that won't get you anywhere. Just recognize it as what it is, a temporary state. Whatever the relaxation exercise, there are three conditions that you must always respect:

1) Always remain active, gently, but still active.

2) Always keep your body and mind connected, through visualization.

3) Make yourself feel good, which is by far the most important condition.

The objective of any relaxation is to reach what I call the "blank page" state. We'll talk about that again at the end of the chapter.

Time to play!

One of the keys of relaxation lies in one of the keys of life: breathing. Learning to breathe is fundamental in order to be able to relax. Let's try out an experiment: ask yourself how your breathing is right at this moment. Don't try to change it, don't judge it. Just observe it.

... ...

Is it fluid, agitated, deep? If it's fluid and deep, you're in the right state to continue the exercise. If it's not, do not stress, do not worry, do not judge yourself. Just "look at" your breathing. Visualize it.

... ...

Then follow the path it's taking in your body, pinpoint where it stops, what's straining it, what's blocking it.

... ...

Are you comfortably seated? Is the position you're in stopping your breathing from being deeper? Are you bent over, twisted, is your belt buckled too tight? Is your energy bottled up by pent-up stress, by unresolved problems? Don't judge yourself, just slowly stand up.

... ...

If you're feeling stress, agitation, worry, gesticulate and yell at the same time for about 10 seconds. Then stop and stay still. Not rigid, still. And take a moment to feel the energy created by the yelling and the movement.

... ...

Repeat the movement and the yelling about ten times. Make sure to take a moment each time to stop still and feel the energy in you. After these last rounds of gesticulating and yelling, stay still for a little longer. Not rigidly. And breathe. Deeply.

... ...

Now continue to visualize the path of your breathing and give a color to the air that you inhale. Choose a color that's warm, soothing, soft and that gives out a little bit of light. Maybe a warm orange color? Sky blue? Light pink? Inhale that color. Deeply. Slowly. Make sure that your stillness doesn't turn into rigidity. If you feel some tension in your foot for instance, very slightly move your foot around. If somewhere itches, scratch yourself. Otherwise, stay still, but not rigid. And keep breathing. Deeply. Slowly. Colorfully.

... ...

Visualize the path that the oxygen's following in your chest and without forcing it, try to guide your breathing down into your stomach.

... ...

Now visualize the particles of oxygen dispersing all through your body. Take your time with each one of your muscles and nourish them with the visualization of colorful oxygen particles.

... ...

Then each one of your organs. Take your time. Nourish them. Internally say hello to all of them. Greet your heart, your liver, your lungs. Thank them for being there, for always being on hand and faithful, nourish them with warm drops of oxygen, in harmonious and fluid waves, with lots of warmth. Take your time. Always. Acknowledge that you're here. As simple as that.

... ...

Breathe into your bones and watch the colorful, warm, soothing, fluid oxygen particles dance around. Say hello to your knees, your ankles, all of the joints. Let the light of the air that you're inhaling flow through them. Feel the wind of the oxygen whirl around them. Thank them for the mobility that they always provide you with. Same for your shoulders, your elbows, your wrists. Your fingers, each one of them. Precisely. Delicately. Here and now.

... ...

Feel the power of your attention when it's concentrated on your stomach, your ears, your brain. This attention is full of light. It's lighting up every part of your body that it touches.

... ...

Go into detail, with your mouth, your ears, your toes, your teeth, your tongue, every nail. Explore each particle of your body, give it your undivided attention, spill liquid, warm, colorful, nourishing light into it.

... ...

Once you've explored your entire body, explore your skin visually. Caress it with your attention, light it up with that liquid, warm, colorful, nourishing light.

... ...

Now feel the connections between each part of your body, still only with attention and visualization. Very gently move your head around and feel the waves of movement that go right to your feet. The waves of movement from your hands to your knees. Play around with connecting, uniting all of the parts of your body. Make them talk to each other, answer each other, feel each other out.

... ...

To finish up, intensify the color of the oxygen that's entering you, follow the path it's taking, make it dance around, make it more playful. Now let it radiate. Let the light that's coming through you shine. Feel your own presence. Feel the awareness that you have of that, which in turn multiplies your presence. Feel your body being coated in a much bigger body, in a body of light, in a body of energy. Your body of energy. Feel it all become bigger, pulsate, illuminate the space around you. Breathe.

... ...

—CUT—

Let's not wait too long. Here's another relaxation experiment/exercise.

Time to play!

Once again after a series of gesticulating and yelling, this one consists of lying on the floor and imagining that it's sand.

… … …

Then, limb by limb, muscle by muscle, feel the weight of your body. Try to use the weight to slowly bring each part of your body a little deeper into the sand.

—CUT—

Come on, one more.

Time to play!

Think of the conditions and elements in your everyday life that put you in a state of relaxation. Blunts, alcohol, MDMA or whatever else do not count here. Ask yourself what makes you feel good, what makes you feel comfortable. Slightly or deeply. A specific type of music? A voice? Peace and quiet? A taste? A texture, a painting, a hand, a smell? Sharpen your sense of relaxation by often asking yourself what soothes you.

… … …

Then test how you can use them in situations where you're nervous. First, use these elements hands-on in stressful situations. For instance, smelling a particular perfume that soothes you during a moment when you're stressed out, and you'll gradually identify the things that work the best with you.

… … …

Then test out the simple memory of one of these elements in a situation where you're feeling tense. Remember the details of the element that you've chosen; its color, its taste, the sound it makes, or their face, their eyes, etc. It might not be automatic, but you'll still be surprised to see that it works quite often. Also use what you learn during your relaxation sessions before playing scenes. Here's an example of something that comes up quite often—and I swear, this isn't a joke: one of the sources of profound well-being that is chosen by a lot of actors that I've encountered is … peanut butter! You see, sometimes all that you need is right in front of you, ordinary, everyday things that you're used to. Stay alert (not rigid!) and use what helps you. Little by little, you'll find exactly what you need to relax and be comfortable on stage. That'll be one step more towards turning *The* Method into *Your* Method.

—CUT—

Quick reminder: despite the many, many benefits that can be drawn from relaxation exercises, practicing being on stage regularly in acting classes with coaches is the best way to desacralize, demystify and thus, to de-stress.

To close the subject on relaxation finally, keep in mind that relaxation is not an end in itself. Maybe that seems obvious to you, but there are a lot of actors (often self-proclaimed "Method actors" actually) that like to display their relaxation on stage. They're watching themselves be comfortable and like to exhibit their insipid satisfaction with that. They no longer worry about the scene, the stakes, its dramaturgy, and are filled with this shallow pride at nothing else besides being able to be relaxed on stage. They're like sad circus animals—well-tamed, but soulless.

The soul of a scene resides in its dramaturgy, which is transcribed by the sources that make up the actor's inner world. The objective of relaxation is not the relaxation itself, it's to reach the "blank page" state that I talked about earlier. Apart from the scenes where he can and knows how to use his nerves, a stressed-out actor is like a page that's been scribbled on, crossed out, doodled on—it'll be impossible to write anything intelligible on it. The "blank page" state is a state of maximum availability, purity, that will allow the actor to kind of "write down" the sources from his inner world and then to physicalize them in the outer world, in an intelligible, touching, and impactful way.

Energization

As we just talked about, one of the clichés of Method Acting classes is to see actors that are so deeply relaxed that they become apathetic.

So, it's just as important to know how to energize yourself as how to relax yourself. To do that, we have a few easy exercises. Just like with the previous section on relaxation, we're not here to make some endless list, but to show actors the path to take. So, besides the exercises that we're about to do, I encourage you to check out books that are specifically about energy and energization.

Time to play!

Once you've reached the "blank page" state, you're available. But if you feel like you lack a bit of energy, all you have to do is gesticulate all over the place and yell, shake yourself, throw yourself into big movements and ample sounds.

That way, you'll finally get back the energy you need to get into a scene, even if you're playing a limp character.

—CUT—

That being said, even though a stressed-out actor can use his stress to the benefit of a character, that doesn't work for a limp actor who has to play a limp character. Just like you have to be very nimble in order to play a clumsy character, so as not to hurt your scene partners or yourself, you cannot play a limp character limply. The limpness cannot be naturalistic, it has to be realistic. It can't just be "ordinary, everyday" limpness, it has to be the essence, the definition of limpness. And acting out the essence of anything demands energy. More or less intense, but energy all the same.

Time to play!

Another way to get energized is by prolonging the exercise where you visualize your oxygen as light. By intensifying through visualization the colors and the speed at which it fills up, travels through and radiates your body, you'll quickly be feeling very energized.

If visualization isn't enough, add some movement.

—CUT—

Time to play!

Be careful not to confuse agitation and energization. For example, a surprisingly good energization exercise consists of moving in slow-motion, a little like Tai Chi. This one can also be used for relaxation. If you're truly invested in what you're doing and your entire body is active, the undivided attention that you're giving to each movement helps you feel the power of the energy that's in you and lets it emerge.

Energy can be born from gentleness.

The caress of a mother's hand on her little boy's cheek, the expertise with which she wipes his tears away ... a drop of oil that's *just* warm enough, that trickles down your back ... Has anyone ever lightly brushed a feather up against your eyelashes?

—CUT—

I'm going to be saying this over and over again, always be gentle with your "instrument," aka yourself. A guitarist can break his instrument at the end of a concert, because all he has to do is go buy a new one. You can't do that.

And yet, there's a particular attitude that seems to be spreading more and more among actors, not so much among actresses—wanting to suffer. Don't fall into that trap and beware of those kinds of actors. They're fakes, who confuse personal investment with egocentric masochism and going in deep with running into a brick wall. In short, all of the trouble they put into demonstrating their so-called perfectionism is actually just a mask that they put on to hide their lack of a solid method, not to mention self-confidence.

He who truly believes in himself and is truly prepared to go all the way doesn't need to demonstrate or prove anything. He believes in himself and goes all the way. Period.

Concentration

Concentration is definitely one of the most misunderstood and misguided facets of acting and life in general for that matter. Try out this experiment: ask some people to concentrate. Eighty percent of the time, they'll start by getting tense. For some obscure reason, the idea of concentration is connected with a type of internal tension in so many mindsets. That's quite a shame, because that tension dooms any chance of true concentration. Here's how we could sum up this type of approach: concentration that's concentrating on concentration. Again, this is a case of the snake biting its own tail. We're dealing with a sort of dead end cycle where energy is present, but is too hysterical. And so it inevitably ends up being completely futile.

It actually works the opposite. True concentration creates a cycle that remains open to outside factors, which in turn intensifies the internal energy. When actors have just started working on a scene, this type of concentration is only possible if they know how to use their stage fright or if they know how to reach the "blank page" state.

You could say that it's a state of being alert, but combined with no panic whatsoever and paradoxically very relaxed. Before getting into concentration exercises, I'll let the cheering crowd in on what they're dying to know: a bit of etymology. Concentration: the root-word "con," meaning "with, together" + "centration," extension of the word "center" = TO BE WITH ONE'S CENTER.

Therefore: *Concentration consists of being grounded in oneself, not imprisoned; this allows an openness, an availability, pragmatically speaking, of everything outside of oneself: meaning the rest of the world, or the pieces of it that you choose spontaneously.*

So when starting the concentration exercises, be aware that it's not sacrificing your openness to the world or the pieces of it that you choose.

Time to play!

Start out by identifying moments in your everyday life when you're in that paradoxical state of relaxed alertness: concentration. Be very careful not to confuse it with a state of tension.

... ...

Active listening, or intense and relaxed awareness of the present moment immediately gets us concentrated. Here is an example that provides absolute concentration: the attacks against the Twin Towers. How powerful and horrible that event was, the impact of the videos, the shock that it inflicted on us, how unreal it seemed ... we were all thrown into a state of absolute concentration. When the two airplanes hit the Twin Towers and they actually crumbled to the ground, hundreds of millions of people around the world were suddenly in a state of ultimate concentration. A state of absolute alert that made them forget everything else and all of their attention was focused on those events and those images. This impact obviously came from an extremely powerful source, which then created what I call "active listening," which in turn created an intense and relaxed state of awareness of the present moment.

In this case, the concentration is not coming from a tense, voluntary inward effort. It comes from extreme openness to external factors. Of course, you can replace this terrible event by something positive and beautiful, like being in the presence of someone you're very much in love with.

Time to play!

Look around you and connect yourself intimately to something, anything. A glass of water, the corner of a room, a window, your cat, a sponge, silence …

If you choose the glass for example, just look at it. Completely, but simply. Without rigidity. Without forcing your gaze. Look at the glass and admire its calm, its shape, how perfect its purpose is.

… … …

Who created it? There had to have been a first glass on Earth. Who were its ancestors? How did it get here? What is it filled with right now? Isn't the perfectly straight line of the surface of the water extraordinary?

… … …

Take it in your hands. Feel the tips of your fingers press against the sides of the glass. Check out the precision of the pressure you can apply or not: a little too much, and the glass breaks. Not quite enough, and the glass slips from your hands. Now lift it towards the light. See the millions of reflections of light on the glass that shift at the slightest movement? Their colors, their suppleness?

—CUT—

Yes, the meaning of things is definitely in our attitude towards them. And that attitude is attention. And attention is concentration. Once again, take your time. Always. Fully apply yourself to everything you do, to the place you're in, to the person in front of you. Maybe most people get tense if we ask them to concentrate because of the way we ordered them to do so when they were children. *"Can't you just concentrate?!"* That order is often unfairly barked at children during moments when they're actually *completely* concentrated. Probably not on what the parent, teacher or whoever else would like them to be, but concentrated all the same. It would seem much more educational to me to "lure" the child's attention, just like an actor's, by gently guiding them towards the subject at hand, rather than tensing them up. Therefore, forever creating a confusion between concentration and tension.[2]

To finish up on the subject of concentration, do you know that as an actor, you actually have a huge advantage? You can't forget or lose your instrument. You take it with you wherever you go. Take advantage of that factor to create as many sources of concentration as possible, sharpen them at any chance you get, always while being relaxed.

---

[2]The comparison between children and actors must not be taken as infantilization of actors. I actually can't stand those who have a habit of babying actors, as well as actors who have the habit of letting themselves be babied.

Try not to swallow the endless amounts of images that surround us. They want to get into your soul. In order to do that, they steal your most precious possession: concentration. Now, can you tell me why it's so precious?

... ...

Because deciding to concentrate is deciding to create your inner world; and deciding to create your inner world is deciding to create your life.

Listening

Like anything that's broached superficially, the Method too went through trends. During the '60s and '70s, Lee Strasberg's approach was all the rage; in the '80s and '90s, Stella Adler's approach came into fashion, and starting in the twenty-first century, Sanford Meisner's teachings made a huge comeback. As I said before, I personally prefer Robert Lewis's approach to all three. As it embraces the entirety of the Method, to me, it remains the most timeless approach and the one that's the closest to Stanislavski's initial vision. Anyway, Sanford Meisner stood out because of the emphasis that he put on listening in the actor's work. It's obviously an essential facet of the Method; however, here's a couple of funny things to point out. First, it came back in fashion during an era when the word "communication" was so overused that it lost its true meaning. Second, the most hardened Meisner fans are often the ones who have the hardest time listening to others. Just like concentration can't be an end in itself, when listening becomes an end rather than a means, it only ends up listening to itself ... and becomes deaf. This is absolutely not about putting down Meisner's contribution to the Method, nor the pertinence of his exercises. It's just a reminder that those exercises are here for listening, and not listening to listening which is listening to listening to listening, in some endless, empty echo that becomes deafening.

Let us also note that the importance of Meisner's precious work around listening is lost when it's taken out of the equation of the other Method tools. As vital as listening is in any good performance, it must include the given circumstances of the plot and the major tool of acting: the internal and external sources that are present or that the actor chooses. That's mostly why diehard Meisner fans are making a huge mistake when they oppose Meisner's work to the Method. Metaphorically speaking, that's like opposing precepts of love to Jesus Christ's teachings. Wrong! Period.

Now that we've gotten that out of the way, let's see what this facet of acting has to share. True listening is definitely essential to the actor. Here's an important detail: listening is obviously not exclusively through hearing, but through all of our senses. Just like with concentration, the best way to sharpen it is to deepen your relationship to everything you do, in your everyday life. Once again, and always, in suppleness, slowly.

Those who actually know how to listen are rare to come by. *Listen*, not hear. To listen. Those who don't have this skill, which is about 80 percent of people, often don't have it because they think that they already know how to do it. Which brings us back to the vicious circle of those who remain indifferent, think they've already done it all, and are as dry as a carbonized bone. That attitude, which is as pretentious as it is empty, is absolutely wrong. But there's worse; it makes them miss out on the most precious knowledge of all—the one that they don't have.

No problem—listening can be worked on. Everyday. In any situation. And that work partially consists of, paradoxically, not working. It's about putting your spirit in a standby state, taking away the burden of anticipation and "I know" syndrome.

Time to play!

Knowing how to listen to someone is having two brains: your own and the other's.

The next time that you have a drink with someone, try out this exercise: listen to the person without giving your opinion. Just be present, without having any prejudice about what's going to be said. This type of experiment can be very surprising and refreshing, because the person you're talking to will be put in a position that surprises them. That position is, for once, not being in front of a type of opposition or validation of what they're saying. Which in turn, will send back what they're saying in their face like a boomerang and might encourage them to be more creative. So you might get even more interesting tidbits from this person, and more directly connected to acting, you'll sharpen your listening.

—CUT—

But, you could counter all that by saying that actors are in a fundamentally different position. They read the play or the script and know not only their own lines and actions to the letter, but also those of their scene partners.

Again, all you have to do to "forget" them is to be deeply connected to powerful sources. And the effect that it has on actors is to submerge them in the ever so precious present moment.

Time to play!

Here's a variation of the experiment/exercise that we just talked about: do a simple action that's familiar to you, without having an opinion. No, I'm not joking! Try it out, don't have an opinion for a while, even if it's just for ten minutes. Not only does it help you work on listening, but this exercise has another huge benefit: it's restful. Really. Deeply. We go through our days having any number of opinions on any number of things, people, ideas, etc. This never-ending flow can often create a kind of internal chaos that literally suffocates listening. Not having an opinion for a few moments releases us from the burden of opinions and lets things just be the way they are. So from time to time, do simple actions while simply listening to what they make you feel, other than opinions and points of view. Just sensations. You'll see that in the beginning, it won't be as easy as it seems. But keep practicing and you'll see that a space of listening will open up inside you, stretch out, be sharpened.

—CUT—

Time to play!

This third experiment on the subject is also extremely simple but can also considerably sharpen your listening skills. Set yourself a simple action to do: making tea, making your bed, getting dressed ... and stop for five seconds between each movement of that action. For instance, if you're making tea, you take out a pot ... stop for 5 seconds ... you place your hand on the water tap ... stop for 5 seconds ... you turn on the tap ... stop for 5 seconds ... you fill your pot with water ... stop for 5 seconds ... you turn off the water tap ... stop for 5 seconds ... etc.

Every time that you stop for 5 seconds, be completely alert, but without tension, to the piece of action that you've just done: the weight of the pot, the shape of the faucet, its temperature, the running water, the sound it makes, the millions of dancing drops that it's made of, etc.

—CUT—

The era that we're in is literally so obsessed with speed, to the point where it actually almost has us at a stand-still. Nothing is worth going so fast if we don't even have time to look *around* us and *inside* of ourselves. Basically, we're zombies. Fast zombies, but zombies all the same. Let us ask ourselves: *We're going fast, but where to?*

The exercise we just talked about not only sharpens your listening, it holds an essential advantage for actors, if practiced often enough: sharpening all of your senses. As Lee Strasberg said, "An actor is someone who feels more." Learning how to feel more will hugely benefit your work in general and specifically the work we'll do with your imagination and your sense memory and emotional memory.

This exercise is also great for sharpening your sense of being in the present moment and, really, listening and the present moment are completely connected. They complete each other in a dynamic and infinite continuum.

Now we're going to talk about an essential facet of listening: active listening. Knowing how to listen without having an opinion can be useful, restful and instructive in many ways. However, in our case, it's basically just an experiment to work on our listening. The thing is that the characters are not Method actors—well, except when they are, of course. Hence, characters are like everybody else, in the sense that they have opinions on (almost) everything. So when you're working on a scene, ask yourself what your character thinks of this or that and physicalize those opinions. Let them express themselves through their/your slightest actions, which will enrich their/your subtext.

Time to play!

Here's a great exercise that can help you work on active listening. Unlike the experiment that consisted of not having an opinion, this one consists of expressing verbally all of your opinions on one action, a person, an idea, etc. Let's go back to making tea for instance. Express your opinion verbally, not only about the action of making tea in general—Yum, I'm gonna make myself a well-deserved cup of tea!—but about every piece that this action's made of. You choose a tea bag—Huumm, Earl Grey or Genmaicha?—you choose Genmaicha—Man, whoever came up with putting rice in tea?—you add some sugar—the hell with the top model in me!

... ...

Did you really try out the exercise? Let's say that you did. Now, repeat the exercise, but this time while expressing your opinions non-verbally. Make sure that you clearly physicalize all of them, but be careful—without starting to mime or overact.

—CUT—

When you're acting out a scene, don't ever be content with just listening. Be actively listening, give your opinion on everything, express your character's point of view in the smallest details. Just the way we do, in life.

Now back to Sanford Meisner. He created a series of fascinating exercises that work not only on listening, but also on spontaneity, reactivity, and the sense of the present moment.

His exercises were mostly based on repetition. Repetition in the true sense of the word: repeating actions, words, or other things over and over.

We'll talk about them here, but I strongly recommend that you read his book called *On Acting*, to dig even deeper into what Meisner was obsessed with: listening.

Time to play!

First, you put two people together and have them say exclusively physical, simple and tangible facts. Try it out with whoever you want.

As for me, let's imagine, for instance, that I'm in front of Mona. One of us will start by stating a simple fact. The other one will answer without changing what was said, except the pronoun used, and repeating it as a question.

Me You're wearing a green jacket.

Mona I'm wearing a green jacket?

We'll repeat this phrase over and over again for a few minutes, until the words themselves slowly lose their initial factual meaning and will be replaced by the relationship between us, the presence of the other, her reactions, and what it all means to each of us. Without ever changing the words of the initial sentence. For example, this can happen:

Me You're wearing a green jacket.

Mona I'm wearing a green jacket?

Me You're wearing a green jacket.

Mona I'm wearing a green jacket?

Me You. Are. Wearing. A. Green. Jacket.

Mona I'm wearing a GREEN jacket?!

Me You're wearing a green jacket!

Mona I'm wearing a green jacket?

Etc.

The idea is to transcend the words, to let what we're actually feeling here and now flow freely and be expressed through the subtext. Without any preconceptions, freely, listening to your partner and to yourself.
Then, without warning, Mona states a simple and tangible truth.

Mona You know I trust in you, right? In us …

No, that's not a fact Mona, that's a point of view. Go ahead, try again.

Mona Uh … You have a Lakers T-shirt.

Me I have a Lakers T-shirt.

Etc.

Now, we'll add a simple opinion on a physical fact.

Me   I like your … blue sweater.

Mona   Hmm … you like my blue sweater …

Me   I like your blue sweater …

Etc.

Then, we add layers to the exercise: actors progress from a purely factual approach to a more subjective approach …

Mona   You're charismatic.

Me   I'm charismatic?

Etc.

… then to an even more personal opinion …

Mona   You fantasize about me.

Me   I fantasize about you?! Ha!

Etc.

… then to a subjective directly intrusive opinion …

Mona   Does it make you nervous that I know?

Me   Does it make me nervous that you know?

Etc.

—CUT—

In Sanford Meisner's book, you'll see how more and more layers are added to the repetition exercises; how little by little, stakes, objectives are included, to the point where you end up slipping into the scene and the character you have to play. This approach can prove to be valuable for working on active listening and your relationship with your scene partners. They kind of work like mantras; the words that are repeated, repeated and repeated lose their meaning little by little, and are replaced by deep listening of the present moment, what's *really* happening here and now.

They can also help break up the rigid preconceptions that actors can sometimes have about characters or scenes that they have to play. Now, having preconceptions is not bad in itself. They can actually be necessary in order to follow the storyline, as long as they're founded by an intimate understanding of the play or the script. But they can never take the place of the truth of the present moment, what's happening on stage here and now.

In my opinion, the main interest of this approach could be summed up like this:

Never act out a character that's in front of another character. Be a human being that's talking *to* and is trying to move *another* human being, a real, palpable human being: the one that's in front of you. All the while including the characters that you and your partner will be embodying. Let me explain. Let's imagine, always of course just as an example, that Mona and I are playing Romeo and Juliet. If we're doing the actions, pursuing the objectives and saying the words of Romeo and Juliet, who's breathing? Romeo and Juliet or David and Mona? David and Mona of course. Same for the emotions. They're David's and Mona's. They're here to serve Romeo and Juliet of course, but that doesn't change the fact that they're David's and Mona's. So when Romeo and Juliet are declaring their undying love for each other, David and Mona must unflinchingly try to move David/Romeo and Mona/Juliet. Whether they're using their imagination, a substitution or reality, whatever the feelings that they have or don't have for each other concerns only them …

The moment to moment to moment ...

Everything that you have lived, are living and will live through, happened, is happening and will happen in the present.

(Eckhart Tolle)

One of the main goals of many of the experiments/exercises that we've talked about up until now, as well as the many others to come in this book, is to create the precious "moment to moment" of the Method, if not of life itself. It is absolutely crucial to any worthy performance. It partially consists of not anticipating. Being, forever and always, in the present moment. Being "busy" enough on stage so that you don't think too much about not only the audience, but also what will happen at the end of the play or the movie, in the next scene, in the next second. As we'll talk about later, every scene needs to preserve the freshness of the first time and that's one of the main reasons why the "moment to moment" is so essential.

Tomorrow the day before I had will run after time

As we've confirmed, and will continue to do so as a voluntary reminder, actors are their own, unique, and only instrument. So their relationship to time in their everyday life will not only influence their relationship to acting in general, but also and mostly their relationship to the "moment to moment."

So many people live in a semi-permanent state of stress and anxiety when it comes to the subject of Time, as if it's this terrible and irreversible *fatum*. As if they were somehow victims of it. But we largely contribute to this stress and anxiety, since we're the ones who make it. This happens when we fall into one of two terrible traps that we inflict on ourselves:

1) Racing against time

2) Living tomorrow the day before.

Racing against time.
Racing against time is simply impossible, since time is merely a mental concept that makes us believe that we're living other moments than that of the present, now. That belief makes us forget the simple fact that time does not go by. Time is.

How is it possible to race against something that is not only immobile, but is also the common ground where ourselves and time stand at each moment? Racing against time makes us leave that common ground where time already is, and then makes us lose all sense of ourselves and of time.

Living tomorrow the day before.

Ahh, regrets! Ahh, projects!

If I had only known ... When I'll have gotten that ... and so many others that propel us to live in the past and in the future: living tomorrow the day before.

But as we've just talked about, the past, the future, the tomorrow, and the day before actually don't exist. That's why the goal of certain "Relaxation" and "Listening" exercises is to reset us in the only dimension where we can actually be: the eternal present. With the help of that but also truly being where you are, when you're there, as much as possible, try to sharpen your presence in the present.³ This will help you out big-time in acting, the moment to moment and, as a bonus, in all aspects of your life.

Since one of the goals of a lot of the exercises that we've already done or are about to do is to create the "moment to moment" exercise, we won't talk about any specific exercises just now.

But, let's talk about an essential element of the "moment to moment" exercise:

Real questions

Acting is about truly thinking in fictional situations.
(Lee Strasberg)

Indeed, really and truly thinking and reflecting on stage is one of the *indispensable* conditions for belief, aka "self-bluffing." To be able to do that, one of the most important ingredients resides in what we call "real questions," which also make or keep your performances alive and fresh. This consists of truly asking yourself all sorts of questions, more or less directly in relation to the play or the script at the exact moment that you're acting.

Speaking of questions, I have one for you: In what world does the play *Hamlet* by Shakespeare simply not exist?

... ...

Which people could not have possibly read it?

... ...

Well, that would be the very people that the play is about. For Hamlet, the play *Hamlet* doesn't exist. The same goes for all characters in all works of art, except of course when the plot puts the characters in a *mise en abyme* or has them break the fourth wall, as an awareness that they're part of a work of art. This simple factor means that the characters almost never know what they're about to say or do, or at least what's going to happen. They also can never be certain of how the other characters are going to react to them, what they have in mind, what they're going to do, what they're going to say or hide. That's why I encourage you to spread real questions throughout your performances. But don't freeze them. Reinvent them according to what your scene partners have to offer *here and now*. This will add very, very rich layers to your performance and will considerably enhance your active listening.

---

³Speaking of which, if you haven't already, I highly recommend that you check out the enlightening work of Eckhart Tolle. He is the author of *The Power of Now* and *A New Earth*, among others. You'll also find a lot of interviews and conferences given by him on the internet.

Plus, real questions nourish the "moment to moment" because they're truly bred from the present moment. It's majorly thanks to real questions that the feeling of discovering events is kept alive, even though you've read the play or the script that's dictating these events. It's all quite paradoxical, because the idea basically consists of helping you "forget" what you already know, all the while repeating it all to the letter.

And the most precious key to be able to do all of this is most definitely what I call …

∗∗∗Sources

"Exploration" is the most important part of the actor's training and "sources" is the most important part of exploration. As you'll see, sources are made up of many elements, but all in all can be defined as this:

Sources are stimuli from the inner and outer world of actors, which breathe true life into their roles.

This other life that actors have truly lived comes from their sources. That's what makes them believe in the motivations of their character, the obstacles that their actions are up against, and the stakes that they're faced with. It will give them the will to physically and psychophysically act out, an authentic desire to reach their objective and, directly or indirectly, emotions.

To be sure that you grasp what a source is, here's a quick exercise.
Who's the person that you love most in the world?

... ...

Did a certain someone immediately come to mind? That person is a source.
Or maybe you're hesitating between different people? Each of them is a source. Whenever you hesitate, you're in the process of what I call selecting a source. This is a fundamental step in working on a scene. But all sources don't necessarily come from our experience, like the ones that we just talked about.
What do you think Gandhi dreams about when he sleeps?

... ...

Again, whether an answer immediately came to mind or you hesitated, you're in the midst of exploring sources. In this case, we're talking about imaginary sources. Whether they come from your experience or your imagination, while working on a scene, you will select them according to the needs of the scene and according to what they make you feel spontaneously.

Let us specify that it's entirely possible to only work with imaginary sources that come with the scene immediately.

−CUT−

Whatever they may be, sources are what give life to your performances. You'll understand soon just how incredibly vital they are to your work.

Sources are what breathe life into the heart and soul of a scene.

They can be composed of images, sounds, smells, textures, and tastes, simultaneously or exclusively. So they need the help of our five senses. That's why one of the prime missions of an actor's training is to sharpen them. As we've just experienced, they can come from the imagination or experience, but also from a mix of the two. Even though sources obviously pass through our brains, we won't have the reflex to ask ourselves what we think about them, but how we feel about them. That's one of the main misunderstandings of those who criticize the Method: they often think that our techniques are *primarily* intellectual. That's where we get our reputation of "racking our brains" from.

First of all, it's worthy to note that the word "intellectual" has become a kind of insult, used most of the time by people who literally don't have access to the part of their brain that allows them to become it. If that zone even exists in them. They're often the same ones who like to play it "*sooo coooooooool*," even though that actually makes them *sooooo stuuuuuuuupid*. So when some low-life calls you an intellectual, remember that that's actually a really good sign. Secondly, let us specify that even though using our thinking process is of course necessary in acting, that's not the only aspect that we're supposed to use and sometimes, we even have to learn how to push it aside a little. This is particularly true when working on sources. They're addressing the sensory part of our brain, which transmits their signals to our five senses. There are five steps in working on the sources of a scene:

1) Identifying the elements of a scene that need a source
2) Selecting imaginary or experienced sources that *could* correspond to the ones needed during the scene
3) Testing out each selected source to make sure that it has the desired effect
4) Repeatedly connecting to each source, to make sure that they're trustworthy
5) Integrating the sources into the scene.

This process often happens partially or completely naturally. But it's good to keep that order in mind for the few times when it doesn't. To truly solidify what sources are and the steps to take, we'll base ourselves off of a scene from a "semi-autobiographical" movie that actually doesn't exist. Well, not yet at least.

Laaadies and gentlemeeeen!!!

Miss M.

Starring

Mona and David

INT/NIGHT — "DAVID'S" OFFICE

In an office lent to him by some friends, David, more inspired than ever, is working on writing his book about acting, accompanied by surreal music composed by consumers of magic mushrooms ... When suddenly, there's a knock at the door.

David (to himself) *Ugghh!!! Arrrggh!* Who's trying to bust my balls!?!

He sprints from his chair and furiously opens the door. Then becomes pale as a ghost. It's Mona. Irresistible.

Mona Hey! I'm not bothering you, am I?

Her slight Romanian accent has some Italian in it, with just a hint of Arabian. All of this intensifies her charm.

David   Uh, hey … Mona. Uh, no, not at all. I …

Mona   How are you?

David   Good, I mean, really great. You?

Mona   I'm good. Well … not really. Are you sure you're ok?

David   Of course I'm ok. Why are you looking at me like that?

Mona   You're acting weird.

David (worried)   Really?

Mona   Really. Seriously.

They lock eyes for a moment, in silence. David definitely seems troubled.

Mona   Well, are we gonna just stand here and count our beauty spots or are you gonna let me in?

David   The two aren't incompatible.

She smiles. He knows that he's just scored a point. She comes in.

To be continued …

Karl

If I was the actor playing the role of David in this scene and Mona was playing the part of Mona, I obviously wouldn't need to select other sources besides the ones that were already being offered to me. But these are still sources nonetheless and it's still good to identify what they are, even if they get offered to you by the scene. Even though you'll be inspired by yourself when embodying a role, that role won't contextually be "the you" that you more or less consciously choose to be in your everyday life.[4] There can and will be a lot of roles that contain elements that speak to you in the same way that they speak to your character. It can even sometimes be possible that you feel the same way about your scene partner that your character feels about his. But there will almost always be elements in a role, sometimes all of them, that don't speak to you at all. It's mostly in these types of cases that I recommend that you choose specific sources and follow the steps that we talked about a little earlier.

So, for this exercise, let's hire Karl, a gay actor who hates Pho soups, tattoos, and books about acting. Not to mention the profound disgust that he feels about Corinne, the actress who plays Mona.

So Karl's about to realize the amount of work that it'll take to be able to believe in the situation, and to play his character with faith and accuracy. This process starts by identifying the elements of a scene that needs a source.[5]

Laaadies and gentlemeeeen!!!

---

[4] That's a subject that we'll talk about more in depth in the book on creating characters.
[5] We'll put these elements in **bold** in the script. …

Miss M.

Starring

Corinne and Karl

INT/**NIGHT**—**"DAVID'S"** OFFICE

In an office lent to him by some friends, David, **more inspired than ever, is working on writing his book about acting, accompanied by surreal music composed by consumers of magic mushrooms** … When suddenly, there's a knock at the door.

David (to himself)   *Ugghh!!! Arrrggh!* Who's trying to bust my balls?!

He sprints from his chair and furiously opens the door. Then becomes pale as a ghost. It's Mona. Irresistible.

Mona   Hey! I'm not bothering you, am I?

Her slight Romanian accent has some Italian in it, with just a hint of Arabian. All of this intensifies her charm.

David   Uh, hey … Mona. Uh, no, not at all. I …

Mona   How are you?

David   Good, I mean, really great. You?

Mona   I'm good. Well … **not really**. **Are you sure you're ok**?

David   Of course I'm ok. Why are you looking at me like that?

Mona   You're acting weird.

David (worried)   Really?

Mona   Really. Seriously.

They lock eyes for a moment, in silence. **David definitely seems troubled**.

Mona   Well, are we gonna just stand here and **count our beauty spots** or **are you gonna let me in**?

David   The two aren't incompatible.

She smiles. He knows that he's just scored a point. She comes in.

If you would've had to play the role of David, would you have identified the same elements as Karl?

… … …

Not necessarily. It all depends on …

1) the natural closeness that you feel to David's character

2) what you actually feel about Corinne, who's playing Mona.

Maybe you don't actually dislike her, maybe she actually has quite an effect on you. Whatever it might be, always stay alert to how you truly feel about your scene partners; this will help you clearly identify what the work you have to do or not is, in order to create the fictional relationship.

Now, we'll let Karl talk, so that he can explain to us all why he identified these elements as the ones needing sources. As you'll see, Karl will mention a few tools from the Method that we haven't fully explored yet. We'll be doing that in the upcoming chapters about the tools in question.

David   Hi, Karl. Thank you for sparing us a bit of your precious time, to tell us all about the work you did on the role that you play in Miss M.

Karl   No problem, Dave. It's a pleasure to share some of my know-how with beginners.

David   Uh … I do work with professionals too, you know, and I imagine that some of them will read this book.

Karl   In your dreams!

David   Excuse me?

Karl   In your dreams! Maybe they'll buy that pile of paper of yours, but they'll never read it! Anyway, I've always appreciated your innocence, kid.

David   Thanks, Karl. Can we get started?

Karl   Sure! But if you don't mind, I'm gonna start with the beginning.

David   Uhhhhh, yeah, good idea! That seems to be a … how should I put this … a good start.

Karl   To start, yes, I prefer to start with the beginning. Did you know that Keanu, I mean Keanu Reeves, during his first flight to Hawaii with Delta Airlines, in … 1987, if I remember correctly, wanted to start with the end. You see what I mean?

David   Not really, but let's talk about that another time, if you don't mind. Right now, we're gonna focus on your fascinating work.

Karl   No problem. So, what does the script say?

INT/NIGHT

Karl   Working at night has an effect on us. The shooting schedule organized by the directing team indicates that we'll be filming on Thursday morning. What kinds of sources will help me believe that it's night-time? I'll get to work on imagining the particular details of the night, like the contrast between the agitation in the streets and the hard-working solitude of the office, etc. Also, David, I'll ask myself what your character did all day. Did he work or did he lay around? Did he get up around sunrise, or around 2pm, like a lot of scenes in the script seem to indicate? I'll then work on the physical state of the character, according to the answers I get. Maybe I'll use a sense memory, you know.

"DAVID'S" OFFICE

In an office lent to him by some friends ...

Karl Even though the script remains discreet on the matter, it's clear that David's character is crashing at this office. I'll have to take that into account in my acting. The thing is, I really don't like the set where we're filming that much, so I think I'll rely on that to create the feeling of not being "at home." So in this case, I'm just using what I feel in reality.

David, more inspired than ever, is working on writing his book about acting ...

Karl Ahh! That's gonna need a source that truly inspires me to commit to the action of writing your book. I cannot directly connect to writing this book for this one good and very simple reason: I hate books about acting. Sorry, that's just the way it is.

David Thanks for the publicity.

Karl Oh please, you can just edit this part out later man, or just say that I hate all acting books except yours. With the big mise en abyme that's so great and can directly train actors live.

David I'll think about it, thanks.

Karl So, for the whole "dude who's writing his book, all inspired as if he's writing War and Peace" thing, I'll have to choose a source that excites me. But don't get me wrong—I'm talking about something that excites my neurons and to my core, see? I know that you don't like it when we reveal our sources, but don't sweat it—this one isn't too private. I think I'm gonna use this particular memory that I have from when I was a kid in high school. I was so fascinated by this homework that we had, when we were studying the flying penguins in Laos.

... accompanied by surreal music composed by consumers of magic mushrooms ...

Karl This type of music seems to have David's character tripping out, but—nothing personal, Dave—that's absolutely not the case with me. You see, I grew up with a mom who believed that we could remain nourished with incense fumes and sitar vibes. So, no thanks. Anyway, as you probably know, when a character is listening to music in a scene of the movie, they often can't actually put on the music on set, for continuity reasons and sound editing. So, just before shooting the scene, I'll listen to some music that puts me in that type of state, that trips me out.

When suddenly, there's a knock at the door ...

Karl Ahh! There's a good challenge—acting surprised! Not easy. I'm betting you already tried out your corny thing with Hamlet who's never read Hamlet?

David   ... Yes.

Karl   I'm going back to the basics here, you know? To be truly surprised, there's nothing like a good old W.W.W. exercise! Here, the action of writing will help me, that and my penguins/your book about acting. I know that if I'm wholeheartedly busy with what I'm writing, I really will be surprised. It's as simple as that.

David (to himself)   *Ugghh!!! Arrrggh!* **Who's trying to bust my balls??!!**

He sprints from his chair and furiously opens the door ...

Karl   Besides the flying penguins, I'll also choose a source to connect to when there's a knock at the door. Being the good crasher that he is, David's character—who at that moment doesn't know yet that it's Mona—is probably nervous about the possibility that his friends who are lending him the office for free could randomly stop by. I think that I'll just use my imagination and connect to that aspect. That rings a bell with me. Or I could also think of my cougar neighbor who's always bothering me. With the first option, I'll specifically imagine my/your friends and the fact that I/you owe them one. If I base myself off of the script, it's pretty clear that you and the wife of this couple of friends always have a lot to say to each other. If I get connected well enough to that, that'll be a plus for intensifying the obstacle and bringing energy to the scene. You see? The details, bro! With the second option, I'll remember specific details about my cougar neighbor that particularly annoy me—her nails-on-a-chalk-board voice, the inventive excuses she comes up with each time to come and disturb me at all hours, her insistence, her loneliness, the awkwardness that just seeps out of every pore of her body. All that just because she doesn't get enough ... well, you get the picture.

Then becomes pale as a ghost. It's Mona. Irresistible ...

Karl   As you know, David, you and everybody in the profession, as well as anyone who knows me: I'm gay. I think my cougar neighbor is the only one who still doesn't get it. Anyway, now's the moment that I choose the most important source of the scene—the one that will get me closer to what David feels for Mona. Not only does my sexual preference not match, but I hate every fiber of Corinne's being and pray every morning that she'll get run over by a convoy of Israeli tanks. So I'll have to substitute her with someone that I know in real life and who really does have an effect on me. That's private and I won't reveal my source. All I'll say is that I can't choose my current boyfriend, even though he's so handsome. Simply because David's and Mona's characters are not yet together at that point in the movie, and the crush feeling that we have with someone that we're with doesn't have the same texture as the crush feeling with someone that we'd love to be with.

Mona   Hey! I'm not bothering you, am I?

Her slight Romanian accent has some Italian in it, with just a hint of Arabian. All of this intensifies her charm.

David   Uh, hey ... Mona. Uh, no, not at all. I ...

Mona How are you?

David Good, I mean, really great. You?

Mona I'm good. Well … **not really**.

Karl *Here, I'm just running over everything we've talked about: the W.W.W. questions, my penguins, the cougar and most of all, my substitution for Mona/Corinne. But when Mona's character says "No," she's not good, I stop running through my source/substitution—it's like a wave or wall just kinda hit me, you know? Now I connect to the real questions that can relate to my substitution, in order to correspond to the questions that David's character is most likely asking himself when Mona admits, after hesitating, that no, she's not good. Maybe she left her boyfriend? Which would mean that she has one. But that's bad for David's character. Maybe she wants to leave her boyfriend but is having a hard time doing it? That's not as bad for David's character, who then might think that he has more of a chance. Is he making a mental list of reasons why Mona might not be doing good? Whatever it might be, I'll have to be asking myself real questions that relate to my source/substitution or other things. Let me underline that David's character doesn't ask Mona why she's not doing good. Maybe he's dreading what the answer might be? This deserves some more thought.*

Are you sure you're ok?

Karl *We can guess, from the dialogue that ensues between them, that that question unsettles David. So, I have to choose a source that can unsettle me. Maybe all I have to do is connect to a detail about my source/substitution. I'll also ask myself, what is David thinking at that moment? That maybe Mona has noticed that he's touched to see her? That he has that psycho face on, that even surprises himself, that he gets when he's inspired? That he's scaring her?*

David Of course I'm ok. Why are you looking at me like that?

Mona **You're acting weird**.

Karl *OMG! David's inner world is going out of control with so many questions at this point: what does she mean by "weird"? She, herself, is unique, peculiar, and weird in her own way. Maybe it's actually a hidden compliment? Mona's character is not conventional, that's why David can't imagine her being with someone "normal." That's good for him! To take care of all of that, I'm gonna prolong the connection to my source/substitution.*

David (worried) Really?

Mona Really. Seriously.

They lock eyes for a moment, in silence. **David definitely seems troubled**.

Karl *Well, this is no longer a scoop: Mona troubles David. But the "definitely seems" indicates just how intense his troubled state is. I'll stay with my source/substitution and* explore what troubles me the most about this person. His dimples? His eyes? The way he looks at me? The scar on his shoulder? And I promise you, everyone will think that I'm obsessed with that girl. You know the rest. You're the coach, man!

Mona Well, are we gonna just stand here and **count our beauty spots** or **are you gonna let me in**?

Karl Now, the scene's finally going somewhere: Mona's making the first move. Or that's probably what David's thinking anyway, as we can guess from his awesome comeback: "The two aren't incompatible." How does that first move make him feel? Which questions arise? Which fantasies? Maybe which fears, too? All of these questions, fantasies, and fears come from visuals. In order to prepare the scene, first, I'm going to carefully choose visuals. Then, I'm going to test out and explore these visuals to make sure that they provoke my/David's character's questions, as well as my/his fantasies and my/his fears. Even though they most likely won't be the same ones, they'll have the same texture. It's not like the audience can read my thoughts, they can only see the effect that they have on me. That's how you establish a natural connection between, on one side, the behavior and vibrations of a "Method actor," and, on the other, an imaginary situation.

David The two aren't incompatible.

She smiles. He knows that he's just scored a point. She comes in.

Karl For this part, I'm just gonna connect to a moment when I knew that a flirt was going in the right direction. I've got a good collection of those. You know, those precise moments when you realize that you just got several points on the guy's mental scoreboard.

David Or the girl's.

Laughs.

David Thank you, Karl. It was great to hear you talk about your work.

Karl Don't sweat it, man.

So? Do you get the point of the first step in working on the sources of a scene?

… … …

What, you think that Karl's crazy? You're right about that. But if you think that he's crazy because of the way that he works on his scenes, then you're wrong. And if you're thinking to yourself "Why all of these questions?" or worse, "Why rack your brains so much just to act?!" I have this to say to you:

1) It's not "racking your brains," it's a game.
2) Just perform a scene for an audience without having worked on it beforehand, and you'll clearly understand why working on it is important, and why this approach is vital to making your performances accurate and impactful.

And obviously, the necessity of this approach is multiplied when you don't have only one scene to play, but *all* of the scenes of a role, with all of the interpretation challenges that come along with it, as well as the character's passions that you must bring to life, the stakes to believe in, etc. Always keep this perspective in mind, because even though the scene we just studied might seem pretty simple to act out, that's almost never the case with many scenes and roles that are worthy of interest.

If you still have doubts about the necessity of all this work on sources, then allow yourself a couple of hours to do the exercise that's coming up. Without a doubt, this one will be particularly appreciated by the slackers, but I'd truly advise everybody to live out this one.

Time to play!

What is your favorite performance given by an actor in a movie or a TV series? And by "performance," I mean a *PERFORMANCE!*, with real acting challenges. A role you could sink your teeth into. Maybe you'll find yourself choosing one of the roles that you would've loved to play or the one that made you decide to become an actor.

... ...

So, did you find one?[6] Great.

Now, go watch the movie or the episode that has that *PERFORMANCE* in it, all the while keeping this question in mind: If this movie or series hadn't been filmed yet and you were the one who had been chosen for that role, would you, yes or no, have quite a bit of work to do?

—CUT—

Well, unless you chose J.R.'s hat in *Dallas* and you strongly believe that that hat should've been at least nominated, if not paid tribute to, by the Academy Awards, then I imagine you've just realized the amount of work that is necessary *AND* how much fun that work in itself is!!!

If you're still not convinced, then there is only one possibility left here: you're an acting genius like we've never seen before. Otherwise, whether you're an acting genius or not, you're aware, just like those who we saw before you, that the game doesn't exclude hard work, just like those who came before you.

It's 1 percent talent, 99 percent work.

In your opinion, whose quote is that?

... ...

All right, here's a clue—an actor said it.

... ...

---

[6]If you haven't, go watch or re-watch *One Flew Over the Cuckoo's Nest* with the inspiring and inspired Jack Nicholson, *A Woman Under the Influence* with the astonishing Gena Rowlands, *Angel Heart* with Mickey Rourke, his magnetic charisma and at the top of his game, or *Star 80* with the terrifying and disturbing Eric Roberts. All of these Method actors worked on their role, and *therefore*, on their sources.

Ok, here's another one: he's considered as one of the greatest actors of all time by all those who know his work, if not *THE* greatest actor of all time.

... ...

Jack Nicholson? No. But he's one of Jack Nicholson's favorite actors.

... ...

Ok, ok, he's a Method actor, if not an absolute *icon* of the Method.

... ...

Yes, that's it!!! Marlon Brando.

So, if Marlon, as Karl would call him, who is *undeniably* one of the most talented actors that we've ever known, if even Marlon thinks and puts into practice his belief of "*1% talent, 99% work*," then why not you?

Mozart was a genius too ... whose father made him practice non-stop from the age of 2, 7 days a week, 16 hours per day.

The five steps in working on sources

Now that Karl has accomplished the first step of working on sources for a scene, which is identifying the elements of said scene that require sources, he has to follow four other steps. Let's see if you can do it, instead of Karl. It's now your turn to take on the part of David's character. Try to find a scene partner who you can share this exercise with and with whom you can truly embody the scene. If you don't find anyone, try it out anyway. We'll work on a fresh, new scene: the one just after Mona's unexpected visit. You'll be able to remain uninfluenced by Karl's choices, all the while being able to use what those choices taught you.

Laaadies and gentlemeeeen!!!

Miss M.

Starring

You and Corinne

OR

(for the actresses)

You and Jack Nicholson, at 37 years old

INT/NIGHT—"DAVID'S" OFFICE

Mona "floats" leisurely around the big room, almost as if she was alone ... She sometimes stops to look at a particular object, brushes her hand against others, with surreal music in the background.

David stays near the door, only a few feet from her. Intrigued and thrilled at the same time, his gaze follows her, with the look in his eyes that men have when gazing at the woman of their dreams.

David So? What's wrong?

Mona (with her irresistible slight accent) Nothing. Why?

David Because you told me you weren't doing good?

Mona I wanted to be sure that you would let me in.

David Good call—I was about to slam the door in your face.

Mona Too late.

David Too late …

They kind of "scan" each other from a distance. David breaks up the moment and heads towards the fridge.

David Do you want something to drink?

(opens the fridge)

I have Coke, or, umm … *Ah!* **Cabbage juice.**

Mona Um, that's very tempting, but I think I'll just take a coffee, if that's ok with you.

David Ah … nope, that's not ok. At all.

Mona (pointing towards the coffee machine) Is it only for the invited guests—female, that is?

David No, it's just that the machine and I aren't speaking.

Mona Then I'll take some cabbage juice. *WOOAAH!!!*

David almost jumps.

Mona (talking about the music) *That's The Fire Rain by Padij Namarapa Swandipak!!!*

She heads to David's computer and turns up the volume.

Mona I love this one!

("playing" *air* sitar)

Dam di dou di dou di dam.

David Sorry, there are no glasses.

He hands her the bottle of cabbage juice, which she doesn't take—she seems to be confused by something on the screen. Realizing that she's reading what he's written, he shoves the bottle in her hands and gets in front of the computer.

David Here, there are no glasses!

Mona (still seemingly confused and a little unsettled) No problem.

David spots, with horror, the word "Mona" written in a bunch of different places in his book file! He nervously closes his laptop—the music suddenly stops. He turns to look at Mona, trying to appear natural … to no avail.

David (pointing towards the cabbage juice) You like it?

Mona Uh, it's … it's … it's cabbage juice.

David slowly nods his head while staring into space, as if she's just revealed the theory of time relativity to him. He's feeling very vulnerable in front of her, since she's seen her name on his laptop screen.

David Yeah. It's cabbage juice.

Silence … Both are uncomfortable.

David Were … were you just passing through the neighborhood?

Mona No.

Silence, again.

Mona So, are you actually writing something or is that just a flirting technique?

David Both.

Mona And does it usually work?

David The flirting or the writing?

Mona The flirting.

He stares at her, while staying noticeably silent.

Mona Ok, I get it, silence validated, 5 stars. So what are you writing about?

David Guess.

She looks at him … then observes a few details scattered around the office—the old map of Paris on the wall, David's mug, the empty package of peanuts, the pack of gum.

Mona About the role of Junk Food in the fattening of the modern male?

David takes that in.

Mona *Joking!* Don't make that face.

David (amused) So, what would you like me to write about?

Mona *Ah, not too bad!*

David doesn't understand.

Mona   Not a bad technique to find out what I think about you. You know, you could just ask me.

She has a small defiant and ambiguous smile that David tries to decipher …

David   Ok, let's get back to my book.

Mona   Ok! What would you like me to like for you to write about?

David   You.

She's caught off-guard by that, touched, almost sad.

Mona   … You're writing about me?

He's not sure that he should admit it to her …

David   No. About acting. I'm an acting coach.

Mona   Ah, you mean you're a failed actor.

They laugh together.

David   No, but it doesn't mean that I'm a good coach either.

Mona   Yeah … that's why you're writing a book I imagine? Because of how modest you are?

David   No, it's … it's for a bunch of different reasons.

Mona (simply, deeply)   You know, I just adored your text.

David   I never texted you.

She takes in that he doesn't remember.

David   *Joking!* Don't make that face. But next time, I'll text you something that really stinks, maybe then you'll answer.

Mona   What did you want me to answer? You already said everything there was to say.

David stops himself from letting out a victory "*Wooow!!!*"

Mona   That's just so French, though.

David   … What is?

Mona   Expecting someone to answer questions that weren't asked.

David   What questions are you thinking of?

Mona   The questions that you'd like me to answer without having to ask them.

David   Which are?

Mona   Well, ask them, that way you'll find out what they are and you'll also get your answers. Unless, like what I'm suspecting, you already have your answers. Which means that I would have to ask you "Why pretend to have questions when you already know their answers, all the while pretending that you don't know them, so that I have to ask you the questions, which would also give you the answers that you already have?" But I haven't even thought to ask you that question.

David   … Did your father invent the Chinese tangram?

Mona   And my mother was a maze architect. We stuffed our faces with sudokus at *every* meal!

They smile at each other, starting to bond.

Mona   Do you need to go to the bathroom?

David   (mentally questioning himself)

Uhhhhh … no, I'm good.

Mona   You're *sure*?

David (amused)   Yes.

Mona   You're sure that you're sure??!

David   Why? You're planning on clogging the toilet?

She smiles, quickly gets something from her purse and leaves the room while winking at David.

Mona   "*I'll be back in a sec*," like the American girls say.

David   "*Dwong buon tsieeeeeeeeeu!*"

(to himself)

… like the Hong Kongese guys say. Umm … Hong Konganese or Hong Kongese? … Whatever, like the guys in Hong Kong say.

Mona's Voice   You ok? Did you say something?

David   No, nothing. Everything's fine.

Now alone, David basks in the vibrations of this unexpected visit and in the glee of the good vibes that they seem to be sharing.

Mona comes back, wearing *RED!* red lipstick and a drop-dead gorgeous smile.

David   Weuh … ow—wow!

Mona   Thaeuh … anks—*thanks!*

David (teasing her)   Do you never flush?

Mona   Oh, you haven't noticed?

(confidently)

I'm a girl—which means that I never use the bathroom just to use the bathroom.

They smile at each other ... Then, Mona's smile slowly fades away, and is replaced by a look of dark seriousness.

Mona I just adored your text, you know ...

David Uh ... yeah, you just told me.

She nods, then lowers her eyes ... He wonders if he should come closer. Too late—she looks at him again, with tears in her eyes, short of breath and shaking.

Mona I ... I'm so scared, David ...

She breaks down, sobbing, and runs out of the office.

With so many emotions boiling over and completely lost, David looks around him ... when something catches his eye: Mona's purse, which she left behind. There's a gun sticking out.

To be continued ...

Whether you're playing the part of Mona or David, try out the five steps of working on sources with this scene too, which I'll list for you here again. Here's a small bonus that I added: it's written as if it were the recipe of a meal that you were making.

STEP 1/ACTING

Identifying the elements of a scene that need a source.

STEP 1/COOKING

Identifying the necessary ingredients in order to make the meal.

STEP 2/ACTING

Selecting imaginary or experienced sources that *could* correspond to the ones needed during the scene.

STEP 2/COOKING

Going grocery shopping.

STEP 3/ACTING

Testing out each selected source to make sure that it has the desired effect.

STEP 3/COOKING

Tasting, smelling, touching each individual ingredient.

STEP 4/ ACTING

Repeatedly connecting to each source, to make sure that they're trustworthy.

STEP 4/COOKING

Re-tasting, re-smelling, re-touching (as we often do) to make sure that each ingredient is just right for the meal.

STEP 5/ACTING

Integrating the sources into the scene.

STEP 5/ COOKING

Cooking.

To be specific, "cooking" up a scene doesn't solely depend on integrating sources, but they still play a *vital* part in the process. We'll talk about other necessary elements in the upcoming chapters, as well as "cooking" a scene.

Time to play!

1) Identifying the elements of a scene that need a source.
Always remember, every scene is a …

… … …

… "Where? When? Why?" exercise, of course!
Now, start by asking yourself the W.W.W. questions according to your character and to the situation. That being said, don't try to "create" Mona or David. For now, let's just imagine that it's you, basically, in these given circumstances. Especially as, at this moment, you don't really have that much information about either character, especially Mona.

However, purposely use the pronoun "I" in the W.W.W. questions, as well as in the answers that you'll give. Sure, it's quite a small detail, but it does help you get submerged in the situation, even if it's just a little.

Where am I?
When is it happening?
Why am I here: what is my objective?
What's pushing me to want to accomplish my objective: what are my motivations?
What are the stakes?
What are the obstacles standing between me and my objective?
What am I doing to beat my obstacles in order to accomplish my objective?

… … …

Maybe there are elements of the situation that spontaneously speak to you? If yes, great. But that doesn't mean that they aren't made up of sources. That means that certain sources spontaneously arise from the situation and in you. That means that the situation echoes within you, it speaks to you.

These sources can come from your life experiences—you could find equivalences or matches. But they can also come from your imagination; they can provoke fear in you, embrace a desire, an urge, a fantasy, etc.

Whatever they might be, write them down.

… … …

But there's always the possibility that other elements of the situation don't speak to you as much. Here's an example. Let's imagine that you're playing Mona, but that you're not at all the type to just randomly drop by someone's place. You'll have to find a source that helps to propel you to do it. Before reading any further, go back to the scene and precisely identify the elements that need source searching.

... ...

—CUT—

Time to play!

2) Selecting imaginary or experienced sources that *could* correspond to the ones needed during the scene.

Now that you've identified the moments that need sources, select which sources you'll need to embody them. If we base ourselves off of the example given earlier—you're not the type to just randomly drop by someone's place—look for a source that could motivate you to do just that.

Maybe all you need is a situation with high stakes? Based on the way she acts at the end of the scene, that could very well be Mona's case, even though she doesn't show it in the beginning of the scene. The question here is actually very simple. What would make you execute the action of randomly dropping by somewhere? Question your imagination, explore your experiences, search yourself.

... ...

—CUT—

Time to play!

3) Test out each selected source to make sure that it has the desired effect.

As always, actors cannot be content with making choices mentally, they must embody them. It's essential to *truly* test out your sources—those that you had to do some research for, as well as those that instinctively arose from the scene and in you. For this exercise, just test out two or three sources, but really test them out.

Many actors are content with identifying sources, coming from the scene itself or from research, without truly *feeling* the actual effect that they have on them. The most you'll get out of them is an accurate portrayal of the right intentions, but that will remain overall superficial. So false, in a way. It remains accurate, but just for show, and that's when I compare actors to circus animals—they do what is expected of them, but without knowing why, besides the peanuts that we throw at them. In this case, they don't act out the true effect that their sources have on them, but rather the idea of the effect that their sources could have on them. Knowing that a source will have so-and-so effect on you is not enough. Again, you must always turn that knowledge into experience. That's why you must carefully select your sources and test the effect that they have on you. Are they appropriate for the scene? If so, that's great. If not, either you haven't dug deep enough into your sources, or you've chosen the wrong ones. Either dig even deeper, down into the details, or search for others.

Really try it out, but not too relentlessly, not here or at any other point in your work. You know why? Because IT DOESN'T WORK. You know why? Because you're not working with a brick and cement wall, you're working with a human being: you.

We'll soon touch on a bunch of different exercises that offer tools to help dig into your sources, get connected to them, and keep them fresh.

... ...

—CUT—

As you may have already noticed, even when you really intend to truly test out a source, sometimes, you might go straight to the result. That's very common and it's mostly due to the fact you didn't randomly choose so-and-so source, you chose it because it seemed like it would bring you the result needed for the scene.

As we'll talk about later, that's one of the main reasons that I encourage actors to regularly research and test out sources, even outside of working on scenes. This can liberate them from the pressure of having a result—because the sources aren't chosen according to a scene, but simply to discover the effect that they have on them.

Time to play!

4) Repeatedly connect to each source, to make sure that they're trustworthy.

To be sure that your chosen sources function and are trustworthy, test them out multiple times before integrating them into your scene. For instance, if you're playing David's character, choose someone who pretty much has the same effect on you that Mona has on David. Then, at different moments during the week, concentrate a little and get connected to that person. Don't worry about having the exact same result each time; not only would that be uninteresting, but it's also just impossible. You're not a machine, and the varying effects that your sources can have on you is partially what helps to keep a scene fresh. Just make sure that the effect of your source is taking the same direction. Knowing that you're using trustworthy sources plays a big part in helping you to stay confident while acting out scenes.

... ...

—CUT—

Time to play!

5) Integrate the sources into the scene.

Obviously, the whole point of working on sources is not seeing that they work outside of a scene, but that they serve it. It's now time to integrate them into the scene. Make sure to stay very relaxed for this step. Sometimes your sources work perfectly outside of the scene, but then behave differently when confronted with the other elements of the scene. Don't panic! Most of the time, you're just going through a period of adjustment, which ultimately doesn't last. But if it does last, that might mean that you haven't chosen the right source, or, as often happens, that you're tensed up because of your expectations of the source. Maybe you're still searching for the result a little too much? Breathe, go back to the relaxation exercises that we talked about earlier and then come back to the scene.

... ...

—CUT—

For this fifth step, let's go back to our acting/cooking comparison. Some ingredients won't need as much cooking as others, some will have stronger chemical reactions than others, etc. Working on a scene and working on a meal have a lot in common: it's all about dosage, listening/tasting, adapting, and adjusting, which ultimately result in its overall uniformity.

Before digging deeper into other matters and tools of the Method that can help you work on sources, let's talk about the two very important reasons that sources are the foundation of any performance:

1) In order to be accurate on stage.

2) In order to have fun.

In order to be accurate on stage.

As we talked about earlier, anyone can be an actor on stage, but what we really want to see is a human being in imaginary situations. And human beings never act like empty puppets—they act once connected to sources that are inside of them. So, everything that actors do must be related to one or more sources. That's mostly what determines whether their acting is accurate or not. Basically, if you don't have a reason to take action, then don't—whether it be on stage or in real life. An actor is like a glass of water. Sources are like syrup. They're what determine the specific flavors of each moment. Wait for the source to take over you before taking action on stage, the same way that we wait for the syrup to diffuse in the water before taking a sip. That's one of the reasons why Marlon Brando became the legendary actor that he is and, incidentally, the main reason for his "slow" acting which many mistook for a sort of stylistic calm. The very idea of giving a fake and soulless performance horrified him so much that he would always wait to be truly connected to his sources before taking action. Though it's still worthy to note that that slowness often corresponded well with the parts that he played. But no matter what, always prioritize being accurate rather than keeping up the pace, although the pace of a scene can sometimes participate in the accuracy. But, since the pace of a scene always comes from the sense of urgency and the pressure of your sources, always privilege them.

In order to have fun.

If you still haven't realized this about life, then hopefully acting will help you out. The actor's profession is demanding. The industry is violent. So, if you don't feel like having fun is a must, then switch professions right now. Seriously. Otherwise, there's a strong chance that you'll end up wasting a lot of time ... I've seen it happen more than you'd think.

But saying to someone "Just have fun!" is completely futile. In fact, the person often gets sucked in an endless boredom, tainted with some kind of bizarre guilt. Except if the person is offered a game that he or she can truly play! In acting and in life alike, the game of sources is one of the most important games to play. Try it out. Play. Trip out.

Time to play!

Choose a simple action to execute. For instance, grabbing your phone to call someone. Now do the action without thinking about anything.

... ...

Your acting might've seemed pretty accurate, but either way, you probably were dead bored while doing that. You probably felt like the circus animal that we were talking about.
Just imagine those that spend their entire career doing that!!!

Bad actors use their muscles. Good actors use their soul, which in turn, guides their muscles.

Now redo the action, but this time after having chosen sources: the person you're calling, the reason you're calling, etc.

... ...

It's much more exciting and alive, isn't it?

—CUT—

Let's imagine that I choose to call Mona. Not only would my acting be alive, I would live out a truly thrilling experience. Especially after her unexpected visit and her unsettling breakdown! Was she running away from me? But then why would she have come? Should I call her right away and ask her to come back? What if she says no? What if she says yes?! What if she never answers me again?

Good acting is not made up of mechanical representations—it's made up of real experiences ... that's why we call it "self-bluff."

You have my word as a coach: get a taste of the pleasure that it is to act with sources, and then acting without them will seem unbearably dull to you. It's a trip, in the literal sense of the word, it's traveling. It's a drug (a non-toxic one!). Why deprive yourself and the audience of it?

The light bulb and the light switch

Don't touch the light bulb, you're gonna blow everything up!
(A haiku about electricity)

You're now about to read the shortest sub-chapter of this whole book. But, in my humble opinion, what's written here is essential. That's the whole reason that I dedicated a sub-chapter to it. When entering a room and you want to turn on the light, you don't press the light bulb, you press the light switch. Well, do the same thing with your sources. Don't look directly for the result, go to their sources. Go to the source of your sources. Find, *in them*, the light switches that will give them life, *in you*. Otherwise, like with electricity, you'll make everything explode.

These light switches are always in the details of your sources.

Always keep that in mind. Press the light switch, not the light bulb.

Internal and external sources

In scenes and in life alike, there are two kinds of sources: external sources and internal sources. When I see Mona, that's an external source. When I think of Mona, that's an internal source. Both are just as powerful. They can also join forces. When Mona randomly dropped by, her presence (external source) gave me visions, images of the relationship and the love story that we could have together (internal sources).

In comparison, when we're looking at a menu in a restaurant, we imagine what the dishes are like before ordering: these are internal sources. When we eye the meals that other people ordered at other tables, those are external sources.

Let's push this comparison a little further; I think this is an example that can speak to everybody, and is the most tangible way to understand taking on sources and the way that we select them. What do we do when reading a menu at a restaurant? We imagine the dishes, we picture what they'll be like, we internally "taste" them. Why do we choose one dish out of all of the possibilities? Because that dish has a stronger effect on us than all of the others. That effect pushes us to take action: ordering the dish. You need to go through the exact same process when choosing sources. Try them out and observe the effect that they have on you. Of course, the effect that they have on you has to correspond to what the scene needs. And once you've found all of the right sources, acting out the scene will feel completely natural to you.

But actors don't dispose of a "source menu." That's why they must create it, or rather, rediscover it, but also stretch it out, nourish it, and broaden it. Conceive your "source menu." I also said "rediscover it," because it automatically already exists in you, because sources are what push you to take action everyday, at every moment, at every second. Stretching out and enriching that "source menu" is one of this book's objectives.

I've often encouraged you to explore the details of your sources and will continue to do so, precisely in order to perfect your "source menu." It's the details that make your sources pulsate inside you, that make you believe in them. That's what will have a strong and reliable effect on you, because:

What is approached superficially will remain superficial, what is approached deep down, can only deepen.

However, it's not only about looking for the "photographic" details of your sources, it's about finding the truly impactful details, the light switches that we were talking about.

Intimacy vs. privacy

Working on sources is almost systematically private. That's one of the reasons why your sources must remain secret, whether they come from your real life, your imagination, or a combination of the two. First and foremost, to protect your private life, your secret garden. Secondly, so that you can stay focused on your sources and not on what others could think of your choice of sources and the way that you connect to them.

When I work as a coach, I always make sure to tell actors that I'm working with them on intimacy, not privacy. Let me explain: for instance, while working on a scene that requires exploring sources in a specific direction—for example, romantic love—of course, we're working on an intimate level. But no one else but the actor should know what source he or she is using. This is the *one and only* way that coaches should be allowed to work with actors!

Unfortunately, there's a type of manipulative violation of privacy that seems to be spreading way too much among coaches. Part of your work is revealing on stage *the effects* that your inner world and sources have on you; however, what's actually contained in your inner world is nobody's business *but yours!* So, if you happen to work with one of these way too intrusive coaches, either put them in their place, or run.

So that the difference between what's intimate and what's private is completely clear to you, let's try out an exercise.

Time to play!

Imagine that a role required you to embody physical and psychological fear of someone. Select, from your imagination or from your real life, the source of a person that heads in that direction. Once again, your source could appear immediately or take a little time to find. That's neither a good thing nor a bad thing. But conceiving your "source menu" over time will help you little by little to find sources faster.

Don't read further until you've found a source.

... ...

You found someone? Ok. Here's a very important note: don't play fear! Play the process. Don't act out the result, look for the impactful details, look for the light switches, not the light bulbs. Take the time to choose them meticulously. What scares you about this person? Their potential violence? Did they ever lay hands on you? In what circumstances? Where? In the light of day? At night? Is it someone who's intelligent? Can you see the look in their eyes? What kind of effect does it have on you? What's the color of their eyes? What do you read in them? Can you hear their breathing? Can you smell them? What's the worst thing that this person could do to you? The worst. Does it include certain instruments? Fire? Blades? Needles? Which are rusty? In your jaw? Under your nails? Acid? On what parts of your body? Etc.

—CUT—

Of course, my questions are intimate, but I have no idea what your source is, what person you're using. Same thing with the types of abuse I named: the questions remain intimate, but I don't know which ones work for you. However, if I were to ask you who that person is—which I would never do—we would be crossing the line into privacy, where only *you* should have access.

I've sometimes asked actors what they were using, but in terms of tools. Whether they were using imagination, a substitution, emotional memory, or others that we'll discover a little later. But I never ask them to reveal the sources that are contained in the tool that they're using. In other words, I know the technical components, but not the private content.

Of course, one of the reasons for this procedure is purely ethical (respecting the privacy of the actor's choice of sources), but here's another one: you can of course suggest sources to actors, the way I just did on the subject of torture. But only actors themselves can truly test out which sources really work with them.

So when you're being directed in a play or on a movie set, don't limit yourself to the sources that are suggested or pushed onto you. Use the ones that impact you and *translate* the other ones into sources that will actually affect you.

It's noteworthy that a lot of actors, supposedly from the Method, like to reveal their private sources. It often seems to come from some kind of need for this useless and superficial exhibitionism. Sure, actors do have a kind of "exhibitionism," but they must always reveal the effects of their sources and not the sources themselves. They reveal their intimacy, not their private life. Always!

Sweat, blood, sex ... and chocolate

As you've probably noticed, I mostly give sources that incorporate primary functions as examples. These elements are brought up simply because they're what we connect the fastest to and, more often than not, their impact is strong and hits us deep down. Also, don't complicate your sources. A good actor can't be stupid, but he also has to know when to use his intellect and when to give it a rest. Do not overthink your sources, it won't get you anywhere.

Look for primary sources, for this one good and simple reason: they work better. Sweat, blood, sex, ... and chocolate. Don't just observe the surface of these words, dig into their deeper meaning and everything that they hold.

Sweat: efforts, difficulty, every kind of obstacle, our will, relentlessness, etc.

Blood: health, violence, life, death, war, peace, our loved ones, survival, fighting, hunger, food, etc.

Sex: desire, love, fantasies, submission, domination, romantic conquest, seduction, etc.

Chocolate: chocolate.

Don't worry, using primary sources won't make you seem or act like a primate species. With painting, all of the colors come from magenta red, yellow, or cyan blue, that's why we call them primary colors.

The magenta red used by Van Gogh or the cyan blue used by Picasso aren't any less primary than when used by any house painter. It's how they choose and dose all three of the colors combined together, which offers an infinite palette and the delicacy in the variations. So:

The intensity of your acting will come from your primary sources; its finesse, from the artful combinations that you'll create.

Two sources of sources, one same approach

> *Don't just say Yuck! ... try it first!*
> **(Our moms)**

There are many ways that you can approach sources: through visuals, music, sense, and emotional memories, substitutions, dreams and living nightmares, imagination, etc. But they can't be exclusively derived from experience or imagination, which we can mix together as much as we want, as we said earlier.

Despite the many debates between the "pro-experience" team (Lee Strasberg and his disciples) and the "pro-imagination" team (Stella Adler and hers), both are equally interesting and useful. Robert Lewis and his disciples, which include me, let actors try all of the possible tools and mix and match as they please, just like Stanislavski.

Don't prejudge ahead of time your preference between using experience or imagination in your acting. Try to truly explore both options. As many times as possible. Stay available and open to both. Don't say "*Yuuuck!!!*" before tasting both. Play the game!

Real-life sources are filled with information that you already know and are familiar with. With imaginary sources, you get to invent everything from scratch. This doesn't mean that you shouldn't go searching for the details in your real-life sources, nor does it mean that imaginary sources always need twice as much work. With both types of sources, there's only one type of approach that's truly effective: looking for the details that impact you. How fast these details appear for you doesn't depend on whether you're using the imagination or real life. Both can also contain heavy elements on the mind and subconscious, but either way, you must always look for the details.

But don't forget—not the photographic details, the impactful details.

By the way, I have a question for you. In your opinion, which profession is the furthest away from the acting profession?

... ...

Newscaster.

Newscasters talk about natural disasters or mass murders with so little detail that they can go from a mass shooting in a preschool to the lottery results in a heartbeat. At best, without batting an eyelid; at worst, pretending to bat an eyelid. The newscaster is paid to present the news and to sometimes bat an eyelid. The actor is paid to embody, with his heart and soul. He can't just vaguely imagine what a mass shooting in a preschool is like—he has to "be there." And in order to do that, he has to go into detail.

While doing the next exercise, take the time to visualize/imagine/feel your answers, even if it's just little by little. I'm counting on you.

Time to play!

What does a baby's pajamas smell like when it's burning? What about a baby? Can you see his little lifeless hand? His name was Benjamin. He just died of suffocation. Can you see his little swollen face? Puffed up because of lack of oxygen. Turned blue of asphyxia. What will his mother say? Are babies measured, in order to build their coffin? Are there ready-built coffins in stock at funeral homes, ready for the next tragedy? What will his mom say? Can you see his teddy bear lying next to him? It looks as if it's crying tears of blood. Benjamin was holding him tight while dying. Maybe he thought that Winnie would save him? How will his mom tell his brothers and sisters? Yes, what will she say to her children? Will she still be able to sing them to sleep with lullabies? What does she make now of fairytales, happy endings, hope, desire? What will she do with Benjamin's crib? Empty. Forever. How will she ever be strong enough to be able to throw away his little belongings, his Winnie, his strapped shoes, the backpack that he'll never use? Right now, she thinks that Benjamin is playing. Right now, Benjamin's dying.

—CUT—

Stalin said this chilling phrase: "The death of one man is a tragedy. The death of millions is a statistic."

No true artist is in the statistics. Every true artist is in the particularities, the case study, a fingerprint, a soul.

The imaginary in real life and the real life in the imaginary

We'll be exploring the work around the imagination as well as real life in different chapters, but it's important to understand that, really, there is no separation between the two of them. There is a belief that is as widespread as it is false, which is that the imagination and real life are radically different.

Widespread, because we're living under an imposed tyranny that promotes an approach to life that's almost exclusively logical.

False, because the imaginary and real life are threaded by the same needle: ourselves, our psyche.

Where else can our imagination come from besides our life experiences? And aren't our life experiences molded, or at least partially influenced, by our imagination? We concretely live by what our vision of the world is, but it remains nonetheless a vision. Our real memories get mixed in with the fantasies of our memory and our projections, for better and for worse. Even the vision that we have of ourselves is woven with two threads—that of our life experiences and that of our imagination. We are the intertwinement of these two sources of sources.

Freely weaving the two together in your acting and anywhere else offers endless possibilities that are a treasure trove of surprises, which are often symbolic. And those symbols can be quite significant, because they are the essence of all things: they not only speak to our conscious mind, but to our unconscious mind as well and inspire us.

Time to play!

You know what a fly is. That's experience. And you know what eating is. That's also experience. But you might not know what eating a fly is. That's the imaginary mixed with life experience. Try it out.

... ...

No, not by *actually* eating a fly! But by asking yourself specific sensorial questions, that are chock full of details.

··· ··· ···

What's a fly's texture? What sound does biting down on one make? We've all seen what a squashed flea looks like and that whitish, thickish texture that seeps out of its body. I'm not too sure, but I think I'd imagine it to be pretty sour tasting. What about you? Taste via the imaginary.

··· ··· ···

It doesn't actually matter whether a fly is sour tasting or not, what matters is whether it has an impact on you or not. If that happens to be the case, then go ahead and write down this source in your own personal "source menu."
Either way, look for others.

··· ··· ···

All of this is related to a subject that we're about to explore, which is about liberating our imagination. A very good way of doing that is intertwining it with our experiences. The amount of possibilities is literally infinite. Often practice extrapolating from your life experience towards your imagination. We already do this exercise quite often without realizing it, most of the time naturally and unconsciously. So what will you find? What can you discover? Try it without letting any complexes get in the way … Nobody knows what your sources are! Have fun. Just let go.

··· ··· ···

How do vampires make love? What does an eye sandwich taste like? And what if you add a little mayonnaise? White sauce, ketchup, mustard? What does a leaf taste like? It probably depends on the tree that it fell from.

··· ··· ···

You've felt what a rush of pleasure or fear is like before, maybe even both at the same time. You've gotten a shot or a blood test before. If you combine that rush feeling with the sensation of a needle puncturing your skin and then your vein, you can imagine/feel what a junkie feels.

··· ··· ···

How many times have you imagined brushing your lips against those of someone that you fantasize about? Is Mona a good kisser? At the moment that I'm writing these words, I don't know yet. But I've kissed women before. And I've also focused on Mona's mouth before. While mixing up the two, I've just felt something very strong. I make it last longer by focusing on the details: her eyes in mine, the silky warmth of her breath … Does she have soft lips? I have no idea, but the slight creases that I've noticed on them make me think that no, not particularly. However, the way that she moves, the way that she gives life to every object that she touches, makes me think that she's an expert at kissing.

… … …

What about you? How do you think your "fantasized" loved one kisses?

… … …

$-CUT-$

Once again, it doesn't matter whether the answers that you've found are true or not, as long as they have an impact on you. Search and test out your imagination and experience "cocktails." Don't remain too rational. Dare to fantasize, to have nightmares, and to dream.
Dare to. Always.
But, while always applying our five favorite safety rules. Get out your pencils, it's quiz time!

Time to play!

Can you remember the five safety rules, without going back in the book to find them?

… … …

$-CUT-$

All right! I'll harp on it one last time, to be absolutely sure that you thoroughly embed them into your research:

1. Do not hurt yourself or others, in any way.
2. Do not grope yourself or others.
3. Do not ingest any alcohol or drugs that strongly alter your state of mind.
4. Never reveal your sources.
5. Always make sure you're having fun in your work.

In order to test out the imaginary in real life and real life in the imaginary, let's call upon our favorite protagonists.

Laaadies and gentlemeeeen!!!

Miss M.

Starring

David (You!)

(for our lovely actresses, turn the tables and imagine that you're playing David too!)

INT/NIGHT — "DAVID'S" OFFICE

David is now sitting down, with Mona's purse and the gun still in it on his desk. Completely still, he looks at her purse with a mix of apprehension and melancholy. He hesitates whether to open it or not … sighs deeply … then looks away, deep in thought …

INT/NIGHT — THE BATHROOM IN "DAVID'S" OFFICE

David tries to relax and splashes some water on his face at the sink … He suddenly freezes when he looks up and sees what's written on the bathroom mirror: "L.O.V.E," then "in numbers" written in red lipstick. He doesn't understand …

INT/NIGHT — "DAVID'S" OFFICE

David doesn't wait any longer and opens Mona's purse.

Besides the gun, which is of big caliber, David finds the usual mess that you can find if you look through a young woman's purse. A makeup bag, phone charger, notepad/schedule, an orange, paperwork, a small water bottle, a facial mask, candy, etc.

He picks up the gun and stares at it for a second. On the handle of the gun, a phoenix is engraved, as well as the words "Mori et Resurgere."

David (whispering to himself)   To die and to resuscitate.

He becomes lost in thought then puts the gun back down on the desk. He rummages around the purse a little more and finds a Russian passport. He flips through it and finds a bunch of different visas: India, Italy, Nepal, Romania, Colombia, Spain, France, Germany, Canada, Tunisia, Latvia, USA … He can't avert his eyes when he gets to Mona's photo, which moves him … However, the emotion evaporates when he reads the name on the passport: Phoenix. Surname: Grof. Nationality: Russian. He puts the passport away.

In the makeup bag, he finds nail polish, eye shadow, makeup brushes, condoms, a small fig-smelling perfume bottle. He gently picks it up and smells it. It deeply relaxes him, immediately. He savors the feeling … then squirts a little on the inside of his wrist.

While going through the notepad/schedule, which is full of her handwriting, crossings-out and drawings, he notices the note "randomly drop by David's place." On another page, he finds a black penned drawing of himself, very well done, with a speech bubble that says: "I love you more than a Pho soup." He smiles.

He goes rummaging through the purse again and finds a silky pouch that has the name Chantal Thomass printed on it, a famous French lingerie brand …

David   Sorry missy, it's for the good of the investigation.

He opens it but is very surprised at what he finds: very tiny plastic bundles. He pinches one of the bundles and white powder bursts out, seemingly cocaine.

David   Ok …

He makes some room on his desk and empties the silk pouch onto it: about a hundred little bundles of cocaine drop onto the desk. He turns very pale.

David Oh, fuck!

He grabs his iPhone and calls Mona. As soon as it dials, the sound of another phone ringing can be heard in the office.

David wonders what on Earth is going on ... then spots Mona's smartphone next to the coffee machine. He grabs it and sees the caller ID, which reads "Teddy Boy" and the option "UNLOCK."

He hesitates ... then chooses "UNLOCK," but a password is needed.

David Shit!

He hangs up his iPhone. The smartphone stops ringing as soon as he does.
As he paces back and forth in the office hallway, he can't stop thinking of all the unanswered questions that he has ... Through the doorway, he can read "L.O.V.E in numbers" or "srebmun ni E.V.O.L," depending on the direction that he's pacing. "L.O.V.E in numbers," "srebmun ni E.V.O.L," "L.O.V.E in numbers." Suddenly, David has an idea!

iPhone in hand, "Teddy Boy" calls Mona's phone again. David grabs it and types in the password.

David L:5, O:6, V:8, E:3.

Mona's smartphone unlocks.

David Yes, nice going Teddy Boy!

But his enthusiasm is short-lived, as he realizes that he can "see himself" holding a phone in each hand, calling himself. He sits back down at his desk, discouraged. He looks at the items spread on the table—Mona/Phoenix Grof's passport, the bundles of cocaine, and the gun.

David Well, your mom isn't the only maze architect here ... Mona, Phoenix Gof, or Whatever.

The orange falls out of the purse, and slowly rolls towards David ...

To be continued ...

Time to play!

In order to work on this scene, see how you can combine sources from your life experience and others from your imagination.

Your "fantasized" loved one has probably already surprised you before. If the answer to that is "No," then don't run after them, you deserve better. You deserve someone who will surprise you. If the answer is "Yes, he or she has surprised me before," then that's a source from life experience.

But did that surprise include illegal elements, that were maybe even dangerous? If that's not the case, then we're working on imagination.

Imagine if your loved one was armed.

... ...

So? How does that feel?

... ...

But not so fast! I don't mean armed with a gun that you see in the movies; a real gun, that sends people six feet underground. And that can get them sent to prison. But not so fast! Not in the prisons like you see in the movies, no sir. In prison-prison. Where rape is just routine, where privacy is nonexistent, where even using the toilet is in the presence of complete strangers. So that all of those elements—death, prison, rape, etc.—are tainted with reality for you, I'll let you explore the details and we'll pick up just afterwards.

... ...

How has your perception of the person changed? I said "has changed" rather than "would have changed," because we're here to really do the exercise, not just think about it.

... ...

Unless you're Pablo Escobar's spiritual son, you've probably never seen 100 grams of cocaine upfront. Now, imagine that while going through your loved one's jacket for clues of his/her unfaithfulness, you were to find 100 grams of some drug.

... ...

How *has* your perception of this person *changed*?

... ...

And when I mentioned unfaithfulness, cheating, what did you think of?

... ...

Did these images and sources come from your life experience, your imagination, or a combination of the two?

... ...

You know your loved one, but you guys aren't together yet. So, *technically*, he/she couldn't have cheated on you. But if you have a pretty "normal" love life, then you've probably already been cheated on?

... ...

No?!

... ...

Are you sure?!

... ...

Absolutely certain?!

... ...

How do my questions make you feel? Are you thinking of experience? Is your imagination up and running?

... ...

What if you had already been cheated on, but you just never found out?

... ...

What if, when you finally got with your loved one, he/she cheated on you?

... ...

But not so fast! Not cheating like in the movies. No. Cheating-cheating. With the stomach aches and, sometimes, the excitement that can come with it.

—CUT—

That last question about your loved one cheating is a combination of experience and imagination, since you guys aren't together yet. That last question probably dug out sources in you. And from those sources came psychophysical actions: questioning yourself? Doubting? Etc. Then emotions might've appeared, right?

Very important! Once again, we didn't work *directly* on the emotions, but on the sources. However, if you really went through with the exercise, then emotions surfaced. So, remember:

100 percent of the time, emotions are the derived products of sources. That's what we search for: the light switches, not the emotions—which are the light bulbs.

Forever and always!

Imagination

Now, it's time to smash one of the biggest misconceptions about the Method into smithereens: all Method actors use their life experience to act. *Bullshit!!!*

The misconception is in the word "all." Many Method actors don't work directly on their life experience, but with their imagination. Even though, as we've discussed, the two are intimately connected. As we've also discussed, just because certain sources haven't been experienced doesn't mean that they aren't just as deeply intimate. And honestly, what is more intimate than our imagination? Isn't it the designer of our deepest fantasies, our wildest dreams, and our scariest nightmares?

New York. I'll never forget that snowy December night. That night at the HB Studio, when entering the classroom, we saw Katharina Sergava, my Master, my mentor, and friend, in tears. Worried by seeing such a powerful, dignified and charismatic woman having a moment of fragility like this, we approached her very carefully. Despite her tears, the brightness of her steel blue gaze was still there, perhaps even stronger than ever. In her Egon Schiele like majestic, wrinkled old hands, she was holding an issue of National Geographic. It was opened to a page that had a photo of a chameleon with very surreal colors. "That's what I'm talking about, when I talk about imagination," she said while staying focused on the creature. "Do you see the unreal texture, these mind-blowing shapes, the range of colors? Can you see the precision, the details, the specificity? Nothing can beat nature's imagination! Nothing can hold a candle to it! And yet, this is the degree of imagination that we need, that we must achieve, or at least reach for, in our work. In our lives, kids! In our lives!"

Now, THAT'S coaching! Invigorating, challenging, inspiring.

Sure, Katharina was teaching us acting, but she was also teaching us about the most important piece of the Method and of life itself: opening our eyes. Seeing the depth of every little thing, seeing the endless beauty that each thing could contain. Widening our potential of wonderment. Understanding the inventiveness of the world around us, whether it be in a roach and its nano-mechanisms, the sky and its infinity, or garbage and what it says about us: letting it all inspire us and nourish our imagination, nourish *ourselves*.

How do we develop our imagination?

Ironically, by looking at fewer visuals.

As we talked about earlier, being non-stop suffocated with pictures and images, constantly forces us to be in the position of a spectator. And an actor must essentially be an actor of life, if he wants to be a human being on stage.

Time to play!

Imagine eating two 28 ounce T-bone steaks, seven dozen fried snails, nine veal cutlets with lots of sauce, three big bowls of mashed potatoes with a side of six plates of fries, two plates of sauerkraut, eight deviled eggs, and, to finish all that off on a sugary note, eleven apple pies smothered in whipped cream and fifteen chocolate puddings.

... ...

Oh, sorry! Forgot the cheese. Here it is. Here *they* are: half a pound of blue cheese, sixteen slices of goat cheese, eight Camemberts, and a pound and a half of Pecorino.

... ...

Now, how about a nice bowl of lentils and sausage, an entire duck pâté with all the crust, and a pint of melted butter to wash it all down?

—CUT—

Desire needs space in order to develop. If we get full, then full again, desire gets burnt out, left behind and "crashes."
It dies, and no longer represents what it's all about: being alive.
It works exactly the same when it comes to imagination.
Imagination needs space. We mustn't force images upon it all the time, so that it can create its own. And when I talk about the imagination creating images, I mean its capacity to create on its own, not regurgitate the images of others.
When I work as a screenwriter/director, I'm always shocked that the first thing that I'm usually asked is to show visual references. It's not that I don't have any, quite the opposite actually! But that's not the first thing that I'm here to offer. And what would be the point of offering it if it already exists?
Have you noticed that more and more often, people will almost always reference other images whenever we bring up something? As if they're search engines. And it is suffocating! The air of this era needs some air.
We all act so surprised that nothing really new has been created. That there are no new movements, no fresh breaths of air, no innovative artistic waves. All we do is repeat, copy and paste, patchwork, compile, best-of.
Sure, we arrived a little late in the history of humanity and art. But I would hope that we're still able to imagine some more.
But for that, we need space. Spaaaace. Spaaaaaaaaace …!

Time to play!

—CUT—

Ok, back to the question that's also the title of this sub-chapter: How do we develop our imagination? And, back to the first answer that I gave, which was: Ironically, by looking at fewer visuals.
Of course, that doesn't mean that you can never watch movies, videos, or see pictures ever again, but it does some good to limit the intake, so that you can at least spend *as much* time imagining your own images. One of the best ways of doing that is and always will be reading books.

Time to play!

Get yourself *The Catcher in the Rye*, the pre-pop art and initiatory novel by the marvelous J.D. Salinger, and read it. Or read it again.

... ...

Once you've finished reading, take in the images that it's left in you. Note them. Dig deeper into them. Live them.

... ...

Follow Holden Caulfield's character doing actions that we don't see him doing in the book.

... ...

For instance, imagine him going to the pool and ask yourself a bunch of specific questions. What kind of bathing suit is he wearing? Is he comfortable with his body? Does he swim well? Is he the type to look girls or boys up and down in their swimsuit? What does he find attractive? Which details catch his eye? What type of disgust does he feel when he senses a hair in his mouth that isn't his? Does it depress him? For how long? Does he judge others? The flabby stomach of the old grandpa who's fallen asleep? The curves of a girl swimmer? The humid footprints of small children on the tiling? The lifeguard's disgusting hairstyle? Etc.

... ...

Try out the experiment multiple times. Follow the character in diverse situations. Take note of the images that work with you, that impact you. Really take note. Keep broadening your "source menu." They'll come very useful to you.

—CUT—

Come on, let's keep up the good work!

Time to play!

Now, choose somebody that you kind of know. A little. Not someone that you know intimately, nor someone who's a total stranger to you. The grocer, a neighbor, someone that you have a crush on. Imagine that person in various situations while, again, asking yourself specific questions and going into detail.

... ...

How does so-and-so cook?

... ...

How does so-and-so clean up his/her living-room?

... ...

Is so-and-so more of a shower of a bath person?

... ...

Does so-and so smoke?

... ...

Etc. ...

—CUT—

Once again, it doesn't matter whether what you imagined is true or not. What matters is the impact that these visuals have on you. Dig into them. Intensify them. Cherish them. Do this exercise as often as possible, with as many different people as possible. Not only does this develop your imagination, but it also sharpens your observation skills, as well as your sense of compassion. Compassion is incredibly important, whether you're an actor or not. We'll talk about its direct link with acting a little later.

Time to play!

Go out and observe the passers-by on the street. Ponder this person or that person. Imagine them in various situations again. Ask yourself questions. Look for the details that have an impact on you. Get past your prejudices. Allow yourself to imagine the part of every Being that's filled with surprises, passion, poetry.

... ...

—CUT—

Stanislavski would tell a story about a woman who lived in his neighborhood, who had a little monkey that she would push in a baby stroller. From an anecdotal point of view, she would simply be considered as crazy. But Stanislavski encourages us to see above and beyond our prejudices and assumptions. He would bring up the possibility that maybe this woman had lost her only child under horrible circumstances. Broken by sadness and mourning, the idea of having another child was too painful and brought back the fear of loss. But her maternal instinct had stayed intact: showy, but stifled all the same. That little monkey filled the empty space in her heart, even though she would be much less attached to it.

Let us transcend the superficial easiness of prejudice and the nauseating vulgarity of the anecdotal. We're worth more than that. Much more.

Time to play!

When the snow melts, where does the white go?

(Héctor Abad)

Now, choose an animal. An elephant, an insect, your cat. How does it see the world? What does it feel when setting its paw on the ground? What does hunger feel like for it? What about affection? Does a cockroach have emotions? Does an elephant dream? Of course it does! But about what? True or false doesn't matter, it's the impact that's important. The point of this experience is to develop your imagination outside of the old beaten track, in extravagant, extraordinary, jarring, poetic ways. It's about broadening its horizons. Breaking down its walls. Ask yourself questions about beings, things, and everything that's around you as often as you can. But never adopt an exclusively materialistic, cold, and factual approach.

How does a rock feel? Is the caretaker of your building an android? Is the butcher an alien? What did Einstein dream about? How was he able to marry his scientific knowledge with his faith in God? What kind of remorse ate him up after Hiroshima? How will you die? How would you like to die? Does being immortal really appeal to you? What kind of loneliness do we feel if we're the only immortal being? Do we come to forget those that we've lost, those who have passed on, if we never pass on ourselves? What do fish think about? Do they have the same awareness of water? Imagine if your skin was made of scales. Imagine the reflections all over them. All over you. Could you eat a human being? If you had no other choice, who would you eat? The person who came to my mind surprised me. What about you? Would you cook them? Would you boil or fry them? What was David Foster Wallace thinking about when he committed suicide? Who draws the clouds? Your bones are fluorescent. You don't yet know your future love. And yet, he/she exists. Where is he/she right at this exact moment? You know that they exist. Is the pain that they're going through right now preparing them to better love you? What about the pain you're going through? How does a flower breathe? Are there lazy ants? Do insects snore? A caterpillar tart. A flying elephant. An enamored jellyfish. Draw me a sheep.

Be surreal! Dare the implausible. Be your own biggest inspiration. Free your imagination. Re-*source* it.

—CUT—

Your imagination will greatly thank you and in return will breathe that precious breath of inspiration into your performances. Once you've started creating your own library full of truly self-created, uninhibited, lively and intimate visuals, then you can dive into the world of visuals that are offered in paintings, in the media, comic books, movies, video clips, the internet, any other platform. But all the while sharpening your critical sense. The point is not to be able to criticize more or better, the point is to be able to make pertinent choices in the sources that impact you.

Time to play!

What types of visuals from the imagination of others speak to you? Which style of painting? Which artistic movement? Where does their beauty, their power, their impact come from? What specific details entail profound reactions in you?

Once again, don't remain a mere spectator, interact with the works of art that call to you. Go inside, via the imagination.

... ...

Don't try to analyze. Feel.

… … …

—CUT—

Nourish yourself with other forms of art. Now that you've become your own inspiration, find inspiration in others as well. But don't swallow everything that's thrown at you. Always stay active, vigilant, creative. Always stay away from the superficial position of spectator and be an actor that participates in things themselves, all the way down into the way that you look at them.

The magic if

It's because of the word "If" that we were able to walk on the moon, invent electricity, discover time relativity, and accomplish many other miracles! Many grand events ended up seeing the light of day thanks to an "If," even if it might've seemed highly unlikely. What if we could fly? Airplanes. And what if slaves had the same rights as free people? Abolition of slavery. And what if there were other specimens in the universe, other civilizations, other worlds entirely? The many conquests in outer space. And what if you got a part in the next John Cameron Mitchell movie? Your decision to go into acting …

Throughout his passionate research of the human soul and his intimate understanding of it, Stanislavski discovered that the word "If" is a very powerful, almost magical, trigger with human beings. That's how he would end up suggesting to actors to work with the "Magic If."

Essentially, it's about bringing up possibilities rather than stating lies.

Time to play!

Say to yourself: "I'm an alien."

… … …

Now, say to yourself: "*IF* I was an alien …"

… … …

Do you feel the difference? Maybe not.

So let's try something else. Say to yourself: "I'm living a love story with my fantasized loved one."

… … …

And now: "*IF* I were living a love story with my fantasized loved one …"

… … …

Now do you feel the difference? Maybe not just yet. Let's try again. Say to yourself: "There's a war going on in the city I live in."

... ...

Then: "*IF* there was a war going on in the city I live in ..."

... ...

- CUT -

The difference might seem very mild to you, but for our imagination, the difference is *major*. If you state something, you close it off. Not necessarily because it's wrong or impossible to believe in, but because that phrasing doesn't let the imagination fly freely. The exact opposite can happen with the "If," and that's why it's so magical.

Time to play!

Try the exercise again, with the same propositions that we brought up or others.

... ...

—CUT—

This time, do you really feel the difference between the statement and the "If"? The first one imposes, the other induces. And our imagination doesn't like to be forced into anything. Not at all! It likes to be flirted with, gently approached, excited. It likes seduction, not rape. The "Magic If" is basically the equivalent of "Let's pretend," something children use naturally all the time and that often brings them to no longer pretend, but to be. One of the main benefits of the "If" resides in the immediacy of its impact on us. Mainly because we often use it, every day of our lives, and have done so ever since we were children. Once again, the Method is based on the ways that we already function naturally: the ways of our psyche, our soul, life itself. So approach your scenes the same way that you approach most of the important moments in your life: with an "If ...."

Oh, one last thing: "And what if you became a renowned actor or actress?" I know, this is a touchy subject. That's exactly why I'm bringing it up. In order to make you fully understand the strength of the very simple tool, that is the "Magic If." A strength that I think is multiplied when you add the word "And" in front. That helps you make a connection, establish a continuity with the already existing reality. So, "And what if you became a renowned actor or actress?"

Do you see the parade of images that that phrasing awakens in you? Say it to yourself again: "And what if you became a renowned actor or actress?" then let the images trip you out. Let their flavors infuse you. Which ones are the strongest? Write them down. Can you see the director telling you that you got the part? Can you picture the scene where you have to kiss? Are you imagining someone? Great. That's the effect of the "If": direct, concrete, gripping, and palpable.

And what if you won an Oscar? Come on, let's be honest ... you know you've already thought about it. Some of you have probably already practiced your acceptance speech in your head, on the subway, in the shower, on the toilet. *"That's* what I'll say when I win my first very well-deserved Oscar." And *if* that happens one day, all of it will have been thanks to a simple "If …."

Living nightmares and dreams

Time to play!

And what if, right now, something horrible was happening to someone you love?

… … …

It's entirely possible. The world is full of dangers. It will happen one day. Maybe even the worst. Maybe even worse than the worst.

… … …

Am I playing with your nerves? Yes, I know, but I didn't force you to be an actor! And what are actors, if not people who play with themselves, their passions, their desires, their fantasies, their nerves?

—CUT—

The "Magic If" is directly connected to dreams and living nightmares. Those are basically the hard-core version of the "Magic If"—they embody our wildest fantasies and our deepest fears. The "What if you became a renowned actor or actress," just as "What if you were the biggest jerk," are part of dreams and living nightmares.

Every day in our lives, we have moments when we get lost in our imagination. Be inspired by these moments, they are great sources of sources. Dig into them. Into the details.

Don't be afraid. It's just to play. It's not for real, but it's true.

Warning: So I've encouraged you to truly try out all of the exercises up until now, but this one is much more tricky. Take your time to think about it before actually doing this one. If it makes you even slightly uncomfortable, go ahead and skip to the next sub-chapter.

To make you realize the importance of choosing the right impactful sources, the internet link just underneath leads to extremely violent images that may shock *even the most hardened ones* among you. I'm not kidding—which is rare—really think about it before clicking on that link.

Don't feel guilty if you prefer to avoid seeing those types of images. But if you do decide to check out the images, at least you'll be prepared for what you're about to expose yourself to. You'll be responsible for yourself.

Time to play!

… Or not …

www.methodacting.fr/extreme-massacres-torture

—CUT—

Are you ok? Are you still here? You didn't faint while looking at those images that simply don't exist? Or, as you've probably just experienced, they do indeed exist, but only in your mind. That goes for those who chose to click on the link just as well as those who didn't. Maybe even more for those who didn't.

What came to mind? What carnage? What horror? What torture? What disaster? And, *always*, which details? Write all of it down, it's very important.

Your mind created images all by itself that were probably more terrifying than any image that I could've shown you. That's what we call the power of imagination.

Imaginary facts

The imaginary fact is one of the simplest and most efficient tools used for sources. For this one reason: the majority of us, besides the few beings who are gifted with superior consciousness, use imaginary facts almost every day.

In common language, we call them prejudices and yes, we all have prejudices. By the way, some of them can even be positive! As we said earlier, judgment is pretty natural and not even that terrible. *As long as the possibility of having been mistaken is included in the process.* What's seriously bad is punishing someone for our own prejudices, without even giving that someone the chance to demonstrate what they're actually made of.

The imaginary fact is a "Magic If" that we project onto one another. When I have two actors work together on imaginary facts that I come up with, I always remind them that these facts might not be that imaginary after all.

Here's a real example that happened with two actors in a class that I was coaching. I had Jean-Michel[7] and Ines stand face to face and I told Jean-Michel this imaginary fact: Imagine that Ines actually thinks that you're kind of dumb, maybe even really stupid. Maybe it's actually even true. Don't ask her about it after the exercise, but really, you and I can never actually know. Who knows, maybe I've just slipped up without knowing.

The "maybe," doesn't impose anything; it induces and then encourages creation *around* it and *starting* from it.

The imaginary fact also has an undeniably playful aspect. Imagining things about others has been, for the best and for the worst, one of the human species' favorite activities since the beginning of time. Spilt tea existed way before tea parties. The "permissiveness" around rumors actually largely contributes to the efficiency of imaginary facts, all the while transcending the vulgarity of gossiping. It can be used to the advantage of something much more noble: creating great acting performances.

Time to play!

Go to a bar, a park, or some other public place and have fun distributing imaginary facts to the people that you see go by or interact with.

... ...

---

[7] Ah, that Jean-Michel! Whose refreshing attitude and dedication make him younger than most of those who are actually at least forty years younger.

Here are a few ideas to try out:
And what if the guy who's sweetly feeding the pigeons just got out of prison?

... ...

Be specific, imagine why he was in prison and for how long he stayed incarcerated.

... ...

And what if he had actually been innocent the whole time?

... ...

What if his whole life had been ruined because of it?

... ...

What if he was a fascist?[8]

... ...

And what if he lost a child? It's a possibility. Maybe you just internally put your foot in your mouth?

... ...

And what if the woman over there abused those closest to her? What if, deep down, she knew that it was wrong, but that she just couldn't stop herself? And what if she would beat herself up, as self-punishment for what she inflicted on her children? What if at night, alone in her bed, she would light up a cigarette just to smash it on her arm?

... ...

What if he or she was a cop? What if, behind his macho appearance, that guy was a sexual submissive? What if he had a serious illness? Which one?

... ...

—CUT—

Imaginary facts nourish your acting big-time, because they naturally induce ultra-active listening. If you create a sort of point of reference and cover your perception of the other with

---

[8]Whatever that word might mean to you.

a sort of filter, every step and movement that they make becomes "analyzed" according to the chosen imaginary fact. To better illustrate this, try out the next exercise.

Time to play!

Organize or go to a party where you know a few different people, who don't know each other that well or at all. After a while, choose a guy and a girl, single or not—according to your sense of humor—and tell each of them that you think, or even know, that the other person has a pretty big crush on them. Whereas really, nothing actually hinted at that.

... ...

Then observe how their behavior changes.

... ...

Whether they're actually attracted to each other or not, this imaginary fact, which might not even be that imaginary, will almost systematically influence how they read and listen to one another.

If you don't want to play with your friends with that kind of subject, which can be sensitive to some, bring a friend to a bar instead. Before ordering, discreetly tell your friend that during a conversation with the bartender, he confided to you that in his past he had spent a few years in prison for having murdered someone with his bare hands. Tell the anecdote pretty nonchalantly. Once again, observe the influence that this imaginary fact has on your friend when reading and listening to the bartender. If you played your part right, meaning that you had sources, your friend will definitely, at the least, give a few "filtered" looks according to the imaginary fact.

... ...

—CUT—

Same thing with your scene partners. In reality, you don't know much about them. And that's great! You'll be able to take advantage of this blank page to imagine everything about them and therefore create a relationship from scratch that serves the one needed in the script or the play.

Actually, once again, the border between what we call "reality" and what we call "fiction" is extremely hazy. What we know from a factual aspect about others influences our behavior around them, but it's just as much, if not more, influenced by what we *believe* about them. When used in acting, the imaginary fact has a strong power of suggestion when it comes to creating the relationships that your character has with the other characters of the plot. Imaginary facts can be created according to the given circumstances of the script or play. But it's important to note that actors themselves can invent imaginary facts that will help point their acting in a specific direction. Here's an example: I was coaching a young actor in a scene where he was playing a teenager who was experiencing generational conflict with his mother. The rage, profound incomprehension and rebellion that he portrayed was very accurate; however, there was something missing from his performance. The fact that all of these feelings were directed towards his mother didn't seem to have been taken into account — it was as if he was addressing a complete stranger. So I reminded him of the given circumstances, which were that he was addressing his mother. But nothing would work. He was still just as accurate in the revolt that he was portraying, but it all remained incomplete as he just couldn't take into account his character's relationship with his scene partner's character. That's when I whispered into his ear to take it easy, because his scene partner was suffering from chronic depression and suicidal thoughts. That imaginary fact immediately changed his acting. Even though it wasn't written anywhere in the given circumstances of the script, it added a touch of attentiveness and precaution to his performance, which could strongly resemble a quality that the character would have in the presence of his mother, despite their disagreements.

Speaking of disagreements …

Laaadies and Gentlemeeeen!!!

Miss M.

Starring

David (You!)

INT/NIGHT — DAVID'S APARTMENT/BEDROOM

Lying on his bed, David is all dressed up and is even wearing his "hottie" Teddy jacket. He's staring at the ceiling and has Mona's smartphone in one hand, and the orange that fell out of her bag in the other.

A series of crossfading images follows: fighting to stay awake gets harder and harder for him as the hours go by … During all this time, he keeps hold of the orange so that when it falls out of his hand, it will wake him and he'll have to go and pick it up … but he still ends up falling asleep, curled up with the orange like a safety blanket.

At that exact moment, Mona's smartphone makes a short ringing sound. David immediately jumps out of bed and reads: "You have 1 message." He types in the password: "L:5, O:6, V:8, E:3" and reads …

Hey Teddy Boy, Congrats! If you're reading this text, that means that you successfully passed the first test. If that's the case, then answer this with the first ten words of the text that you sent me … and that I LOOOOVED!!!

David types: "Beyond ideas of right and wrong, there is a field …" and makes sure that there's the right number of words.

David   1,2,3, blah blah blah, 10.

He sends the text … then receives:

Ok, it's really you. Re-congrats! You also successfully passed the password test. Not bad!

He can't help smiling and answers: "Hahaha! But what are you playing at, daaaaamn …"

Then he receives:

You ok? I'm not bothering you?

He's entertained by this non-answer that's made up of such "normal" questions … and answers: "Yeah, I'm ok. No, you're not bothering me. But what are you playing at?!"

Don't tell Min-Mân, you know, the boss of the Vietnamese place, that you're in contact with me.

David (to himself)   Min-Mân? Why him?

He hesitates … but decides to not take it further. He just answers: "Ok."

Are you alone?

David impatiently sends: "Yes."

Ok then listen, well, I mean, read: I'm sorry to have left like that. Don't ever ask me any questions about my life. Don't ruin everything. We don't know each other that well, but you are the most important person to me right now, David. Well, you … and Lassie!

He's astonished, touched, hurt, bewildered, all at the same time.

David   Lassie??!

(trying to decide what to answer)

Uh …

(talking out loud while typing)

Alright, you'll tell me later what the deal is with Lassie, uuhhhh … Unless I'm not allowed to ask you any questions about your zoophilia either.

He proudly sends his text.

David   Take that! In your face!

(hottie-like)

Still cool though.

He waits for her answer … which doesn't come.

David   Shit! A little too hard on the face …

So he sends: "Are you there?"

There's a knock at his door at the exact same moment. David can't believe what he's hearing. Suddenly on cloud nine, he runs to …

INT/NIGHT — DAVID'S APARTMENT/DOORWAY and HALLWAY

… the door to his apartment. He opens the door, with the excitement of a love interest in a romantic comedy … but loses all enthusiasm when he sees three really sketchy guys who look like gangsters.

SKETCHY GUY #1

(with a really heavy New York accent)

I see you already got your jacket on? Great, we just wanted to take a walk with you.

David looks defeated. The three have a smug smile on their faces.

SKETCHY GUY #1

Police, dummy.

To be continued …

Before we talk about sources that come from life experiences, let's finish off this chapter by using the tools of imagination to act out this scene. Truly embody it! You can pull it off even if you're all by yourself, since you don't actually need a scene partner until the arrival of the three sketchy dudes.

Time to play!

Create your W.W.W. questions of the scene.

… … …

Follow the five steps of working on sources.

… … …

Take it one step at a time. No pressure. See what works with you.

… … …

Keep going!

—CUT—

Experience

> *When an old man dies, a library burns to the ground.*
> **(An African proverb)**

Until that fatal day, keep exploring the endless shelves of your library: there are so many sources in stock there for actors. And that stock is valuable. So valuable. According to some researchers, including Carl Gustav Jung and Stanislav Grof, we receive drastic amounts of information from the very moment that we're conceived. Probably even before that. In order to avoid going absolutely insane, we sort through and select which bits and pieces of information to take into account. Some of it evaporates into thin air, some stays with us and shapes who we are, consciously or unconsciously. Sometimes in a very visible and explicit way, sometimes hidden deep down inside us. In some ways, you could compare us to the way a computer works. And rightly so, as computers mimic the ways of functioning of human thoughts: the information that we can't see on the screen exists just as much as what's on the screen. Working on sense and emotional memories consists of digging up information from past experiences, in order to literally reactivate, *relive* them, to serve a role. It's the same phenomenon as that of "Proust's madeleine."

The emotional memory technique is unequivocally the most criticized part of the Method—in my opinion, for mainly three reasons, one good and two bad. The good reason: Some Method actors and coaches turn that technique into a religion. The two bad reasons:

1) It's scary

2) It's risky.

The good reason: Some Method actors and coaches turn that technique into a religion. Nothing in acting or in the Method, whether it be this one or any other, must be taken too seriously. Nothing! That goes for Meisnerists too. When passion rhymes with submission, it becomes the prison that crushes itself. When dedication rhymes with tension, it becomes the venom that poisons itself.

Let's come back to the two bad reasons:

It's scary.

"*Well!* How about that, digging up their own past life experiences. Those Method guys are absolutely crazy!" But where else could actors find that, but in themselves? They are their one and only instrument, their own well of sources, their own library. Honestly, imagination isn't any less treacherous than experience. If you're afraid to dig deep into yourself, here are a couple of tips that I have for you: either get yourself lobotomized or become a cashier at a toll highway. But in any case, forget about becoming an actor. Why look to expose yourself if you just end up hiding? And should I say: isn't it impossible to reveal oneself when you're hiding from yourself? I'm not saying that you absolutely have to use your life experiences in your acting. I'm just saying that if you're afraid to at least go and take a look, not only are you missing out on you, but also, that fear is probably hiding something. Most of the time, it's hiding something very precious for actors: a fascinating inner world that wants nothing more than to be outwardly expressed. I am convinced, and many different experiments have proved it to be so, that it is much more toxic to keep emotions bottled up inside us, rather than expressing them.

It's risky.

You have a point there. Or to be more specific, you have a bit of a point there. That's why the first researches concerning emotional memory in acting were conducted with the help of vigilant specialists: therapists, psychologists, psychiatrists, and behaviorists. As we continually do today, they always recommended the use of painful emotional memories that dated, at the least, from three years prior. Besides the fact that they would generally be more reliable, they would entail much less of a risk for the actor.

Yes, nature is well built and our memory is made to build a kind of wall of protection between our past pain and the present. That's one of the elements that allows us to overcome it and move on. So when the actor is able to reactivate certain memories, it's not that the wall has been blown up, it's just that the door in that wall has been opened.

But let's be completely clear and honest: it's not down to an exact science. There's always a risk. A small one, if not a pretty insignificant one, but it's still there. It's actually common in a lot of professions, especially when it's a passionate one. A cashier doesn't get the same kind of goose bumps as a mountaineer. Because the mountaineer took the chance to follow his passion. And the same goes for every true artist, including actors, who *probably* didn't choose their job just to be cows that watch the train go by. They have to give themselves wholeheartedly and that can be "risky": not a lot, very rarely, but not absolutely never. But there's a question that I'd like you to truly ask yourself. Really, what creates the most damage, the risks that we take or the fear of taking them?

… … …

To me, and in a large majority of cases, it's unequivocally the fear of taking risks. But I'm not talking about stupid or blindsided risks, I'm talking about the risk of leaving the old beaten track, discovering oneself, becoming one's own master. Because *over*protection not only turns you into a sleepwalker, it also makes us terribly weak. **Basically, the only truly tragic risk in one's life is to not take any.**

After coaching hundreds of actors, yes, I've witnessed some be shaken after having used a painful emotional memory. But I've never seen anyone not get over it relatively quickly. Here's a reminder of one of our five safety rules, which is my personal favorite: "Always make sure you're having fun in your work!" The Method also has a selection of exercises, made to help the actor feel better and come down from using a painful emotional memory. So, let's not dramatize this approach and, as we'll see in the sub-chapter dedicated to emotional memory, let us not forget that this is all just a game.

Like life. Just like life.

Whether you're an actor or not, I highly recommend reading the major masterpiece by Alan Watts, *The Wisdom of Insecurity*.

Sense memory

Arm yourself with thoroughness!

Whether you decide to use emotional memories in your acting or not, don't deprive yourself of working with sense memories. These, however, are not risky whatsoever, are very useful, extremely enriching, and often hilarious. You'll need them in a lot of scenes for many reasons, like playing hunger, sexual urges, a headache, the cold, the heat, etc. Just to name a few.

When I coach actors, I use sense memories first and foremost to help them create real sensations that are appropriate for the scene. But I also do it to help them sharpen their own senses in a broader way. But why sharpen the actor's senses if it's not to use them systematically to create real sensations that are appropriate to a scene? Well, the point is to make them more expressive, more carnal, more present, basically, more *sens*itive.

Honestly, our senses are solicited so much and sometimes even so attacked by all of the messages that we or the society that we live in offer them, or impose onto them, that they end up "laying themselves off." They put themselves in a kind of sleep mode. Being that actors are their own instrument, I'd highly recommend that you allow yourself to limit the intake of information that you and your environment sends to you; thus, inevitably, what you and your environment sends to your senses. No, I'm not encouraging anyone to lead the life of an ascetic. **Because anyway, how can we embody all of mankind's passions if we further ourselves from them?** But from time to time, creating a bit of distance between yourself and the agitation of the world allows your senses to *re*-awaken. Maybe you already know how to do that and put it into practice. Either way, regularly practice sense memories and your senses will be quicker and quicker to answer and will be clearer and clearer.

Time to play!

Choose a meal that you only eat at a particular restaurant and that you really like. Really, really like. Now, go to that restaurant, order that meal and eat it. Seriously. That's the exercise. Well, at least that's the first part of it. The second part can't be explored until you've been to the restaurant.

Enjoy! I'll see you later.

… … …

—CUT—

So? Did you enjoy your feast? Great. We'll talk about that again later, but for now, let's explore what happened within you between the moment that I asked you to mentally choose a dish and the moment that it was actually served to you.

Maybe the choice of dish was completely obvious to you. For me, a Pho soup from Min-Mân's place immediately came to mind. Or maybe you had to choose between a few different dishes—a Bo Bun, a nice rib steak, maybe couscous? Whatever it turned out to be, at some point, you chose one of them. In a matter of fractions of seconds, your brain kind of had your senses "taste" that dish. Images, smells, tastes, a temperature, and maybe even sounds flooded you. That's pure sense memory. We go through them every single day.

Time to play!

It's very easy to pinpoint the most powerful sources that this sense memory is composed of. All you have to do is ask yourself this question: What do you love so much about this dish?

... ...

We'll use my Pho soup as an example. I especially enjoy the way that different temperatures and cooking methods are mixed together: the boiling hot noodles, the warm broth, the thin slices of half-cooked, half-raw beef, cut up by Min-Mân's saber. The chopped onion that just barely cooks in the broth, the raw, cold coriander leaves. My mouth is watering just thinking about it.

What about you? What details in your dish do you particularly enjoy?

... ...

Be specific. What makes you salivate?

... ...

Just like when working on imagination, don't look for all of the details. There's no need to make a documentary about your own Pho soup, just keep the impactful details in mind.

... ...

With the Pho soup, I also like the smell of the steam that it gives off. It's sweet and acid at the same time, which is pretty paradoxical. And that smell marries itself splendidly to that of the freshly cut coriander. Yuuum! I could go on forever, but you get the picture. If the sources of your sense memory are truly impactful, they bring out tons of sensations. Here and now. Really and truly.

... ...

—CUT—

Always make sure that you're not heading directly to the result, that's the exact way that you won't find it. Remember, when you want to turn on the light, you don't press the light bulb, you press the light switch. These light switches are and always will be in the details of your sources. And those details are always sensory. That's why when you work on a sense memory, you shouldn't ask your mind questions, you should ask your senses. You shouldn't be thinking of the idea of your dish, but rather of its specificities so that your senses can "taste" it. You just experienced it. Write down what worked with you, which specific details, which smells, which tastes, which visuals, etc.

Maybe the restaurant that serves the dish that you had chosen was closed. Or maybe you just didn't play the game and simply didn't go. Or if you really did go, you weren't able to just teleport yourself over there in a second. Whatever it was, you didn't have to take a bite of that dish in order to awaken and feel the sensations that it gives you. And yet, the sensations were truly there, just as tangible, true, physical, and palpable as ever.

Basically, the desire for the dish is at least as strong as the dish itself. That's the power of sense memories. The important details are stored in us, as well as the most impactful ones, which is a major advantage for the actor. Which means that you have an endless stock of sensations and that you can call on any one of them for any one of your roles. It's noteworthy that one of the reasons that sense memories work so well is that they call on pleasure, desire. It's majorly those factors that recreate those sensations. Of course, that's not the case if you have to act out a headache, for instance. But again, if you go into detail, if you thoroughly question all of your senses, you'll be able to recreate that physical state just as meticulously.

And if you're the one who created it, then you'll definitely be able to get rid of it when the scene is over.

Sense memories don't only have to be put into place when it's clearly and explicitly written in the script or the play. We are constantly in a specific sensory state, even if it's not particularly powerful. That's why I encourage actors to always ask themselves what their character's sensory state is, during every scene that they act out.

While you're reading this book, you probably neither have a bullet in your head, nor are in a heavy alcoholic coma state. But if you really think about it, you'll see that you're inevitably in some kind of sensory state.

Time to play!

What is your sensory state right now, at this exact moment?

... ...

Do you have lots of energy? Are you tired? Have you smoked a cigarette, more than one? Are you thirsty? Are you comfortably seated? A little too comfortably? Are you close to falling asleep? Etc.

—CUT—

Whatever it might be, you're always in some kind of sensory state. If not, you're in pretty bad shape. Very. That's why you must always ask yourself what your character's sensory state is in each scene.

That doesn't mean that whatever state you're in is the most important thing about the scene. But it will definitely help you out in giving physical life to your role. It will help out your presence, and give it a certain truth. Plus, working on sensory states, no matter how minuscule they might be, is a very efficient way to get concentrated. And since you have to start working on a scene somewhere, and that "somewhere" is the W.W.W. questions, remember to answer the question "Where?" and the question "When?" in a very precise and sense-oriented way. Asking yourself sensory questions is an excellent way to enter the fiction, because in this way, it's taken on in a very simple, physical, and tangible way. Thus, this approach is an excellent "springboard" for belief.

Poetic sense memory

Even though sense memory is one of the founding tools of the Method, many actors and coaches use it much too literally, in my opinion.

Let me explain. Sense memories can of course help you embody certain physical states, like the cold, hunger, etc. But it seems to me that an overly "documental" approach to these states is neither the most efficient, nor the most fun. And since it also seems to me that fun is one of the best "springboards" toward believing, it would be a huge shame to not take advantage of it. To give you a good idea of what I mean, try out the two approaches in these next two exercises: first, try out the "documental" approach to a sense memory. Then, try out the adaptation of it that I came up with, which is the poetic approach to a sense memory.

Time to play!

The documental approach to a sense memory.

Work on a simple sense memory. And when I say "simple," I mean "pure"—for instance, the cold. In order to do that, ask yourself detail-oriented questions and let your senses answer for you.

... ...

Start by reminiscing about a moment when you were very cold. Then, go into detail, what parts of your body were hit the hardest by the cold? Your face? Your hands? Your feet? What specific parts of your face? The tip of your nose? Your ears? Was it humid cold? Dry? Etc.

... ...

I'm rambling on purpose—let your mind ask the questions and your senses answer. The more precise your questions are, the more it will encourage the reactivation of those memories.

... ...

Concentrate on the details: how the cold feels on your nails, on the tips of your fingers, how your shoes feel frozen by the cold, how your toes feel in your cold socks, etc.

... ...

Take at least twenty minutes to explore that sense memory. Don't go directly to the result. Repeat the questions for your senses. Give them the time to remember the sensations.

... ...

If you've never done this type of work, don't expect too much of yourself. Don't put pressure on yourself.

... ...

Arm yourself with patience. Arm yourself with thoroughness.

... ...

Don't force anything.

—CUT—

Did it work with you? At least just a little? If that's not the case, don't worry. Your senses will assuredly end up answering you. Learn to "seduce" them. Give them the time to sharpen up.

Time to play!

The poetic approach to a sense memory.

Work on another sense memory with the cold, but this time, with a more poetic approach. This is what I mean: ask your senses specific questions again, but this time while being mixed with more imaginative sources. Imagine sources that are less directly connected to the factual aspect of the experience that you're remembering. Less "realistic."

... ...

For instance, imagine that there are ice cubes in your socks.

... ...

To stay with the theme, now imagine that there's a freezing iron plate touching your back.

... ...

Imagine that even the bones in your body are an icy blue color.

... ...

That your lungs are filled with ginger ice cream.

... ...

That you're wearing dental braces that just came out of the fridge.

... ...

That your tongue is pierced with a very sharp, tiny tube of dry ice.

... ...

Imagine that vapor is continuously flowing out of the tube and is becoming embedded in your tongue, your throat, your teeth.

... ...

Visualize the particles of vapor of dry ice that are holding onto the nerves in your molar teeth.

... ...

—CUT—

Do you see the difference between the documental approach and the poetic approach? Which one speaks to you the most?

For me, it's the second one. I find that by using analogies that sum up the essence of a particular sensation, poetic sense memory can reactivate it in a more impactful way. I've noticed, throughout hundreds of sessions of working on sense memories with actors, that the poetic approach often works better and a lot faster. And I think that's because the documental approach has something just a little too school-like. Whereas the poetic approach directly encourages us to have fun. When using the first approach, the actor kind of falls into reporting facts, sometimes becoming stuck with scientific accuracy. When using the second approach, the actor becomes a creator that can fantasize completely freely. They can launch themself from a poetic springboard to call upon and excite the magical memories of their senses. With the first approach, a lot of the actor's concentration is used up.

It's also interesting to note that we often use images to illustrate our sensations: "It gets me going, almost like I got an electric shock," "It's so irritating, it's like I'm being jabbed with a needle over and over, right here," *"Wooow! This shit is so trippy, man …. I really feel like I'm floating on a wave!"* etc.

It's no coincidence that a lot of expressions that we use to describe how we feel are largely made up of poetic imagery or are allegories.

Time to play!

Let your senses explore these expressions by visualizing, very literally, the images that they portray:

"Having your head in a vise."

... ...

"Having a frog in your throat."

... ...

"Having your eyes burn."

... ...

"To have pins and needles in your foot."

... ...

"To have your blood boil."

... ...

"To have your stomach in a knot." *Ugh!* Aren't the details of that one particularly unsettling?

... ...

"To put your head in a noose."

... ...

"To smoke like a chimney."

... ...

"To have blood shed."

... ...

"Your head is about to explode."

... ...

"To be in seventh heaven."

... ...

And, last but not least: "Shitting razor blades."

... ...

Truly imagine the sense-oriented details of that last one. If you can really tell me that you don't feel anything, then I officially invite you to change professions.

... ...

—*CUT*—

These expressions, as well as many others, can be excellent sources of inspiration. What, you found that *far-fetched*?! Be careful, I've been *on edge* ever since those so-called cops came knocking on my door! Since we're talking about expressions, notice how we say "*source* of inspiration," which really sums up perfectly all of the work that we do around sources. It's about looking for the ones that inspire us, whether they be from our experience or our imagination.

Speaking of experience and imagination, we could assume that working on sense memories would be exclusively based on experience. However, you might've noticed that in the sub-chapters dedicated to sense memory, I also encourage you to use the imaginary. Both create our inner world by lacing themselves together. They are two semicircles that end up forming the same circle by melting into each other, becoming one. Keep that idea in mind as we slowly start exploring the slippery slope that is the ever-criticized emotional memory.

Emotional memory

Since this territory is about as slippery as an ice-skating rink smothered in oil, we might as well add a few banana peels to the whole thing, nice and ripe if you please. We'll start out with a quote from the most attacked of the biggest defenders of the use of emotional memories in acting:

> *People who have had bad childhoods have a better chance of becoming great actors.*
> (Lee Strasberg)

I really like Strasberg, not only because he has made a lot of enemies, but also because I have enormous respect for his work and realize the precious contribution that he has given to the Method. However, his statement is false. Well, it can sometimes be true, but definitely not always. Fundamentally, it's not about whether you had a bad childhood or not, it's about how you take things: with a distance or with your heart.

If you're not an actor or an acting student, but are reading this book out of sheer curiosity about the inner workings of the human being, I'd advise you to take events with a certain distance, with a certain perspective. There are quite a few exercises that I suggest here that can help you with that. But for actors, I'd advise you to take things, as much as possible, quite hard. But hold on! That doesn't mean that I'm asking the non-actors to behave as an undaunted refrigerator throughout life, nor does it mean that I'm asking actors to bask in some kind of emotional hysteria. No. It's about the non-actors being able to get the perspective needed in order to fulfill a profound serenity. Not unbreakable, not cold, just profound. And it's about actors being able to achieve that same serenity through "absolute" availability and maximum compassion. So if you didn't have a bad childhood—which is pretty rare nowadays—don't think that you've missed out on something essential that would've made you the next Jack Nicholson. It all depends on your availability. That's one of the reasons why, in the beginning of this book, I emphasized so much how important it was to not be indifferent. Because being indifferent doesn't mean being able to create a certain distance with some events, it means closing yourself off from them, stopping yourself from feeling them, and ultimately, being unable to reunite with and express those feelings. Creating a distance is being able to choose whether something affects you or not. Being indifferent is emotionally castrating yourself. But again, I will insist upon the fact that it's still not about encouraging actors to become hysterical Drama Queens coming down from a coke binge every time they see an insect fly … or perishing from an alcoholic coma after taking a kamikaze dive into a Bloody Mary bath. No. On the other hand, if you take the time, you can see just how fascinating the nano-engineering that lets an insect fly is. Just like its microscopic glam-rock death can be touching … But otherwise, no, it's just about remaining emotionally available, vulnerable, and in a way, kind of "thin-skinned."

Isn't that a beautiful expression? "Being thin-skinned."

… … …

Which goes well with being an actor, because as we've said before, an actor is somebody who feels more. So let us get rid of our *supposedly* protective armor so that we can immediately feel lighter, more human. Available. Truly. This piece of advice is quite intimate, but that is what you're playing with after all: your intimacy.

We already talked about the very low risk of using painful emotional memories. In order to almost completely annihilate it, remember that every use of an emotional memory, painful or not, must fill this condition: containing a share of pleasure. First of all, because it makes the needed emotional memory more accessible. Second of all, no matter how obvious it might sound, it's always good to remind actors and everyone else that acting is a game. That notion is fundamental in any kind of work on emotional memories, as it helps to avoid any kind of deviation towards psychoanalysis or masturbating psychodramas that often come with it. Acting classes and books about acting are not meant for that. Also, remember that even when we're working with intimacy, only you must be in on your privacy, only you must know the sources that you're using. Period.

I've often been asked what kind of pleasure could you possibly have when working on a painful emotional memory. I often start by answering that an "s" should be added to the word "pleasure," since it can come in different forms. It can be the pleasure of expressing repressed feelings, the pleasure of expressing the forbidden, the pleasure of self-exhibition, the pleasure of transcendence, of pushing your limits or those of social conventions, the pleasure of taking revenge on the feelings because we're able to handle them and so, in a way, dominate them, the pleasure of playing with fire, or even a masochistic pleasure. Because the very essence of masochism is feeling pleasure from suffering. That is when and only when the paradox of acting must come in: when a character is suffering on stage and the actor is suffering just as much, but then experiences pleasure at having been able to express that. That pleasure also often comes from having been able to choose that source of suffering. That's why the form of masochism that can sometimes be present is healthy. Let me explain. When using a painful emotional memory, the pain is not being forced onto the actor; it's not coming from the will of a third person or from some kind of uncontrollable compulsion. Not only is it coming from a very conscious choice, but it's your choice and you have to make sure that it holds a share of pleasure. Even if it's just a tiny bit. As children, didn't we all play at "hurting ourselves," sometimes until there was blood, with a baby tooth that was ready to fall out, a splinter in our foot, or some other kind of scratch? Taboo is so present in our adult world that we often end up treating ourselves like children … but without the games. So much fun … We make such a big deal about pain, when in fact, it's not really that far from pleasure. Of course, as long as it has been chosen completely consciously! When working on emotional memories, if they're painful, have fun with them with no complexes, freely. And if that's not doable, then use a different emotional memory. With all of that being said, let's remember that emotional memories are also used to call on joyful memories, happy, serene, and pleasurable.

I tend to privilege the poetic approach to the documental approach when working on sense memories. However, I make it systematic when working on emotional memories. You know why? Because, whether we want it or not, when it comes to emotions, our memory is always subjective, so *in extenso*, poetical. Which means that it's filtered not only by our own vision, but also by the feelings that we have about the emotions that we've experienced in the past. In this way, every emotional memory is a poetic and subjective allegory of reality. It inherently contains conscious or unconscious symbols of our own vision of the world. That "unintentional" poetry is sometimes of quality, sometimes it stinks. But that really doesn't matter, as long as the sources that actors choose impact them.

Lastly, there is no emotional memory without a sense memory. The platform between us, here and now, and our past resides in our five senses' memory. They're the five doors that we can go through to access our memories. They're the five doors that memories can spill through into the present.

Time to play!

Choose a music piece that played an important part in a specific moment of your life. Ideally, choose a song that was *THE* song during a romantic relationship. The one that became your "anthem," for both of you.

... ...

Now listen to it. Without looking for anything in particular. Listen to it, that's all. Let the music take over. See you later.

... ...

—CUT—

So? How was it? Only two things are possible: either you felt something, or you didn't. If you felt something, maybe it was what you were expecting to feel or not. Both cases are absolutely valid and are both just as useful for the actor. If you didn't feel anything, either you weren't concentrated enough, or the source—in this case, the chosen song—doesn't affect you anymore or maybe that effect is hidden behind a wall of protection. If that's the case, then redo the exercise with a different song, a different story, another anthem.

You probably won't be able to listen to the song when you're playing the scene (although some actors actually do, with the help of an earpiece). But this exercise is mainly here to show you that there's a never-ending stock of memories inside you, which you can bring to the surface as you wish. Actually hearing the music can help, but you'll see that, with practice, you'll be able to access that stock through the memories of your senses. It's a muscle that should be kept in shape and you can do it anywhere, at any time.

The goal is the path.
(François Grelley)

Just like with sense memories and any other type of sources, don't look for the result directly. Always go to its roots: look for the light switches that are going to let it become alive in you. As always, those light switches are in the details of your sources. Those details are sensory-oriented. If you can't find them, dig deeper and deeper. And deeper! Still nothing? Try again tomorrow. *Still nothing?!* Ok. Change sources—maybe you didn't choose the right one. Or maybe you need to approach it differently. Are you looking for the result that you assume it's going to provoke in you too much? Are you anticipating it too much? And yet, you know a very simple way to stop doing that: exploring the details. Being thorough. Be more preoccupied by the path, not the goal.

You could sum up the right attitude to have like this: *Have the will to not have one.*

The challenge lies in choosing to use a past event because of what it has to do with the emotion that you want to reach, without worrying about the emotion that you want to reach. That last point is important for two reasons:

1) You could be surprised.

2) You can't force an emotion.

You could be surprised.

We conceptualize a lot of things. Some things need to be, others not so much. We have a tendency to conceptualize who we are, our relation to certain events, our history. We even go so far as to create what we like to call our "identity." But all of that is just part of a mere story that we tell ourselves. It's all prejudices about ourselves or what we "should" be, our relationships with others or what they "should" be, our past or what we believe it was. When you shed yourself of that supposed knowledge, you make room for the magnificent opportunity of surprising yourself.

That's why when working on emotional memories, if you haven't just randomly chosen one, you shouldn't focus on the desired result. Because it can turn out to be far different from what you would've imagined. Don't *plan* anything. Connect yourself to the sensory details of the event, let yourself feel and just *see* what happens in you. If you were expecting fear and instead found amusement, that's great! You'll have broadened your "source menu" and you'll be able to use that emotional memory in the appropriate scene.

That's why I always encourage actors to work on emotional memories outside of working on scenes, just as an objective in itself, that of discovering sources without the pressure of a result. You can then store them in your "source menu." When that's done, actors have multiple sources at their disposal that they can call on whenever they need to. Without any stress. All ready to go, because they've been prepared.

You can't force an emotion.

Good actors are "seducers," bad actors are "rapists."

We've all attempted to fall in love with the "right" person, or tried to laugh at a joke that wasn't funny, to cry at a funeral when (to our surprise) we're just too drained to, to be happy for some "good news" that we just don't care about, to belt out "Happy Birthday!" with an enthusiasm that we don't have. It doesn't work. At best, it looks cheap, we feel it and everyone with at least one eye can see it. At worst, it seems completely fake and you don't even have to see it in order to feel it. Anyway, it does not work and anyone can see it. It's even worse for actors, because their very job is to embody a role—we analyze their slightest movements and gestures, the slightest micro-expression, even the breaths that they take. To top that all off, remember that the world of cinema has the capacity to zoom in at least a thousand times on a face, a look in the eyes, a mimic. And the camera and the video projector don't lie. One registers what it's given, the other reflects what it receives. Times 1000!!! So, cheap just becomes cheap under a magnifying glass. Truth becomes sublimed truth.

So never try to force your emotions, seduce them. The difference, allegorical of course, that there is between a bad actor and a good actor is the exact same as that between a great seducer and a dirty rapist. Yes, emotions are exactly like the people that we want to "win over"—difficult, delicate, demanding, sometimes even locked shut.

If you try and rape them, nothing good will come of it. You could also try screaming at them *"Love me!"* ... it doesn't work either. But when we try to seduce them, without it seeming too obvious, delicately, with just a touch of nonchalance, we have a much better chance of getting our prince/princess charming. It works the exact same way when working on emotional memories. When you've chosen a specific event, don't pounce on it like a junkie who needs his fix, but rather, approach it slowly. Don't go directly to the result, flirt with the sources. Tease the light switches. Turn on the light by pressing on the details. Yes, yes, again and again, always and always.

Lee Strasberg compares emotions to a gourmand child who you would yell "EAT THAT CAKE NOOOOW!!!" at, with, may I add, a speakerphone only a centimeter away from his ears while he's suffering from a severe ear infection. There's a strong chance that the child will run away, terrified. So Lee brings up the possibility of slowly approaching the child, even slightly teasing him, like: "Who's this yummy cake for? No, it's not for you. It's for me. Yum!" Of course, now there will be a strong chance that he comes running to you.

Stanislavski compares working on emotional memories to an expedition to find a precious diamond in a small box. You'll have to make a few mistakes, follow a couple of false leads, retrace your steps, before finally finding the town where the jewel is hidden. But once you've found the town, you'll have to find the neighborhood in the town, the street in the neighborhood, the building on the street, the floor of the building, the apartment on the floor, the room in the apartment, the piece of furniture in the room, the drawer in that piece of furniture, and finally, in the drawer, the small box that contains the diamond: the emotion. Don't be discouraged! The path is often a lot easier than that. When that's not the case, don't be discouraged either—look for the details. One of them is a diamond, one of them is the lever of that emotion. To sum it all up: *Search and tiptoe around the lever of the emotion, not the emotion itself.*

And for a good reason: it can't exist if it's not levered. Also, don't look down on any of the details, you might be surprised to find out that the light switch is hidden in one that, at first glance, didn't seem to be of that much importance.

Didn't hurt, nah nah nah nah nah!

I remember being surprised at having been able to leave a very passionate romantic relationship, which I was very anxious about ending, without any remorse whatsoever. Nada. I could go to the places where *we* went, no problem. I could listen to *our* anthem, no sweat. I could reminisce about *our* most defining moments, not the slightest trace of nostalgia. I became absurdly proud of feeling nothing, of being stronger than ever and *I'm Still Standing* by Elton John became *my* anthem. Weeks went by. Then one day, by accident, I found a pair of leather gloves that my princess had left at the back of my closet ... which unleashed an earth-shaking tsunami in me. I almost drowned in my own tears, the top model inside me became worried about my loss of appetite and even Elton couldn't do anything for me. I wasn't still standing at all and whatever was left of me had to be scraped off the ground.

That pair of gloves definitely wasn't a major symbol of *our* story, but yet it was the explosive light switch to *my* breakdown. When you find yours, don't start analyzing them. It's completely useless and might even distance them a little, a lot, or completely from you. As Louis Pauwels would say, don't be like "Those academics who pick apart a watch in order to know what time it is," because when you'll have finished, the time will have disappeared.

Tarzan

Time to play!

Choose a past event that had a strong positive impact on you.

... ...

Don't focus on the result that you felt at the time, but *re*-dive into the sources.

... ...

Where did it happen? With whom? What temperature was it? Ask your senses' memory these questions, not your intellect. Pause at each detail and let yourself be taken over.

... ...

I already said that we shouldn't reveal our sources, but since I'm not an actor[9] and because it can work for the book, I'm going to reveal the event that I'm connecting to here. It's actually not really that "private." This is mainly to show you clearly how to approach an emotional memory. Once you've read the story, reconnect to that past event that had a strong positive impact on you and follow the steps in your own emotional memory.

When I was a kid, I wanted more than anything to have a dog, especially a Bobtail, but my parents were totally against the idea. No matter what strategy I tried—asking, sulking,

---

[9]Not because I failed, as Mona seems to think, but because I quickly became very passionate about the other side of things—coaching, writing, directing, and producing.

pleading, talking about my past life as a sheep dog, barking, eating from a bowl on the floor, it was no use—no dogs allowed.

Lucky me, at the age of ten, I got severe peritonitis that almost left me for dead on the operating table. I still wasn't doing too good while leaving the hospital, but all of my pain suddenly disappeared when I saw my father waiting for me with Tarzan, a Bobtail sheepdog puppy who celebrated my arrival, as if he at least recognized my canine origins ... which were completely made up.

When I dig deeper into that memory, I can remember the repeated negative answers of my parents in specific situations: in the '70s-style kitchen of our apartment, in my mom's Austin, in my dad's Jeep. The photos of dogs that I would tape onto the fridge or the washing machine, the ones that I would hide under the blankets on my parents' bed, the type of fridge that we had, how cold the washing machine felt, the fuzziness of the bedcover, its texture, its weight, the radio alarm clock next to their bed, etc.

Same with the clinic. Blurrily regaining consciousness in that yellow hospital room, the pain in my lower stomach, that feeling of having been "kidnapped" and the intrusion of that surgical intervention. I'm not looking for the result, I'm basing myself off of the sources and I'm trusting their power. The depressing meals at the clinic, the bleak taste of that lukewarm soup, of the sugarless yogurts, the fat and very pretty nurse's reassuring energy, her big smile, her words, her voice, her way of downplaying the situation (again, thank you for that!), her encouragement, my crutches, the black string that sewed up my scar, etc., etc., etc. It's almost as if I was back there.

While still and always questioning my senses, I'm reliving the sudden shots of pain that I would feel at every step. I would never have expected it, I can see the image that would come to me every time that I moved an inch—a fishing line that was pulling from the inside of my wound. Just by writing these words, I'm surprised by the impact that this image has on me. I'm not looking for it, but I can clearly see the image ... and *"Ouch!"*, the feeling is there. Really. Now. It's no longer a memory, it's a *re*-experience. It's not just an idea, it's feelings. I'm not heading directly to the feelings, I'm looking for the light switches. The one with the fishing line is working marvelously. As soon as I connect to it, I can feel my stomach tense up and a kind of apprehension takes me over, a sort of anticipation of the pain ... Hold on, I'll be right back.

... I went to walk around a bit and it's absolutely crazy: my body answered and wholeheartedly believed in the details that I was sending it. I wasn't looking for weakness, I was weak. But as soon as I let go of my sources, I would start up a very poor imitation, I would start pretending. As soon as I became specific, the belief would immediately set in. As I said before, our bodies, our minds, and our spirits only ask for one thing: to TRIP OUT. But on the one condition that we don't take them for idiots.

Once I've reached the post-operation state, my mind is going to concentrate on the dog that I'm about to discover. That's obviously a mistake, since I didn't know that I was going to discover anything, so anticipating the discovery won't let me truly live it. So I'm going back to focusing on the fishing line that I imagine pulling from the inside of my wound. *"Oooooouuuuuuch!!!"* It's working! I'm trying to put one foot in front of the other. I can do it, but it's hard. I remember the feeling of those crutches, the warm plastic of the handles in the palms of my hands. The nurse's warm, chubby hand holding my arm. Her voice. The kind look in her blue eyes. Her pink cheeks. The sense of eternity in her timeless presence.

Her soft reassurance. I think that I can see tears in her eyes. That detail especially affects me. She's sort of hiding, and as if it was already agreed upon, I pretend not to notice ... we engage in small-talk, but we don't talk about what's essential. Real questions about her go through my head. Why is she about to cry? Is she going through something difficult? Who takes care of her when she suffers? Is she an angel? All of those questions come back to me, in that hallway of that clinic of the '70s. I can hear sounds, I see gurneys, chrome everywhere. I'm mad at myself for not being brave enough to put my arms around her. She helped me so much. I feel cowardly. I feel stupid. I feel as useless as she was useful. I'm a little ten-year-old boy with a fishing line that's pulling on the inside of my wound and a feeling of discovering a certain injustice that even I'm capable of. I wasn't looking for that feeling. I promise you, I had completely forgotten it. But there it is. Intact. Surprising. Terrible. And that's when I see my father, his mustache and Ray-Ban sunglasses, with that little black and white ball of fur who jumps up and down at the sight of me: Tarzan. I forget about the nurse, out of cowardice and out of joy at the same time. I touch my dog. We know each other. We recognize each other. We've never laid eyes on each other before. We already love each other. It's obvious. It's love at first sight. I feel his fur. Long, soft, lush. His smell. Simple and deep, just like a mother's milk. I can really smell him. It's not an idea. It's a feeling. I can still smell him. Here and now. Like a baby's breath. Like freshly cut grass. I'm smiling. Really. I'm not acting a smile. I'm not using my muscles. I'm using my soul. That's what's guiding my muscles. You see how it works?

... ...

Ok, your turn now. Take your time. Let yourself be surprised. Don't anticipate. Dig into the details. It can never be said enough. Those are the keys to your beliefs, those are your precious diamonds, the jewels of your performances.

... ...

—CUT—

Don't count up the results of your emotional memories like some greedy real estate broker. It's the quality of your emotions that counts, not their quantity. Here's what Strasberg used to say about that: "A little bit of coffee is still coffee." Behind that seemingly ordinary haiku is a simple but quite important truth concerning the approach to emotional memories and to acting in general: basically, a drop of coffee isn't any less made of coffee than an ocean of coffee. Just one of your eyelashes contains the entirety of your DNA and a hint of emotion isn't any less of a strong emotion than a whole ton of emotions. And that's always the case, no matter whether you're playing Randy the wrestler or Romeo the lover.[10] What counts is how pure your emotions are. And when I say "pure," I mean that they aren't cheap or fabricated. To sum up: *Acting isn't weighed by the pound, it's weighed by the feather.*

---

[10] By the way, the two certainly aren't incompatible. Mickey Rourke's breath-taking performance of a love-stricken wrestler in *The Wrestler* proves it.

Time to play!

Practice that exercise for emotional memories often, with every type of past event that you've lived through, no matter how insignificant they might seem. But never forget: when you're working with a painful past event, always make sure that it's dated at least three years prior and ask yourself what kind of pleasure you could get out of reliving it. Curiosity? Transcendence? Surpassing yourself? Another type of pleasure?

... ...

Really ask yourself that question!

... ...

If, before even starting to explore the chosen event, you can't find or feel any kind of pleasure, choose another one.

... ...

Then go into the details.

... ...

Pinpoint those that have an effect on you.

... ...

Then go through the same emotional memory a few times over the course of a few weeks. But hold on! Don't expect yourself to reach the *exact* same result each time. Let yourself enjoy the little variations that it can contain and that it will offer you.

... ...

If each and every time, the emotional memory heads, more or less precisely, in the same direction, if it has the same more or less powerful type of effect on you, you can then validate it and incorporate it into your "source menu."

... ...

—CUT—

Ok, I'll be back in just a minute, I need to go remember the first time that I'll kiss Mona. Once again, it's totally possible (just like we do in real life), to mix up your experience (I do know Mona) and your imagination (I've never actually kissed her).

Hopefully, we'll find out more about her in the next scene ...

Laaaadies and gentlemeeeen!!!

Miss M.

Starring

Really Sketchy Gangster-looking Guys

and

David (You!)

INT/NIGHT — INTERROGATION ROOM

David is seated with a black bag over his head and is handcuffed in the back. In the background, he can hear indistinct muttering …

The bag is pulled off of his head. In front of him are the three really sketchy guys who look like gangsters, with two others in (what looks like) a police interrogation room — there are a few desks, paperwork scattered, a bit of a mess, photos and blueprints covering the walls, weapons.

The New Yorker Do you know someone called Zoe?

David grumbles something incomprehensible, even though he isn't gagged.

The New Yorker (to David) What did you say?

David grumbles even more, while trying to point to his hands with his chin.

Sketchy Guy #2 I think he can't talk without his hands.

David confirms, by grumbling and nodding.

The New Yorker Yeah, I get you. Me neither.

(to Sketchy Guy #3)

Alright, take off the handcuffs. This bird seems harmless.

Sketchy Guy #3, who uncuffs him, has a big hearing aid in each ear, which adds to the disturbing weirdness of his massive face.

David Thanks. That's really nice.

The New Yorker Come on, we really are nice, you know?

Sketchy Guy #4 That is, if you answer our questions.

The New Yorker *That's* for sure! So, Teddy Boy, you know someone called Zoe?

David No, and I can't know for sure whether you guys are policemen or not either.

The New Yorker What, you want us to send you our résumés?

The five of them laugh.

David   No, but I am allowed to see your badges.

Sketchy Guy #3 punches him hard.

The New Yorker (to David)   Ouch. Choose your words carefully, Joel here is hard of hearing and just a tad dyslexic.

(to Joel, previously known as Sketchy Guy #3)

What did you hear this time, Jojo? The guy said "I'm allowed to see your badges," not "to be jabbed."

Joel (calmly but very loudly)   Woah, sorry.

The New Yorker   Don't worry about it Little Jojo.

(to David)

So, now that you know that we're really cops, do you know Zoe, yes or no?

David   Fuck no.

Joel punches him again, which cuts open his brow line this time.

The New Yorker   Oh, forgot to tell you—swear words make Jojo's hearing aids crackle. He doesn't like it. So?

David   No, I don't know anyone who's called Zoe.

The New Yorker   What about Aurora, Aurora Bloom?

David   No.

The New Yorker   Or maybe Angela?

David   Uh, nope.

Bam! Super-punch from Joel. David bleeds even more.

The New Yorker   He didn't say "dope," he said "nope."

Joel   Woah, sorry.

Sketchy Guy #4   Ok then. What about this pretty stunning Czech girl, an insurance saleswoman, with a flame tattooed on the back of her neck … You know her?

Joel starts massaging David's scalp, to break the ice a little.

David   Uh … yeah, I know about a stunning girl with a flame tattoo.

Sketchy Guy #4   But?

David looks nervously at Joel, who gives him a big tense smile which reveals these really complex-looking braces. He keeps massaging him.

David   (to Sketchy Guy #4)

But she's not Czech and she doesn't sell insurance. She's Turkish and she works at a lingerie store.

All of the sketchy guys smile cunningly at one another.

Sketchy Guy #4 (to the New Yorker)   We got her.

(to Sketchy Guy #5)

We can start the confession.

Sketchy Guy #5 gets behind a typewriter.

The New Yorker   Last name?

Joel   You have really soft hair.

David   Confession? What confession?

Sketchy Guy #4   That's what you're gonna tell us.

The New Yorker   Last name!?!

David   Barrouk.

The New Yorker   First name?

David   David.

Joel   You have really soft hair, David.

The New Yorker   Profession?

David   Acting coach.

The New Yorker   Ah, you mean you're a failed actor.

All of the guys laugh, except Joel, who's very focused on his scalp massage.

The New Yorker   Anyway, you can't learn to be an actor, either you got it or you don't.

David   Really?! Who's your favorite actor?

The New Yorker   De Niro in *Heat*. Nah, nah, wait! De Niro AND Al Pacino in *Heat*.

All of the guys comment: "Yeah, Pacino's hair looks so smooth!", "You're talkin' to me?" over and over again, "Those Italians, man, they got it!"

David   Well, they both … sorry, but, but can you ask him to stop massaging me like that?

The New Yorker   Come on, Jojo, that's enough. He needs his scalp to talk.

Joel obeys, expressionless. David notices that the tattoo on Joel's forearm is a replica of the engraving on Mona's gun: a phoenix and the words "Mori Et Resurgere."

Joel   Woah, sorry.

The New Yorker   So, you were talking about De Niro and Pacino.

David   Thanks. Uh ... yeah! Both of them took classes with acting coaches. *You know, even Jack Nicholson was coached!*

The New Yorker   Really?! I gotta say, that's a surprise. They seem so natural! But anyway, who'd wanna coach actors, besides a failed actor?!

David (immediately getting carried away)   *WHO!?!* Stanislavski, Strasberg, Lewis ... me!

The New Yorker   Don't know them.

He looks at his colleagues, questioningly ... they don't seem to know them either.

The New Yorker   Whatever, they're probably failed actors, just like him.

David   An acting coach who's worthy of that name is someone who's passionate about the human soul and its ways of working. The light that's in us, just as well as our share of darkness.

The guys are all looking at David kind of mockingly, all except Joel, who's been won over.

David   Someone who knows that this supposed reality, as well as the identity, are mere lures, limits, censoring compromises. Worse—self-censorship? He gets up, getting carried away, despite the dripping blood on his face. *A Hollywood style music comes on, underlining this unexpected flood of emotion.*

David   Someone who recognizes that factual truth will never be worth more than the poetry of our inner world and that of the outside world, as long as you know how to see. That it's fundamental to explore it, to explore oneself, to become unbridled, to "uncensor" ourselves, to undo our complexes! Basically, to allow ourselves to be. He or she is also someone who wants to embed knowledge into the flesh and flesh into knowledge. Joel is moved. David now has everybody's attention, which makes him even more passionate. *The music gets even more intense ...*

David   Someone who believes in the salvation of Transcendence. In its power! In its magic! Someone who knows that we are our own playing fields, our own galaxies, our own universe!!! And that we can see infinitely in only two directions: beyond the horizon and in ourselves. Maybe sometimes through the eyes of someone else ... Mona, Phoenix, Daphne, or Joel.

Joel shyly holds back his tears.

David (adding onto the effects of his speech)   But, maybe, most of all ... he or she is someone who knows ... that to turn on the light bulb ... you have to press the light switch.

That last sentence hangs in the room and takes a long time to sink into the five guys' brains ... before miserably floating back to the top.

The New Yorker   Well, that's just what I was saying! A failed actor. Like, *really failed!*

Sketchy Guy #4 (pissed off, to David)   Ok, we've heard enough bullshit, fat-ass! Where did you put that girl's fucking purse, if it's not at your place or at your office?!

David   Which girl are you talking about, Zoe the Czech who sells insurance, or Krikri the Swiss girl who deals crack on Mars?

The New Yorker   *Hey! You wanna play, coachy boy!?!*

David (imitating him)   I'd love to! I can also coach you if you wanna pretend you're a real cop! Yeah, with fewer clichés too, you dope!

An ultra-supreme punch from Joel sends David flying across the floor. The New Yorker holds him by the collar …

The New Yorker   *"Real cop!?!", "Real cop!?!"*… and drags him towards an open steel door …

The New Yorker   And is this custody room real enough for you?!… then kicks him hard in the balls, throwing him in the cell.

To be continued …

Even though it really doesn't seem likely that our ever-hopeful main character will kiss Mona anytime soon, let's take advantage of this scene to put our sense memories and emotional memories into practice.

Time to play!

Start this next process even if, for lack of scene partners and special effects, you're not able to embody it:
Create your W.W.W. questions of the scene.

… … …

Remember to not answer the W.W.W. questions mentally, but *with your senses*.

… … …

Follow the five steps of working on sources, while identifying the moments when you'll be able to use and test out a sense memory or an emotional memory.

… … …

For instance, you'll probably need a sense memory in order to embody the physical state of having been beaten up, with conviction.
That doesn't mean that you have to know, from experience, what it's like to be knocked around. No. For example, you can be influenced by the state of being drunk to act out the state of someone who's been beaten.

... ...

By the way, what are you going to use to act out the powerful impact that Joel's ultra super-sonic punches have? Maybe just imagining the power of the punch will be enough, but maybe not. In that case, I strongly advise you to dig into your inventive potential with a poetic sense memory. To do that, explore images that are likely to have an almost instant shock effect on you. Look for ideas yourself, I'll give you a few ideas of my own just afterwards.

... ...

What about being just underneath a spaceship's jet engine at the exact moment that it takes off? And a pair of scissors being suddenly shoved deep into your nostrils? Ouch? That was your idea?! Then keep searching.

... ...

Also, even though our humble Barroukovitch's poetic declaration obviously contains quite a few quirky and satirical elements, what would you choose that could make you get carried away like that? Let us insist upon the fact that the quirkiness and satire will only come out if you play that moment with passion and faith. Not by playing the satire and quirkiness themselves, as so many self-proclaimed comedy actors do. We'll explore the subject about the tone of a scene a little deeper in the sequel of this book. But for now, let's get back to that poetic declaration. Once again, it's totally possible that the character's point of view speaks to you. If that's the case, don't look any further and let yourself be inspired by the scene itself. If that's not the case, then you'll have to find a subject that gets you carried away like that.

... ...

—CUT—

The last element of the exercise that we've just worked on, which is changing an element of the scene and replacing it with an element of your life, is a precious tool of the Method. We've already briefly skimmed by it on more than one occasion, including once with our friend Karl. It's called ...

Substitutions

As we said earlier, some scenes include sensations or emotions that you've never experienced. If you're playing a heroin addict, you obviously shouldn't inject a shooter in your arm to see what it feels like. No, Method actors aren't uninventive half-wits who have such a severe lack of imagination that they have to experience *verbatim* everything that their characters experience. If that was the case, all of them would've died as one of their characters and that would have been it. They would've either killed themselves or had themselves killed. So when you're playing a sensation or an emotion that you've never experienced, that's when you can possibly use substitutions. And I say "possibly" because, again, always try to see if the imaginary aspect of the scene inspires you enough to rely only on that.

Not only does this tool work with sensations or emotions that you've never experienced, substitutions also work when your character's passion doesn't speak to you at all, if it doesn't resonate with you.

Here's the thing about that totally false idea about Method actors, which is that they have to live, literally, everything that their character "lives." That card is often used to ridicule and to discredit the techniques of the Method, by those who know nothing about it. The fact that those ignoramuses, whose main character trait is to think that they're intelligent, take us for ignoramuses is actually a pretty good sign. However, what's a real shame is that a lot of people, including actors, actually believe that bullshit. Don't listen to them. Ridicule is a weapon often used by those who don't have any valid points or arguments. It's also an admission of powerlessness of those who have no curiosity. Method actors who decide to live everything that their character "lives" do it with discernment, all the while following our five safety rules, which include: "Do not hurt yourself or others, in any way; do not grope yourself or others; do not ingest any alcohol or drugs that strongly alter your state of mind." Let us pay tribute to those whose curiosity allows them to dare to explore territories and experiences that are unfamiliar to them.

Here's an example of how a substitution can be useful and when and how to use one. In *The Missouri Breaks* directed by Arthur Penn,[11] Marlon Brando had to play a state of deep concern in one of the scenes. In his memoirs, Brando revealed the source that he used: he substituted his character's concern with one that he truly had at the time, which concerned the nuclear weapons tests that were being carried out by the American army in the Pacific during that time period. And just like that, magic happened! Just to be clear, even though it's important to not reveal sources in general, it's mostly crucial to not reveal any sources that are related to the actor's private or "secret" life. His or her life must stay that way.

Now, let me insist on an essential condition that needs to be met when using substitutions: the quality of the chosen substitution has to match that of what's being substituted. For example, if a scene contains physical desire, the substitution has to be chosen according to that desire, that same *type* of desire. For instance, the actor wouldn't be able to substitute it with the desire for knowledge, which would be more abstract and less frontally sensual. But you can still remain open when choosing a substitution. While staying with the theme of physical desire, you could use a culinary substitution.

So it doesn't matter if the substitution isn't an exact copy of what's being substituted, what matters is that they share the same quality, which attributes the kind of importance that it has. When Brando used the nuclear weapons test as a source/substitution, he was acting in a western movie that was taking place in a time period when no one could have had any idea of what it was. The freedom in the choice of sources, substitutions, and other tools, which an actor can always use in a convincing way, is bound to a very simple but essential truth:

---

[11] Who's also the director of the "cult" *Bonnie and Clyde*.

The camera doesn't film the actor's inner world, but the visual and perceptible effects that it has on his body.

And when I say "visual and perceptible effects," I mean the ways that it can resonate with the actor on physical, energetic, emotional, and sense-oriented levels. That's not only the case with the camera, that's also the case with an audience at the theater and with every human being that we meet (for better or for worse?). It doesn't matter how clever we think that we are, we can't read someone's inner world. Which, in my opinion, is rarely for the worst, but mostly for the best.

Here's a true story. A Jewish Austrian actor emigrated to the United States, to flee the rise of the Nazis. However, in a cruel twist of irony, he would be hired to play a hard-core Nazi soldier, because of his strong Austrian accent. How could this man, whose own family was persecuted by the Nazis, possibly be able to identify with his worst tormentor and adopt the motivations of someone who had made his life a living hell?

Time to play!

Put yourself in his shoes and ask yourself what you would've done?

... ...

—CUT—

I'm sure that you probably found a substitution that works well with you. But listen to the brilliant, ingenious magic trick that this actor came up with. He imagined that once the war was over, the victims of the concentration camps simply reversed roles with their torturers, in order to exact revenge. That's how he was able to embody his worst nightmare, with cruelty that was hardly acted. In this type of case, we can easily imagine the cathartic, almost therapeutic, pleasure that the actor must've gotten out of that.

As you can see, substitutions are not only useful and efficient, they contain an element of fun that should be taken into account. When actors use a substitution, they need to be the only ones to know what it concerns, just like with any other source. That kind of "secrecy" accentuates the feeling of having performed a sleight of hand, kind of like a magician, having a "thing." A feeling of amusement is drawn from it, just like the games we would play as children. It's a sophisticated version of hide and seek. Paradoxically, it's a conscious illusion, because there's a consciousness of being illusory—a voluntary distortion of an agreed-upon "reality."

Time to play!

See if you can remember moments of your life and maybe even in dreams that you've had when you've used a substitution.

... ...

Did you find anything?

... ...

As the saint of debauchery, Oscar Wilde, said, "Every sinner is a saint who doesn't know it." The opposite might also be true.

Substitutions can be used in any number of cases. They can be used in order to create a relationship with your scene partners, that is appropriate to what's needed in the script, just like what Karl did with Corinne in *Miss M*. They can also help you believe in an objective that doesn't resonate with you, but that your character is pursuing. The same goes for obstacles, motivations, places, circumstances—hence, the Jewish actor who had to embody a Nazi.

But you can also use substitutions completely freely, in ways that are as absurd or as eccentric as you want, just like with all of the other tools that we talk about in this book. Never forget, the Method is not an end in itself, but a means to get yourself inspired, liberated and to broaden your horizons creatively. So for instance, try to blend the substitutions that you use with poetic sense memories, you'll get astonishing results pretty quickly.

Here's a good example. I was coaching an actor who had to act painfully shy in the presence of the girl of his dreams. He was fairly accurate, but whenever he had to act with his scene partner, his shyness would be flat—he would act it in the bad sense of the word. I can't be sure, but it seemed to be a sort of conscious strategy to show the beautiful girl that, in "real" life, he was a "real" man. I didn't get involved in what his personal motivations were, but I helped him explore past situations when he might have felt uncomfortable. The results would be pretty good, but everything would come crashing down when he'd be faced with the dreamy hottie. I then decided to try another strategy. I told him, in front of the girl, to imagine that he had just shat himself. Since I gave him that very elegant indication in front of her, he could no longer escape it by playing it off as being a hunk. Plus, the simplicity of the tool that I suggested to him and the visuals that it offered had an immediate and very strong effect. And to get to that, I would keep insisting on the details: was it hard, soft, or diarrhea-like? Could the beautiful girl smell the charming odor from where she was standing? Etc. That also made him ask himself a series of real questions.

Before using substitutions or other tools from your experience, always try first to base yourself off of the imaginary world of the script or the play that you'll be acting in. If it still doesn't work or doesn't work deeply enough with you, try again by truly digging into the details of the situation, by embroidering around it ... Still nothing? Then don't hesitate to use substitutions and emotional memories.

Still, there's a possible trap that you can fall into when using them, which is losing your ability to listen. When you're concentrated on a substitution or an emotional memory which is an internal source, always make sure that part of your concentration stays with the here and now, in order to not stop listening. You might have a hard time juggling both at the same time at first, but with practice, you'll soon have no problem.

The substitution is actually not too far from how we naturally and intuitively behave. More or less consciously, we often project our own perceptions onto people, places, or situations. In those moments, we substitute naturally, as we substitute an objective reality with our own subjective, internal visions. This has a connection to the imaginary facts that we were talking about earlier.

Sometimes, even our sleep is filled with substitutions. Have you ever dreamed of someone very specific, but with the physical appearance of someone else? Once, in one of my dreams, I had a very realistic-sounding conversation in French with a cat, who was very clearly my mother (to me at least). What's pleasant about artistic creation is that you don't need to over-analyze the symbols of our inner worlds in order to play with them. I highly encourage that way of creating anyway!

Stanislavski's dream was to be able to connect to the creative unconscious and master its ways of functioning. But he never went as far as to over-analyze it, because analyzing it would mean losing its magic. I believe he managed to succeed in his objective and generously decided to share with us how he did it. Have you gotten a chance to read his books, like I suggested in the first paragraph? I'm bringing it up again, because they are truly endless wells of inspiration, not only for our work, but also for our ethics, our aspirations, our lives.

Thank you, Constantin.

Reflex sources

Reflex sources and more specifically, *your* reflex sources are sources that have an immediate effect on you. They do so because they're deeply anchored into your psyche. That's why they contain almost always primary or unconscious elements.

No matter how old you might be, there's probably experience or imaginary sources that have had an almost-immediate effect on you ever since your childhood. Those are reflex sources.

For example, from the very first time that I listened to Mozart's *Requiem*, it has always had an immediate and profound effect on me. Every time that I listen to Mozart, he carries me away, turns me upside down, turns me around, and makes me believe in the beauty and transcendence of art, its genius, and the human being's potential. That's one of my reflex sources. I have some unshakable feelings for Julie, my soulmate and writer sister, even when she annoys me (which is fairly often). Also, bring in any Vietnamese dish at any hour of the day or night and you can be sure to get a good reaction from me! There you go, those are some of my reflex sources. Your turn!

Time to play!

This one will probably contain a share of experience and imagination for most of you (I apologize ahead of time). Have you ever eaten someone else's vomit while it was still warm?

... ...

Did you dip some bread into it?

... ...

And what if you swallowed that slice of bread smothered in lukewarm vomit down with a glass of caterpillar juice?

... ...

Ok, I'll stop.

—CUT—

If you felt something while reading that, that means that these primary sources are reflex sources for you, like for a lot of people. If you feel like throwing up, then go read the sub-chapter called "The shower." You'll see how easily that exercise of the same name can work to help you feel better.

Are you ready to come out of "The shower"?

... ...

Time to play!

Now look for reflex sources.

... ...

Just like the example we talked about where you swallowed a slice of bread with vomit spread. Oops! If it had an effect on you a second time, that means that it's a really strong reflex source for you. Write it down.

... ...

So, back to what I was saying, search by asking yourself simple questions. What do you love?

... ...

What gets you *over*-excited?

... ...

What would you be ready to kill for?

... ...

Really kill. Not like killing in a movie, in slow-motion. That's the director's job, not yours. To kill. To take away somebody's life. To see the light in their eyes disappear. To feel their last breath on your skin.

... ...

Now, what would you be ready to die for?

... ...

To not be a part of this world anymore. To never again touch the hand of the person that you love the most.

... ...

To never feel the rush of excitement again, to never taste your favorite food, to never feel the suspense of seeing a new movie …

... ...

Dinner with friends? That's over.

... ...

Who will take care of your belongings, left like still life in your bedroom? What will your loved ones do with them?

... ...

—CUT—

Basically, ask yourself simple questions in relation to things that are elementary, yet profound. Pleasure, death, sickness, family, love … acting?

If you ask yourself simple questions about those types of subjects, you'll discover an endless array of very tangible reflex sources that you can use for any one of your roles. But be careful! Don't make your questions too conceptual, like: Why do we chase pleasure? Even though those types of questions and their answers can be fascinating, they're rarely useful as sources and much less as reflex sources.

Time to play!

So? What are your reflex sources? What touches you, incurably and directly? Truly search them within yourself and test them out.

... ...

Make sure that the sources that you come up with don't have a short-lived effect. It's not that they aren't valid, it's just that they shouldn't be put in the "Reflex sources" section of your "Source menu."

... ...

Did you find some? Yes, I know, we can change, thank God for that actually! But what is just so anchored inside of you that it's absolutely unchangeable?

... ...

The affection that you feel towards your mom? Or the hatred towards her? A mix of both? A Van Gogh painting? That woman or that man that you saw in the subway quite a long time ago and that you didn't have the courage to go up to, who has forever left in you a feeling of regret, of a chance that you didn't seize?

... ...

—CUT—

Identifying and knowing how to activate your reflex sources will be very useful to you on set and on stage. But they'll be even more useful during auditions when casting directors ask of you, more or less reasonably, immediate results. But still, never forget: don't chase after the result, go after the details. It's been a long time since we brought that up! Knowing how to identify and how to use your reflex sources will give you a lot of confidence while acting and in many professional situations.

The first contact

> *Lord, forgive me, I lived mechanically, I do not remember anything.*
> **(Cardinal Jean-Marie Lustiger)**

Most of the sources that work with you at least once have the potential to work multiple times. When a source suddenly doesn't seem to work anymore, it's often due to the fact that actors know what effects that particular source has on them, and they want to go directly to the result. That mistake can happen with experience sources and imaginary sources alike.

And that mistake is connected to our way of living. Yes, I know, again, we're dealing with something intimate here, but you, as an actor, and I, as an acting coach, are playing with intimacy to begin with. When I say that this mistake is connected to our way of living, I'm talking about the overdose of stress that we deal with on a daily basis. This often causes us to miss out on the ultra-precious present moment — to miss out on life, on others, and ourselves. That's often when the pathetic habit of acting indifferent comes in. Often, we then proceed to fall into two traps. We just accept that horrible feeling, or we hysterically chase after new sensations.

Obviously, it's not about denying ourselves the intense pleasure of having new experiences. That's actually a *must* for any self-respecting artist and human being! But we also need to make sure to treasure the "little" things, and the actions, relationships that we live with day to day. It's about not going to the result, but to the source, touching the light switch and not the light bulb, privileging the process and not the aim. Let us be reminded of that wonderful motto by the wise François Grelley: "The goal is the path." When we're able to get to that, we sharpen our ability to be present and we stop running a race that we cannot possibly win: the one against time.

I encourage actors to have the exact same attitude when it comes to their sources. Take your time, as I already said. Always reinvent the path. Rediscover it. And the best way of sharpening that attitude is to have it in everyday life. Not only is it a big advantage for the actor, it's also a great way to have much more fun being alive. Much, much more.

Our lives are partially made up of repetitive actions. Everyday, we take a shower, we brush our teeth, eat, go to the bathroom, open the door to our apartment, get dressed, sleep, drink, talk, think, shake hands, kiss, etc. But very often, we do these things mechanically. I actually find it to be disastrously sad.

Little by little, we become dried-out ideas of ourselves, and sadly, we then become indifferent to the point of making ourselves disappear and morph into robots, zombies, idiots. Of course, that's highly detrimental to anyone, but especially to actors. It's a sure-fire way to become insipid, empty, heavy. So, inevitably, a bad actor. As I've said before, an actor must literally become someone who feels more. And in order to do that, actors must sharpen their senses. And in order to do *that*, they must live to the fullest. Not only on stage, but in everyday life. How can they know how to truly live out their feelings on stage if they don't know what living truly is? To feel. To rejoice. To create at every moment.

Acting, just like every other art, is not merely a profession, it's also a way of life.

All we have to do is call on our ultra-precious potential of amazement. But be careful! Again, I'm not talking about overdone, forced amazement. I'm not asking you to scream *"Oh my God!!!"* every time the new collection of H&M socks comes out. Nothing's further away from amazement than fabricated amazement. Instead, I encourage you to give yourself fully to everything that you do, without looking for the result and without becoming falsely hysterical over the slightest thing. Make *each* time the *first* time. In life, in scenes and with sources alike, you have to retrieve the path, refresh it, in order to successfully attain the goal.

The next experiments might seem like a joke to you at first. If they make you laugh, that's great, but they're not jokes. Unlike most of the source experiments that we've done since the beginning, these are not as hands-on. I like to call them satellite exercises. Do them. Really. You'll have sharpened your work as an actor since you'll have sharpened your senses, your amazement potential, and your power to be totally present. Your essence. Your senses.

Time to play!

Take a shower. Try to completely forget the goal, which is to become clean—just like when you work on sources. Take a shower just to take a shower.

... ...

Take the time to do each action and each sub-action that the global action of washing yourself is made of.

... ...

Feel the weight that has been lifted off of you, after getting rid of your shoes, your shirt, your pants, etc.

... ...

Then just stay like that for a moment. How does your body feel? The air that's dancing around on your skin, the temperature, the feel of your feet on the floor. Is the floor colder than the air? Warmer?

... ...

Now, open your eyes. Well, they probably already are if you're reading these words and they probably will be when you actually take a shower. What I meant is, *really* open them. Open your eyes in your already opened eyes. Without tension, without forcing anything, and *discover* your bathroom.

... ...

Yes, you've probably already been in this bathroom hundreds, maybe thousands of times. You know it by heart. But truly take in the colors, the textures, the shapes.

... ...

Take in the reflections that are on the shower faucet for a moment. What are they made of? Play with distances. Get closer, get further. See how the reflections of all of the shapes on the shower head dance around with you, how they follow your every movement.

... ...

Now, look for at least one detail of your bathroom that you had never noticed before. A piece of chipped paint that looks like a face on the wall, the streaks on the shampoo bottle cap ... anything ... but you must:

Look for newness in the "known."

... ...

—CUT—

I encourage you to go through the same process when working on chosen sources that work well with you. To freshen them up with your power of attention to detail. Without tension. Loosely. In the present moment. Just like the first time.

Try to redo that approach to things and to actions as often as you can. For instance, you can wander around visiting your own city as if you were discovering it for the first time. But again, don't be looking for the result. Don't look to be amazed, don't play it, don't lay it out. Look for the sources of amazement.

Time to play!

Do not feel any pressure to do this next experiment, unless you truly feel comfortable with it. The next time that you see a loved one of yours (family, friends, lover, etc.), hug them. Like I said, you might think that this is a joke, but I promise you that it isn't. And you might as well combine what's useful with what's pleasurable, right?

... ...

One thing though: don't tell the person that you're doing an experiment. It'll most likely ruin the magic of the moment and also the very point of the experiment. But the share of pleasure and the share of magic will only come in if you *really* hug that person, just like the very first time that you ever hugged ... or as if it was the last time.

... ...

—CUT—

Even though this approach is obviously much more pleasurable than mechanically hugging a loved one, you could be very legitimately asking yourself what all of this has to do with acting. Well, a lot of things, but mostly with the process surrounding sources that work with you. They worked once and will continue to work if you always refresh them. Which means approaching the details as if it was the first time.

If you take the time to redo the path, *gently*, with the passion of a first hug or first contact, you'll once again find its beauty, whether it be with your loved one or with your sources. If you can't find the passion, at least give it your attention and that might bring the passion back ... then its beauty.

> He who masters the grey everyday is a hero.
> (Fyodor Dostoyevsky)

In order to be able to defeat the dreariness of the gloomy daily routine, I only see one solution: to not approach it like a routine. Most of the time, it's neither objects, actions, nor relationships that grow old, it's us. Or to be exact, it's our vision of objects, actions, and relationships that grows old. But it is in our power to change that. We can refresh our vision. Even if you've used the same source for the 1207th time. Even if it's the 1207th time that you've hugged your boyfriend or girlfriend (for example), it's the *one and only* 1207th time that you've hugged your boyfriend or girlfriend! Isn't that beautiful? It might sound lame, but I really do find that beautiful. Don't you? Unless your heart truly isn't in it anymore. It can happen. But in that case, ask yourself this question: Are you taking the path too quickly and jumping on the result too fast, or does your source really no longer affect you, for one reason or another? Basically, are you lazy and mechanical or is the magic really no longer there?

Let me specify something: Please don't take the example used above as me lecturing you. I just want you to do everything with passion. Whether it be the first or millionth time that you're doing something, whatever it may be. It's very useful for understanding sources and much more exciting, in every sense of the word.

The wear and tear of certain sources

As we just said, certain sources and certain relationships can become "worn out" without it being caused by a kind of mechanism on your part. You keep trying with all your heart, but your heart just simply isn't in it anymore.

As we also said before, this is even more understandable as actors are their own instrument and this instrument evolves and changes. So when you've made sure that your approach to the source is neither lazy nor mechanical, and that the source really no longer works with you, change sources. I call this process "verifying a source," which needs complete, vulnerable honesty.

During this verification, actors have to be able to truly question themselves in order to make sure that the problem's not coming from them. Besides being a magnificent virtue, honesty will help you save a lot of time in your work. Because finding a new source to replace one that once worked can turn out to be a very long and foggy process.

It's now time to put to the test *ALL* of the tools that we've worked on in the W.W.W. questions and on "Exploration." In order to do that, let's dive back into the adventurous world of our main character ... who, right about now, is kind of feeling like a real loser ...

Laaaadies and gentlemeeeen!!!

Miss M.

Starring

Really Sketchy Gangster-looking Guys

and

Hemanovitch

and

David (You!)

INT/NIGHT — CUSTODY ROOM and POLICE INTERROGATION ROOM

Despite his bloody face, David is sitting cross-legged and seems very relaxed. His eyes are closed and he's deep-breathing. He's holding what seems to be an imaginary bowl and is inhaling the invisible smells that are coming from it.

He has a series of visions — coriander leaves, onion slices, fuming broth, Min-Mân, the old Vietnamese guy from the restaurant, the way that he expertly cuts the meat in mid air.

When David opens his eyes, he can see an appetizing Pho soup in a bowl that has finally appeared in his hands.

David   AHH!

The New Yorker's Voice   *Shut up, over there!*

David's vision of his Pho soup suddenly shatters.

David   OH!

The New Yorker's Voice   *Shut up, I said!*

David can hear the sounds of punches and painful groans. Then he hears the New Yorker's voice yelling some more.

The New Yorker's Voice   *How about that? "Real cop!?! Real cop!?!"*

David is getting worried.

The New Yorker's Voice   *And is this custody room real enough for you?!*

The cell door suddenly opens and the New Yorker hits a guy with a groin shot that sends him flying across the cell, before heavily crashing to the floor.

Without batting an eyelid and despite the fact that he's all bloodied up too, he gets up immediately, with an anxious David staring at him. He's a living replica of He Man: extremely body-built, blond pageboy haircut, with tiny shorts and a low-cut tight shirt. He has a very strong Bulgarian accent.

Random Guy   JOEEEEEEEEEEEL!!!

He lets out a thundering laugh and gives David a friendly handshake.

Random Guy   Dragan, but you can call me Hemanovitch.

David Uh … David.

Hemanovitch What you here?

David Ugh … because of a girl.

Hemanovitch (not happy) *You rape?!*

David *No no no!* Me just meet a girl and, and, police come over.

Hemanovitch Me same.

He gives a friendly tap on David's back which makes his whole body waver.

Hemanovitch Me magnificent girl.

David Me same.

Hemanovitch Me girl better. Girl magic!

David Me same.

David takes Mona's orange out of his jacket.

Hemanovitch Impossible. Not magic same. Me girl like no other girl. Beauty magic. Eyes magic. Spirit magic. Everything magic. But magic special.

David looks at the orange affectionately.

David Me same.

Hemanovitch Stop say "me same"! You not same. Me girl with magic smell. Tattoo magic. Girl so magic that me draw my body like her. Look.

He parts his hair away from the back of his neck and reveals the exact same flame tattoo that Mona has on hers. David drops his orange.

David Me same. I mean, her same. Uh, I mean … nothing.

Hemanovitch laughs loudly and picks up the orange.

Hemanovitch *Hahahaha!* You say anything for you friend with Hemanovitch.

He starts to peel the orange, which saddens David … Nevertheless, he decides not to complain.

Hemanovitch You what job?

David Acting coach.

Hemanovitch Ah, you failed actor. *Hahahaha!*

David (discouraged) Yes, failed actor yeah. Totally.

Hemanovitch Hemanovitch origamist. Look.

He gives the orange back to David, carefully takes something out of his pocket and proudly shows it to David, who goes white ... Hemanovitch is holding a paper sculpture in his massive hand that is a perfect replica of the engraving on Mona's gun: a phoenix and the words "Mori et Resurgere."

Hemanovitch   Me make this for magic girl.

David (unenthusiastic)   Ah ... it's ... bravo, that's great.

Hemanovitch (poetic)   A phoenix for Phoenix!

David rolls his eyes.

Hemanovitch   But only Hemanovitch know real name Phoenix ... Pamela! Like Pomelo but for girl. And also Clementine like little orange.

David produces a weak laugh.

David   Yeah. Or Zoe, like a zoo, but for a girl.

His weakness turns into irritation. He approaches Hemanovitch.

David   Or Aurora, like the Northern lights, but prettier.

His irritation transforms into aggressiveness. He gets right in Hemanovitch's face and challenges him.

David   Or Angela, like an angel while you're at it!

He pushes Hemanovitch, who stays as still as a statue.

David   *Or Mona like MONAAAA!!!*

He screams and hits the frozen beast's chest hard ... And he hits some more, some more and some more.

David   *Magic girl mine, you understand, Dumbovitch!?! MIIIIIIIIIIINE!!!*

He ends up falling to his knees, sobbing, while 7-feet tall Hemanovitch stares down at him, expressionless ...

Hemanovitch   No. Mine.

He hits David in the face with his massive knee, who screams in pain while bleeding relentlessly. Then suddenly, there are other screams outside of the cell.

For a second, David and Hemanovitch forget that they're fighting and look at each other questioningly. Suddenly the steel door busts open and sends Hemanovitch crashing into the wall.

It's Min-Mân, armed with his bloody kitchen knives. His face and clothes have blood on them too.

David   *Min-Mân!*

Min-Mân *David!*

(telling David to follow him)

Quick, quick, come!

A little suspicious, David feels like he might be missing something. Min-Mân takes him by the arm.

Min-Mân *Quick!*

The New Yorker's Voice *Asshole!*

A shot is fired! David's shoulder has been hit.

David *Uggh! My jacket!*

The New Yorker is lying in a pool of his own blood. He puts his gun down and takes his last breath.

The New Yorker *God damn it …*

Min-Mân and David escape while stomping all over him.

Min-Mân *Take that!*

All of the cops have been left to agonize in their own blood. Only Joel remains alive, but both of his arms have been cut off.

Joel *SAMANTHAAAAAAAAAAA!!!*

To be continued …

Time to play!

Once again, do the following exercise even if you can't fully embody the scene, for lack of scene partners and special effects.

Create your W.W.W. questions for the scene.

… … …

Remember to not answer the W.W.W. questions mentally, but with your *senses*.

… … …

Follow the five steps of working on sources.

… … …

Identify the moments where you can use the imagination or experience, magic ifs, imaginary facts, a sense memory or an emotional memory, substitutions, reflex sources.

... ...

—CUT—

Try. No pressure. Without tension. Without looking for the result. And, *last but not least*, while having fun. Freely. And remember, even though any true acting requires huge amounts of work and research, you should do it all while having fun! Use the tools of the Method more as a springboard for your inspiration, rather than seeing them as rules written in stone to follow blindly.

The shower

It can happen that a source leaves a trace in you, an echo, especially if it was used successfully. If that source is positive, then there shouldn't be any problem. However, if it's negative, then there's no problem either, because we have the shower!

The shower is an exercise to help actors concentrate on a new source that would erase any leftover effects from the negative source. This process can prove itself valuable even for non-actors, during many types of unpleasant situations of everyday life. But in order for the exercise to work, the shower-source or salvation-source needs to be at least as strong as the source that you want to get rid of. For example, if you want to get rid of a nasty taste in the mouth, the best way of doing that is replacing it with a good taste. But again, it has to be at least as strong. You can't, for instance, get rid of a coffee and cigarette taste just by eating a grain of white rice. But you can get rid of it by drinking water and then chewing on some mint leaves or slices of lemon. Or both, while adding a drop of sugar ... delicious!

The same thing goes with sources. So always have powerful shower/salvation-sources on hand. You don't have to look too far to find them. They often lie in simple, ordinary pleasures.

Time to play!

Which taste deeply relaxes you? Which smell? Which type of chocolate? You have my word as a coach, for a lot of people, chocolate is a shower-source that works great. Try it out and find other ones. They can sometimes be very helpful.

... ...

—CUT—

There you go!

And that's just the beginning of exploring the infinite possibilities of sources. Always remember that they are what breathe life into your performances. Sources of life, sources of inspiration. Without them, whether you're an actor or not, we would be cold, soulless machines. So look for sources, everywhere that they are. Within you, within others, their eyes, nature, the universe, life as a whole.

6   Aaaaaaaaaand Action(s)!!!

Without sources, actors, as well as human beings, remain cold machines. However, without physical and psychophysical actions, they remain lifeless mollusks. A mollusk can feel sublime or tragic emotions and, internally, live through magnificent experiences. But that doesn't change the fact that it's still a mollusk and as far as I know, a crying oyster has never made an audience cry. I'm not saying that the concept isn't moving, it's just that the poor oyster can't fully express what it's feeling without actions.

Sources are the heart and soul of any good acting performance. Actions are the bone structure and muscles. Without them, nothing can hold up for long.

The average person's belief is that an actor's job is, at worst, to pretend to feel emotions and to convey them and at best, to truly feel emotions and to convey them. While that's true, the wording of that belief has a disastrous effect on the actor. Because for an actor, as well as any human being, nothing creates fewer emotions than the pressure of wanting to create them.

First and foremost, the actors' job is actually to identify the actions of their role and to execute them. When you think about it, it's no coincidence that we say "Act-or" and not "Emotion-or" and certainly not "Speak-or." That's why every director in the world yells "*Action!!!*" and not "*Emotion!!!*" or "*Lines!!!*" and why our art is called "Act-ing," not "Emotion-ing" or "Speak-ing." Let me also remind you that we often talk about *embodying* a role, which means literally living it through the movement of our flesh, thus through actions. In his third book about the Method, *Creating a Role* (which was published posthumously), Stanislavski explains just how important the action is. He even created a work process around it, which is definitely not as well known as it should be, called active analysis.

Physical actions

To avoid confusion for actors and acting coaches alike, the Method divides actions into two major categories: physical actions and "psychophysical" actions. A physical action is an action that necessarily involves one or more objects being used in its primary function. Here's a few examples. While I'm writing, sometimes I drink from the glass of water that's on my desk. That's a physical action. The same goes for when I open or close the window, when I turn up or turn down the heater, chew some gum, etc. However, even though I'm using my computer in one of its primary functions, writing is a psychophysical action. *The physical actions form the skeleton of a scene.*

Time to play!

Look for other examples of physical actions, based on the ones that I just gave you.

… … …

Remember what defines them: using one or more objects in its primary function.

… … …

– CUT –

Are you finding some? Here are other examples of physical actions: loosening the cap on a bottle, opening a door, closing shutters, pouring water into a pot, cutting onions, wiping down a table with a sponge, cooking, etc. This might seem trivial, but don't underestimate this type of action. In reality, they're incredibly useful to acting, mainly for these three reasons:

1) Physical actions are partially what structure acting.
2) Our inner world echoes through them.
3) Physical actions help us believe even more in fictional situations.

Physical actions are partially what structure acting

Physical actions help in structuring acting and make for good psychological marks, simply because of how visual and tangible they are. They make your performance materialize little by little.

Our inner world echoes through them

A mere physical action, by itself, is not of that much interest. But here's the thing: it's almost never *merely* physical. Physical actions are one of the sounding boards for our inner world and are kind of what helps it spill outwards. The main sounding board being our body itself. They don't always have a meaning of their own, but they allow what's contained in the inner world to be expressed and to become visible *in* and *to* the outside world. In other words, physical actions are a part of the embodiment of our inner world.

To see if you understand, try out this next experiment.

Time to play!

Choose a very simple physical action that's familiar to you, like entering your place and taking off your jacket. Actually do it. We'll call it "Entry 1."

... ...

Now connect to an imaginary or experience source. You ran into your "fantasized" loved one in the street and they were really happy to see you! They almost seemed moved ... As always, be specific. Go into the details that make you feel that.

... ...

Maybe they were looking for the right words to say? Were they seemingly nervous, but trying to hide it? Which tangible elements let you see how they were feeling and allowed you to believe in it? Are you there? Are you connected? Stay connected. Now, enter your place again and take off your jacket. That's "Entry 2."

... ...

Now, redo the experiment, "Entry 3." But this time, imagine that you ran into your loved one but that they were cold as ice, didn't seem to care that it was you; they may have even seemed annoyed to run into you! *Ugh, woe is you!* Stay connected to your sources, enter your place and take off your jacket.

... ...

Do you see the differences between your three entries? If that's not the case, then try entries 2 and 3 again while going into even more detail with your sources.

... ...

– CUT –

There should definitely have been tangible differences in the ways that you enter your place and that you take off your jacket. These differences come from how your sources affect your physical actions, according to whether your run-in with your loved one was ideal or nightmarish. And these differences are tangible precisely because they're expressed through physical actions. That doesn't mean that a human being's inner world can only be expressed when they're doing physical actions. But they truly help the inner world to become visible and without being too demonstrative. Physical actions might not have a meaning of their own, but they allow the meaning(s) of your inner world to be expressed.

Physical actions help us believe even more in fictional situations

Just do it.
(Nike)

The beauty of physical actions is that we can't pretend to do them. We either do them or we don't. Period. It's simple, pure, potentially meditative and that makes them a great help to our acting. You can't really pretend to do the dishes, move a chair, or empty an ashtray. Physical actions are often neglected or taken for something trivial, which they shouldn't be. Because in reality, they contain bits of pure truth. That's why they're even more precious for an actor, as they offer a unique, simple, and very accessible entrance to the belief and truthfulness of fictional situations. They propel you towards a much deeper belief, the psychological belief. As an actor, when you execute actions on stage, you send a specific message to every particle of your being: I'm really doing what I'm doing. *That's* where the "self-bluff" starts, when you truly live out an experience on stage rather than *represent* it.

So always look for physical actions that you can add to the scenes that you play. What kind of objects surround you? What does the character have in their pockets, their bag, etc.? What can you *realistically* and *simply* do with them? Then do it. But, be careful, it's not about doing physical actions just for the sake of doing them, or even worse, in order to fill a void. They should always be motivated *by* and *in accordance with* the story of the script or the play. No, deciding to peel some potatoes or to clip your nails during the famous "To be or not to be" speech by our dear Hamlet would obviously not be appropriate. However, characters in classical plays can have physical actions. Less than in contemporary plays, for sure. But there are always some physical actions.

Here's an anecdote about that. When I was studying in New York, I went to see a play by the Royal Shakespeare Company. They were playing *The Merchant of Venice* and Dustin Hoffman was playing the role of Shylock! I was already a fan of Dustin Hoffman (so maybe a little biased), but I still asked myself: Why does Hoffman seem more alive than his scene partners? He had probably done deeper, more humane work on sources, but there was something else that I was having trouble pinpointing … Then, *Eureka!* I was hit with a very simple truth: it was because he had physical actions. Of course, he didn't start putting together IKEA furniture in the middle of a monologue. But he would do things like adjust his clothing when he sat down or got up, wipe his forehead with a tissue when he was hot, make sure that his kippah was adjusted to his head right, etc. That's not where the entirety of his genius resides, but that's certainly what partially makes his performances so truthful.

Here's another anecdote, but to illustrate the exact opposite. I went to see *Romeo and Juliet*, directed by a French so-called director and in which there were some so-called actors. No point in naming names. During this delirious "adaptation" of the play (as if bringing Shakespeare's vision to light wouldn't suffice), this pseudo-director ordered the poor actress who was playing Juliet to brush her teeth, during the famous balcony scene when Romeo declares his undying love for her. That choice of a physical action completely distorted the meaning of the scene and rendered it completely trivial, if not killed it. Therefore, it completely *belittled* the meaning of the entire play.

However, here's the exact opposite of that exact opposite. There's *Romeo and Juliet* directed by Baz Luhrmann, who only adjusted the time period during which the story takes place and yet respected its meaning *to a T*. Here, Romeo brandishes a gun instead of a sword, which corresponds perfectly to the initial meaning. However, he doesn't start chewing on old tobacco when he's angry, which would be a bit of a stretch from what the brilliant Shakespeare had intended.

Psychophysical actions

A psychophysical action is expressed through an active verb. It's directed towards someone else or towards yourself. It is driven psychologically and is communicated through the body. In other words, *psychophysical actions are the keystone in body language*. As you might already know, psychophysical actions are actually already known as "psychological actions." There's a reason that I choose to rename them as "psychophysical actions." After working with many actors, I often noticed that the original word didn't necessarily encourage them to express their psychological actions physically. It's as if they assumed that the movements of their inner worlds could be read without explicit physical movements. When I renamed them as "psychophysical," I almost systematically achieved more physical implication.

Side note: Whether it be physical or psychophysical, actions must *always* be activated by one or more internal or external sources.

Without a source, an action remains mechanical.
Without an action, a source remains lifeless.

Here are some examples of psychophysical actions: to learn, to seduce, to take care of someone, to threaten, to demand, to beat around the bush, to apologize, to make a decision, to convince, to plead, to taunt, are all psychophysical actions.

Al Pacino is a great actor because when he eats, he eats.

(Harold Becker)

Well, that sentence kind of falls flat, unless you understand it as a whole. After having directed a certain number of movies with Al Pacino in it, when Becker says that, he's saying that Al Pacino never pretends to be doing anything, whether it be physical or psychophysical actions. That's partially where the truthfulness, the presence and the power of his acting come from. As we said earlier, it's harder to pretend to do a physical action than it is to pretend to do a psychophysical action. But pretending will just make it seem fake and superficial. So always make sure to *really* do the psychophysical actions that your role calls for. Again, that's also how you'll have a lot more fun! But first, let's make sure that you clearly understand what psychophysical actions are: *psychophysical actions form the muscles of a scene*.

Time to play!

Base yourself off of the examples that I gave earlier and find ten other psychophysical actions.

... ...

Warning: we can't consider the verbs to think, to hear, to see, or to talk as psychophysical actions. In a way, they are. But they remain much too general in the sense that they are or can be contained in every psychophysical action. They have no precision, no specific meaning, and most of all, they can't all be clearly translated on a physical level. They're merely a potential part of a psychophysical or physical action. If you still have doubts, you're probably confusing these action verbs with others that mean the same thing, but that are much more specific and relatable. Instead of "to hear": to listen, to detect a sound, to lend an ear, to listen through the door, etc. Instead of "to see": to stare, to observe, to examine, to look someone up and down, to look down your nose at someone, to peer, to leer at, to zoom in, to focus on, etc. Instead of "to think": to make a decision, to doubt, to convince yourself, to weigh the pros and the cons, to philosophize, to search for an answer, etc. Instead of "to talk": to argue, to lie, to disclaim, to debate, to claim, to exclaim, to butter up, etc. Do you see the difference? Ok, back to the initial exercise about psychophysical actions. Look for ten.

... ...

Are you finding them? Otherwise, ask yourself this question: What are you doing here and now? You're reading. Yes, that's a psychophysical action, but it's a little vague, just like thinking, hearing, seeing, or talking. What do you do when I encourage you ("to encourage" is a great psychophysical action!) to search for psychophysical actions? Stay simple. That's right! You're looking for an answer, that's a psychophysical action. Maybe while reading, you're saying to yourself: *"Barrouk is really annoying me with this book!"* If that's the case, woe is me and maybe woe is you too, but let's take advantage of the situation to figure out what the psychophysical action behind that sentence could be.

... ...

Did you find it? To blow off, to drag yourself through, to complain, to make fun of, to patronize, to disparage are possibilities.

... ...

Back to the psychophysical action of reading. I said that it was a little vague, because according to the interest or disinterest that you have in this book, you do so-and-so psychophysical action. Again, take the time to figure out what psychophysical actions you've done at certain moments of reading this book.

... ...

If you can't find them, imagine that someone was watching you. Behind the psychophysical action of reading, that person would be able to identify your relationship to what you were reading, not only through your emotions but also and above all through your psychophysical actions. So? Have you found your actions behind that of reading?

... ...

There you go! To validate, to criticize, to agree, to try to understand, to suspect, to question, to look for mistakes, and, of course, to appreciate, to devour, to praise, to put on a pedestal, to admire, to idolize. I'm kidding obviously, but those last ones really are psychophysical actions. Just like "to make a joke."

... ...

—CUT—

In the chapter about physical actions, I specified that the verb "to write" is not a physical action, even if I'm using my computer in one of its primary functions. It's a psychophysical action, but it remains vague, just like "to read." It also potentially contains many other psychophysical actions in itself. Among these actions, you could find: to hesitate, to get carried away, to impose, to provoke, to look for an idea, to make a decision, to validate, to correct, to have fun, to tease, etc.

Is it a little clearer?

Let's start from the objective, which is the target that we want to reach. The desire to reach your objective is partially what provokes physical and psychophysical actions, in life just like on stage. It's pretty simple, when we have a physical objective, we execute physical actions in order to reach it. When we have a psychological objective, we execute psychophysical actions in order to reach it.

Time to play!

What do you do when you're hungry and you want to eat? That's a physical objective.

... ...

You go grocery shopping, you go to a restaurant, you eat. Those are physical actions. And what if you stop yourself from eating, because of the top model inside you? That's a psychophysical action. So, for instance, if you take out your jar of chocolate spread and hesitate to eat some ... then decide to throw it in the garbage, taking out the jar is a physical action doubled with a psychophysical action: to indulge. To hesitate is a psychophysical action. Deciding to get rid of it is a psychophysical action, which then is followed by the physical action of throwing it in the garbage.

Ok. Now, for instance, what do you do when you want to improve your acting? That's a psychological objective.

... ...

You inform yourself, you study, you work, you practice, etc. Those are psychophysical actions.

... ...

—CUT—

I want to get a role. I want to become a star. I want to marry Mona. I want to get revenge. I want to beat up Hemanovitch. I want to help my family live in better conditions. I want to be done with this book. In order to reach any psychophysical objective, you're going to have to use one or more psychophysical actions.

Time to play!

Choose one of the objectives above and try to find the psychophysical action(s) that you would use to reach it.

... ...

Did you find them? Now connect to one of the objectives that you have in your life at the moment and try to identify what you do actively and psychophysically in order to reach it.

... ...

To help you out, let's call on your loved one. Whenever you see him/her, what do you do besides your physical actions? What do you do psychophysically?

... ...

Do you tease him/her? Do you flirt with him/her? Do you play hard to get? Do you play the mysterious type? Do you look to create complicity?

... ...

– CUT –

Whichever one it might be, those are all psychophysical actions. Here are more examples of psychophysical actions: to mock, to judge, to punish, to approach, to encourage, to bear with, to coach, to concentrate, to awaken your senses, to apprehend, to keep your guard up, to impose, to belittle, to show off, to impress, to patronize, to break through, to heal, to tend to, to take care of someone, to caress, to coddle, etc.

It's noteworthy that a psychophysical action can be embodied in many different ways and is very often adjustable. These different adjustments depend on the internal and external sources that the scene offers. For example, you can caress a face with your hand or simply with a look in your eyes. A mother who's finished comforting her child after a nightmare can caress her child's face from a distance, while leaving the bedroom. That doesn't necessarily mean that the mother will act out the gesture of caressing her child's face, but that gesture can simply be present in the look in her eyes, a slight tender nod or even just the blink of an eye.

Also, remember that there's never a moment when we're not in psychophysical action. *Never!* We do psychophysical actions even when we sleep. Even though the actions are much more obvious when we're sleeping next to someone, it's just as true as when we're sleeping alone.

Time to play!

Time for a guessing game! Which psychophysical actions do we do when we're sleeping?

... ...

Come on, you can do it. That's it! To snuggle up, to loll around, to sprawl out, to rest, to try to relax, to tense up, to toss and turn, etc.

... ...

―CUT―

Here are a few actions that are not physical actions, but psychophysical actions, despite the fact that an object is being used in one of its primary functions (just like reading or writing): to point a gun, to whip, to draw, to paint, to play music, to undress someone, etc.

Our physical actions are often tainted by not only our sources, but also the psychophysical actions that come with them, as was demonstrated in the exercise with entries 1, 2 and 3. When Mona randomly dropped by for the first time, the details of her personality were external sources for me. What I think of her and the way that I would've liked the night to turn out were my internal sources. For example, when I closed the door behind her and when I gave her some cabbage juice, I wasn't doing purely physical actions, they were tainted with my sources. So, inevitably, with the psychophysical actions that came with them.

Time to play!

Get a bottle of something, two glasses, and your loved one. He/she isn't free or you doubt that he/she will want to contribute to one of your acting experiments? Too bad for them! Get seated at a table and imagine that he/she is there with you, seated across from you.

... ...

Again and as always, connect yourself to the details about them that strike you.

... ...

I'll use my Mona as a source. Her mysterious smile, which is always a mix of gentleness and teasing. The small spots scattered around her eyes. Her fig perfume. Have you connected to the details of your loved one? Ok. Now pour him/her a glass.

... ...

Then do the same experiment while imagining someone who has the exact opposite effect on you. Someone who you don't like, to say the least.

... ...

Get connected to the details that make you not like this person and when that's done, pour him/her a glass.

... ...

– CUT –

You were probably able to feel and identify the differences between the two people that you poured a glass for? If you were connected to your sources in both cases, they'll not only have influenced you emotionally but they'll have also influenced the physical action of pouring a glass of something. It changed the psychophysical action, which in turn, influenced the way that you do the same physical action.

With your loved one, you could've filled his/her glass while doing one or more of the following psychophysical actions: staring, trying to figure out, show your intensity, etc. However, with the person that you dislike, you could've filled his/her glass while doing one or more of these psychophysical actions: to look them up and down, ignoring, putting them down, patronizing, etc. Since we're always in psychophysical action, defining which ones you're using in each scene will help you to sew together an "emptiness-proof" moment to moment. And that will help you to never, *never!* conk out on stage, since you'll always be busy doing actions. Hallelujah!

I imagine that you've now not only understood the definition of psychophysical actions, but also their importance in acting. Just to make sure, let's test out what you've learned with a new scene.

Laaaadies and gentlemeeeen!!!

Miss M.

Starring

Min-Mân and David (You!)

INT/NIGHT — RESTAURANT *MIN-MÂN'S PLACE*/KITCHEN and DINING ROOM

On a flaming stove, there's a big old pot with broth and huge unidentified bones boiling. We can hear screams of pain. They're coming from a bloodied-up David, who's sitting on a chair, while Min-Mân is pulling the bullet out of his shoulder with a rusty pair of pliers.

David   *AAAAAAAAAARGH!!!!!!!!!*

MIN-MÂN   There you go, David. It's finished, finished!

David isn't doing too well and is about to faint … Min-Mân heavily sprays his wound with alcohol from a bottle that contains a very strange stem.

David   *WAHAAAAAAAAAAA!!!*

Min-Mân gets his knife from the kitchen, which was heating up on the fire. The blade is flaming red. He presses it onto the wound, which smokes up immediately.

David   *GAWAAAARH!!!*

Min-Mân puts his leg around David's neck to stop him from falling from the chair.

Min-Mân   There you go! *THEEEEEERE YOU GO!* It's done.

He releases David's neck from his leg and takes the knife away from his smoking shoulder. David is rocking back and forth and groaning from the pain. He still ends up fainting.

We can hear police sirens in the distance.

CUT TO ...

The sounds of the police sirens seem to be closer and can be heard throughout the whole scene.

David is now seated at one of the tables in the empty restaurant, still out of it and with a bandage on his shoulder. Min-Mân gently covers his bloody face with a relaxation mask that's made of this cold, bright green fluid and which makes him look really weird.

Min-Mân   Wake up, David.

Min-Mân snaps his fingers in front of David's face, but he remains out like a light. He puts on traditional Vietnamese music, nothing. He turns up the volume, nada. He puts on some hard Vietnamese rock, still nothing. He jumps up and down on the table and yells/sings over and over again in an irritating manner:

Min-Mân   *Failed-actor-failed-actor-faaailed-actor-faaailed-actor!!!*

Nothing. Min-Mân is getting really worried … until an idea comes to him!

Min-Mân comes back from the kitchen with a big bowl of hot Pho soup. He puts it in front of David and waits … The seductive fumes of the soup reach David's nose and just like that, he opens his eyes.

David   Aw, Min-Mân, that's so nice!

Without realizing that his checkered shirt is soaked with blood, he puts a napkin around his neck and starts eating. He doesn't realize that he's wearing a bright green mask either, and because of that, three quarters of each spoonful spills onto the table.

Min-Mân   I fucked up, David.

David   Oh, I certainly don't think so, the soup is great!

Min-Mân realizes that David is still a little bit out of it.

Min-Mân   I killed four cops and made the fifth one armless, David!

David   … Oh, that does sound familiar.

Min-Mân   Finish your soup and let's get outta here.

He takes off his kitchen clothes and while he's changing, David sees that he has a tattoo of Mona's face on his chest, with the inscription Bào-Châu.

Min-Mân   Yes, me too. It's really for her that I saved you.

David (still a little drowsy)   Really? But you got it wrong, Min-Mân, her name isn't Bào-Châu.

Min-Mân Very funny. What's her name then?

David tries to remember.

David Uhhhhh …

Min-Mân You see!?! Bào-Châu — Precious Pearl!

(very serious and moved)

You know, you're very important to her …

David Me?

Min-Mân You, David … well, and Lassie.

David pretends to not get it while Min-Mân puts on a strange wig and a big black hat. These are the final touches to his orthodox rabbi costume.

Min-Mân There we are! No one will be the wiser. Come on, let's get outta here.

David But what about my soup!?

Min-Mân Who gives a fuck? It was just to wake you up, David.

He gets behind the cash register and takes out a few guns.

Min-Mân Half of the world's cops are chasing us down. Soup or no soup.

(throwing a gun to David)

Catch!

David catches the gun and notices that it's the same type as Mona's gun.

Min-Mân Come on, come on!

Min-Mân is at the door, ready for action as an armed rabbi.

Min-Mân So, you coming or not? Quick, David, cops are coming!

Gun in hand, blood-soaked shirt and with a bright green mask on his face, David hesitates …

David No. I think I really deserved that soup.

Min-Mân You think of top model in you? All chubby guys have one.

David Yes. He can go fuck himself.

Min-Mân Shalom, then!

He leaves and disappears into the dark, yelling:

Min-Mân's Voice BAO-CHÂÂÂÂÂÂÂÂÂU!!!

To be continued …

Time to play!

Choose one of the characters and define what his psychophysical actions are.

... ...

I'll help you out a little with an example for each one. At the beginning, Min-Mân's psychophysical action is to "ease out the bullet." No, it's not a physical action, but a psychophysical action that contains physical actions. We'll come back to that a little later.

As for David, he's trying to keep it together. That psychophysical action is provoked by a physical state, which needs work around a poetic or sense memory. Now define all of the psychophysical actions of the character that you've chosen. Really do it, it's one of the many major tools of the Method and one of the most helpful.

... ...

– CUT –

So? Did you find them? If that's not exactly the case but that you still tried, don't worry, it can take time to fully understand and we'll talk more in detail about how to identify a character's psychophysical actions later.

Ok. Now, here's another question for you: Is kissing someone a physical or psychophysical action? What about making love? Of course, both are psychophysical. To be clear, every time that you're in action in the vicinity of another living being, your actions are always psychophysical. So when Min-Mân eases the bullet out of David's shoulder, it's a psychophysical action that happens to contain physical actions.

Here's an important question about psychophysical actions that should be taken into account: If they're naturally provoked by our sources, what's the point in defining them, rather than merely defining our sources and letting them take care of it? Well, mostly for these next three reasons:

1) In order to add variations, range and precision to your performances.

2) Because the characters that you play impose specific actions, but not the sources that will push you to do them.

3) To create characters.

In order to add variations, range and precision to your performances

When discovering the work process around psychophysical actions, many actors have a hard time naming them at first. It's often because they haven't yet understood how to identify them and still confuse them with non-active verbs. They confuse them the most often with what we call emotion verbs, like for instance: to love, to cry, to laugh, to hate, etc. Which is often due to the false conception around acting that we talked about earlier: actors who think that they need to feel emotions before anything else. Once they free themselves from that error and all of the pressure that comes with it, they're given much more room to concentrate and *feel* what psychophysical actions are. Not to mention their fundamental use in acting.

When that's done, most actors have a hard time perceiving the range of psychophysical actions that are at their disposal and can only identify those that are familiar to them. They identify those that they're used to doing or seeing in everyday life, which is normal. So in order to widen their range of psychophysical actions, defining them and naming them helps open up a much broader and more diverse horizon of possibilities. Hence, their acting becomes much richer.

It's noteworthy that some psychophysical actions that are part of the same category can be defined with even more precision. This helps to sharpen and diversify your performances. That's one of the reasons why we encourage actors to clearly define and write down the psychophysical actions of each scene, not merely in order to be a good academic. Here are examples of psychophysical actions that contain their own specificities, despite being in the same category: to seduce, to flirt, to sweet-talk. When these specificities have been understood and identified, they bring in various colors and precision to your performances.

Time to play!

Search for psychophysical actions that are part of the same category and then do them while being connected to well-chosen sources. Pay attention to the differences that there are between each of them, no matter how subtle they might be.

... ...

Ok, I'll help you out a little: to warn, to alert, to caution are all part of the same category but each contains nuances. The same goes for: to pamper, to coddle, to soothe, to cuddle, to caress. Your turn. Identify, connect, act.

... ...

– CUT –

Because the characters that you play impose specific actions, but not the sources that will push you to do them

During the acting experiment that we did earlier with your loved one where you were serving a drink, we started with your sources in order to pinpoint the psychophysical actions that they provoke. But when you have a role to embody, you go through the opposite process. The role imposes very specific psychophysical actions and it's up to you to define the sources that will allow you to execute these actions in an accurate and motivated way. In other words, your character's psychophysical actions form a context that defines the choice of your sources. So it's very important to first identify and specifically define what you're going to act, meaning the psychophysical actions that the role imposes. Then you'll be able to select your sources accordingly, which will then provoke the needed actions (whether they be physical or psychophysical).

To create characters

This is an extremely vast subject—we'll be broaching it from a pretty general point of view. Again, despite many widespread misconceptions, what defines a character's personality (as well as any human being for that matter) is not the way that they walk, their clothes, haircut, or any other physical attribute. It's not their social status, their ancestry, culture, their job, etc. It's mostly the psychophysical actions that they do. Even if the rest is still a lot of fun to figure out and very important to work on, it's all of secondary importance, no matter what the role is! For example, the reason that we describe someone as "shy" is because they make themselves smaller, hesitate, avoid direct eye contact, apprehend, search for others' approval, etc. It's the combination of a character's psychophysical actions that makes up what we call their conscious or unconscious strategy. In other words, their approach to the world, to themselves, to anything, and any type of event. So when we "analyze" a character, we identify their psychophysical actions, which is a fundamental basis of any good creation.

We are what we are because of what we do. And when I say "what we do," I'm not talking about a profession, but psychophysical actions. Observe the way that you more or less intuitively define another person in everyday life. What they say, the way that they dress, where they come from, makes up around 10 percent of your opinion. The 90 percent left is based on what they do. And if that's not the case, then you're severely mistaken in the way that you read others. Becoming an expert in psychophysical actions can be very useful in life in general and in your relationships.

So, clearly identifying your character's psychophysical actions is a huge help in embodying their personality, without overacting or artificiality. Actors who don't know how to create characters or just do it badly (but who aren't necessarily trash) usually just lack knowledge about psychophysical actions. They tend to make the mistake of depending on the emotion. Emotions are obviously important, but they definitely aren't everything and they need actions in order to be expressed in their entirety.

Psychophysical actions are an essential support system made to give your performances a tangible structure and humanity. They are to acting what movement is to music. They make up the paths that your characters take in order to achieve their objectives. They are the arrows that the characters use in order to reach their targets. Many psychophysical actions are dictated by the objectives, but there are other elements that can influence the choice of actions: motivations, obstacles, the character's unconscious mind.

1) The relationship between motivations and psychophysical actions.

Let's imagine that your character's objective is to kill someone. The motivation that's pushing them to want to achieve that objective will deeply influence the choice of psychophysical actions. If your character is motivated by revenge, their psychophysical actions will vary accordingly. If they're motivated by a form of pleasure that they get out of the murder in itself, other psychophysical actions will occur. If they choose to kill in order to save their own life, yet more psychophysical actions will appear. Not only do motivations influence your choice of psychophysical actions, they taint the way that you execute them.

2) The relationship between obstacles and psychophysical actions.

Even if a character does psychophysical actions in order to achieve their objectives, being confronted with external or internal obstacles can of course influence and even change their actions. We'll again use the example of a character wanting to kill a specific person, let's say out of revenge. Their education, the fear of punishment, or the fear of remorse can be obstacles that change up their psychophysical actions. Even though they were sure about it at first, your character could start doubting, questioning, having trouble making a decision, looking for inner motivation, etc.

3) The relationship between your character's unconscious mind and psychophysical actions.

We mentioned earlier the fact that we're constantly in psychophysical action, even when we're sleeping. That means that certain psychophysical actions come from the unconscious mind. But unconscious actions can arise at other moments besides being asleep. Human beings (so the characters that you'll embody) have many inherent personality traits, which can dictate some of their psychophysical actions, whether they want it or not and whether they realize it or not. Among the causes can be education, trauma, fears, beliefs, etc. That being said, since you have to be conscious (ironically) of your character's unconscious mind, the choice of actions must be rigorous and based on a detailed analysis of the deepest parts of your character's soul. If you choose sources that truly impact you and motivate you to do your character's psychophysical actions, you'll be surprised to feel the emotions bubble up by themselves.

7   How to ~~Rehearse~~ Create a Scene

I am taking my time, for I am in a hurry.

(Lao Tzu)

That notion is major to any worthy creative process, whether it be Van Gogh's or nature's works of art. Let's start out by correcting a common mistake—the concept of a rehearsal. Rehearsal, which leads to repetition. That word actually has nothing to do with the work that a good actor does during that time. Yup, a bad actor rehearses. They rehearse and rehearse and rehearse. They mostly rehearse their mistakes! They triumph in repeating the same choices over and over again, or rather the same lack of choices. Some of them are even comfortable remaining on the surface of things. That way, they'll never have to reach their true depth. Not to mention that the repetition can induce a completely counter-creative attitude. An attitude that implies that as soon as we start working, we already know where we're going. It can be deeply uninteresting.

> *Mediocre actors rehearse in order to represent life; good actors explore it, in order to create it.*

But there's an even worse attitude "rehearsing" can induce: not working at all. Some actors will show up without a care in the world. It comes to them "instinctively." I might sound harsh, but so many pseudo movie actors justify their laziness and pretentiousness by claiming that they avoid working on their role beforehand, so that it remains "fresh." But I'm sorry, what "freshness" can they possibly be talking about? When all they do is keep serving us the same old dish?

Unlike what most people think and assume, encouraging actors to work on their roles does not tense up their performances. That exploration is not supposed to be a prison, but a springboard. The reason that we so highly encourage actors to use Stanislavski's tools from the Method is precisely to help their creativity blossom! And that blossoming happens when, after working on a role for a while, it becomes a second nature that's truer than nature. Almost like magic.[1]

During a fascinating international conference organized at the Beaubourg museum in Paris, called "The Stanislavski Century," I was lucky enough to meet and talk to a few major figures of the Method, including the brilliant Robert Lewis, the genius Stella Adler, and the charismatic actor Ben Gazzara. Gazzara talked quite a while about his work with John Cassavetes. For those who don't yet know his work, what a treat you have in store! John Cassavetes, who is an actor, acting coach, screenwriter, director, and producer,

---

[1] I know—that could be a very bad coach's catchphrase. We'll talk about that more in detail a little later.

is without a doubt an unmatched genius. He's known for independent American movies, as well as internationally. The acting performances in his movies are famous for being breathtaking, exciting, inspiring, free, magical! They are so fresh, that a myth has been created around them: that Cassavetes only has his actors improvise. "Bullshit!" said Ben Gazzara. "Apart from his first movie called *Shadows*, which was in fact based on improvisation, John worked so much with his actors on their roles, for each scene, that it was all so anchored in us so that we felt completely free." All is said right there about the purpose of working on roles beforehand. The deepened exploration of roles creates tangible guidelines, which puts actors in confidence and dotes them with profound freedom. Ironically, we obtain spontaneity by working relentlessly on our role.

Really, there's a very common conceptual error that opposes upstream work and improvisation. And that error partially comes from a belief that freshness can only be found in newness. That's *also* bullshit! Improvisation (in scene work anyway) can actually only be possible when it's based on prior work. We don't improvise just whatever, completely randomly. But rather, just like jazz, we improvise starting from a set partition. Thus, to be able to improvise with it, we need to start by getting to know it, studying it deeply, and then truly mastering it. It's really not that much of a coincidence if it just so happens that great actors like Marlon Brando, Jack Nicholson, Meryl Streep, or Zendaya do that kind of work. So … why not you? Stop systematically making yourself choose between prior work and spontaneity. The two go hand in hand.

The principles of the Method are not made to *control* your performances. They're made to give you so much confidence that they *liberate* your performances. By the way, don't mix up freedom and artistic blurriness. And so when you hear great actors like Mickey Rourke, for instance, say that they improvise, know that they've reached that freedom by intimately understanding and knowing their character. Basically, they don't get there with the help of the Holy Spirit, but by working hard. Based on what Stanislavski would say all the time, maybe we should actually specify that the Holy Spirit of inspiration is ready to come to you if you're ready to welcome it. It'll come to you if you've laid the proper foundation that will allow it to freely express itself. And hence, bring that vital freshness into your performances.

First reading, first impressions

Now, we're going to explore the work surrounding a scene, without yet going into all of the different facets of creating a character. Even though that process starts naturally, with all of the acting choices which are made.

From a blank page to infusion

Trust your first impressions, they have so many gifts! Well, under two conditions: that the play or script is good *and* that the role, even if it seems very far from you, resonates within you. If that's not the case, then you're in a sticky situation and we'll talk later about the solutions to that kind of problem. To be able to trust your first impressions, you have to make sure that they're pure. And when I say "pure," I mean stripped of any parasite, prejudice or anticipated concept. Basically, from a blank page state.

In order to avoid any type of distortion whatsoever, I encourage you to turn your first readings of scripts/plays into a ritual. Reading a scene without knowing its context (which is the entire script) is completely pointless. So make sure that you have a few hours to kill, maybe even an entire day, get by yourself, don't talk to anyone, turn off your phone, get a drink—preferably non-alcoholic! Then get into a relaxation session. Once you've reached the "blank page" state, when you truly feel available, then you can start reading.

Stanislavski always insisted upon practicing this kind of ritual, which, according to him and also myself, has the potential of putting the actor in a state of responsiveness to the story and to the role. That way, those elements can fully permeate throughout the actor's inner world—imprint it, inspire it. Now that's a good start!

When you've finished your first reading, don't immediately throw yourself back into the agitated outside world. I promise you, it can still hold on a little longer without you turning your phone back on. Wander around your place a little and feel the traces that the story has left in you, its characters and their passions ... Maybe start out by taking some notes, without forcing it too much. Just let the pen guide you. Maybe you'll come up with a drawing, or a quote, or names of well-known people or people from your dreams, or both. Let yourself digest all of it and, ideally, let yourself sleep on it. You'll see the world will not have forgotten about you yet. Anyway, keep these first impressions alive in you or on paper, they are the soil from which your performance will bud.

Just in case the play or the script isn't good or doesn't resonate within you

As I promised earlier, let's talk about the case in which the play or the script isn't good or doesn't resonate within you at all.

Option number one: decline the role.

I've often coached actors starting out their career who, once getting a part in an awful play or film, would ask me if I thought that they should take the part. In this type of case, my first answer is always unequivocal: I'm not the one putting food on your plate every day or a roof over your head every night, so it's up to you. Ethically, it's true. But yes, it's a very trivial answer and it usually doesn't satisfy the person who asked me the question. So they insist. Then, I give my second answer, which is less superficial: Decline the role. Then, I'm almost always hit with the same expression on their face: it's kind of as if I've just suggested that they gut their entire family and then sell their organs on eBay. That's right! You are allowed to decline roles when they're simply not worth anything. When they're coming from plays or scripts thought up by pseudo-brains who don't even deserve a pseudo-name. There's no law that forbids young actors to decline roles. But the mass hysteria of formatted success is sometimes so strong that it instills a kind of pressure in some, who didn't even have that anxiety in them in the first place. Some kind of illusory thirst, an injected void.

No, the point is not to encourage you to live a sacrificial life of being a cursed artist. As if being an artist was somehow a pledge to be perfect. No. But there are other solutions that can help you do your profession, rather than putting up with crap. It's hard, it's complicated, but it's very gratifying and it helps us to look at ourselves in the mirror.

Here's a great example: Matt Damon and Ben Affleck were so tired of running after mediocre auditions, that they wrote *Good Will Hunting,* where they were able to give themselves the main characters' parts even though they were basically unknown. Once again, I'm not saying that it's easy, but it's certainly worth it.

With all of that being said, there is another option that's available to you. Option number two: substituting everything. If, for one reason or another, you still decide to take the part— which is your right to do so—you have the possibility of substituting everything. It's a lot of work, but it definitely pays if it's done right. So you'd have to substitute the given circumstances of the play or the script with ones that inspire you more.

In that case, there's one problem that could still arise: if the director or others actually want you to act like shit. It happens more often than you'd think. That's the favorite strategy used by a lot of morons who have turned their limits into choices and try to impose them onto others. If you decide to follow them, neither the Method nor I can help you. It's between you and self-worth.

I've seen actors who, despite the lack of ambition of a project and the team responsible for it, bravely try to do their best and who are mocked for that. If that happens to you, please don't take it to heart. Mockery towards the passionate is one of the favorite weapons used by the truly incapable and is the exact expression of their vulgarity. There's a lot of them in our profession and the times that we're living in often give them credit. But even if their mediocrity manages to climb the steps of the hierarchy of merit, remember that their "throne" shall be swallowed up by the trivial crap that they created, erased without even having existed.

Giving life to what's in white on the page

As you've probably noticed, I use the word "create" when referencing the work surrounding a scene. You could legitimately counter that by saying that, technically, it's impossible to *create a scene* since it already exists. That's true, but also false. Let me explain: it's true from a *literary* point of view but it's *literally* false from an acting point of view. The scene does exist on paper, but its entire embodiment has yet to be created.

That's exactly what I mean when I tell actors to not act out what's written in black on a page, but rather what's written in white. And since there's nothing written in white, that it's up to them to create it.

First, let us clarify that not all scenes are the same and that even though I encourage you to follow the steps that we'll see in just a minute for most of them, there are obviously some exceptions to these "rules." Once actors have digested their first impressions of the first reading, here are the steps that I encourage them to follow (most of the time) in order to create what's in white in a scene:

1) Breaking the scene down into sections.

2) Starting active analysis and defining the psychophysical structure.

3) Making choices, then testing them out by physicalizing them.

4) Loosening up the psychophysical structure.

We'll review certain terms like "active analysis," which for now might still seem a little obscure to you. So that you fully understand each of the steps of giving life to what's in white on a page, we're going to work on it together with a new scene, so that you'll be able to do it by yourself later on with others.

Laaaadies and gentlemeeeen!!!

Miss M.

Starring

Ahaaa! Surprise! and David (You!)[2]

INT/NIGHT—RESTAURANT *MIN-MÂN'S PLACE*/DINING ROOM

Once again, police sirens can be heard throughout this entire scene and they sound even closer than in the previous scene. David is seated at a table. With his "hottie" jacket around his shoulders and his face still covered in a bright green liquid mask, he's playing a Vietnamese electric sitar that was hanging on the wall as decoration. He's playing a Vietnamese-variety sounding melody, which is childish yet touching. He masters the instrument but can't carry a tune in a bucket.

David Failed actooor, you won't go tooo faaar … That's whyyy you started coachii-ing … Oh, failed actor, yeah! Failed actooor …

---

[2]Unless you choose to work on the role "Ahaaa, surprise!."

Then, we see that he's actually singing along with the lyrics of a karaoke video that's pretty corny and tasteless. But it's still pretty touching, despite the very bad actor that looks like a Vietnamese version of David and the just as bad actress who looks like the Vietnamese version of Mona.

David   You could siiing tooo … Unless yooou're a faailed singer … Oh, failed singer, yeah! Faailed singer … So you'd become a varietyyy coach … Who would teach a few beautiiies … But who would have no affeeect on yooou … Because you only think ooof Mona! Phoenix! Zoeee, yee hah! Aurora! Angela! Krikri the crackhead from Mars! And Pamelaaa! Clementine! Samanthaaa! Let's not forgeeet Bào-Châuuu … Or that yooou're … a faaailed boyfriend … Oh, failed boyfriend, yee hah! Oh yeah, failed boyfriend …

A single tear drips down his bright green mask … when suddenly, he can hear someone clapping.

He turns around to see Mona. She also has a bandage on her shoulder and seems to have gotten beat up too. But that doesn't take away any of her unique charm.

Mona (without her accent)   You might be a failed actor, but for the boyfriend part, that has yet to be seen.

David   Ah, there you are, you ungrateful bitch!

She turns pale as a ghost.

David   Don't make that face. Kidding! And, I admit, I just needed to vent a little. Where did it go?

Mona   What?

David   Your accent.

Mona   I never had an accent.

David (suspicious)   Kidding?

Mona   No, that was a fantasy of yours.

David   That's definitely possible, but you still had an accent.

Mona   If that's what makes you happy.

David   Ok, we'll get back to that later. God damn it, where were you?!

Mona   Your place.

He stares at her, trying to figure out if she's telling the truth …

Mona   By the way, I read your book.

David   That's impossible, I'm still working on it.

Mona   Of course it's possible, otherwise how could I be saying the lines that are written in there?

David Don't get too excited, I'm still not sure if I'll put this scene in. It might be more private rather than it is intimate.

Mona Private? Don't get too excited either, I'm still not sure if it's a sure win yet.

David For you or for me?

Mona For us.

Silence … He puts the sitar down and takes off the mask. She's happy to see his face again, even if he's also all bruised up.

Mona What happened to you?

David (pointing at her own bruises) You're one to talk.

Mona I slipped on a banana peel. What about you?

David I ran into a few guys who really wanted to know where you were.

Mona I can see that. Do you have it with you?

David Of course! I just love walking around with 100 grams of cocaine on …

Mona Not that, the phone, my phone.

David Yeah.

She comes and stands closer to him. They lock eyes, both a little overwhelmed by this proximity …

Mona Hand it over.

He gives her the smartphone and she goes to throw it in one of the fish tanks of the restaurant.

Mona There! Now no one else can mess with you, since no one can know where you are.

(discreetly, like it's a secret)

It's tapped.

David Thanks, I got that. By the way, thanks for making me take the risk.

Mona I needed to be able to find you.

David Well, you have my number. You know, a lot of people do that. They each have a number and they call each other. You should try it, it's pretty practical.

Mona I really thought that it would be too risky to call you on your phone.

David You've got a point, as you can see, everything worked out really well. I only got completely wasted by cops who seemed to be fresh out of the nuthouse, then by a

7-foot Bulgarian dude in shorts, then just to be shot in the shoulder which, as icing on the cake, made a hole in my favorite jacket.

Mona   I'm so sorry. Seriously.

David   It sure seems like it. Ok, now you've got some explaining to do.

Mona   No prob.

She goes behind the bar to get a bottle of Saigon Export and drinks directly from the bottle.

David   What's the deal with the phoenix tattoo on the deaf cop's arm? Well, the deaf cop's ex-arm now, the one who calls you Samantha?

While he's listing everything that he has questions about, we see flashbacks of the things that he's talking about.

David   How interesting, a phoenix with the words "Mori et resurgere," just like the engraving on your gun. Ahh, there's another one, a phoenix just like the name on your Russian passport, Mona from Romania.

While he's talking to her, he goes to sit down at the bar.

David   Again, the same words as on the origami, how interesting! A phoenix made by Hemanovitch, who calls you Pamela-like-Pomelo-but-for-a-girl, and also Clementine-like-a-little-orange, for you. How interesting, an orange just like the one that strangely rolled over from your bag toward me. How interesting, the Bulgarian origamist has the same flame tattoo that you have on the back of your neck. Again, how interesting, just like Min-Mân, who calls you Bào-Châu, who has your face tattooed onto his chest.

He gets behind the bar to face her, literally and metaphorically, and looks like he definitely expects answers.

Mona   I do want to answer you, I'm just not sure if I get the part about the rolling orange.

David   Forget about the rolling orange. Talk about the other stuff.

Mona   Well, first of all, I don't have a flame tattoo on the back of my neck, or anywhere else for that matter.

Seeing how suspicious he is, she turns around on her bar stool and pushes her jet-black hair away from her neck, where there isn't, in fact, any tattoo.

Despite how bewildered he is by this discovery, David can't stop himself from savoring the fumes of her fig perfume.

She turns back around to look at him and sees that he's tripping out a little.

Mona   Are you ok?

David   Yeah, yeah, I'm fine. It's just that I love your perfume!

Mona Ah, that must be another one of your fantasies, just like the accent and the tattoo—I never wear perfume.

David (mockingly) Oh, really? And the one that's in your bag is just for decoration, I suppose?

Mona That's not my bag. And what's in it doesn't exist. There's really no bag anyway.

David Is that so? What's this then?

He "brandishes" the bag from beneath the bar counter.

Mona Uh … my bag.

He nonchalantly sets it on the counter between them.

David And everything that's in it? Are those fantasies too?

Mona No. A gun …

She takes it and with precise and quick gestures, checks if it's loaded.

Mona That's loaded, a real fake passport, very real coke and … my perfume.

David What kind of perfume?

Mona (with a slight smile) Fig.

David *So?!* Fantasies, huh?!

She holsters the gun in her belt, squirts some perfume on her neck and her seductive accent reappears.

Mona The two aren't incompatible. But even though I'm truly, sincerely flattered that you went through my bag, those are the only answers that you'll ever get, Barroukovitch.

David Just like in the text that you sent me, right? No questions about your life?

Mona That's right.

He gets lost in thought. She observes him.

Mona You wanna know why I never answered that text that I told you I loved so much?

David To make me want you even more? You didn't need to.

Mona Kind of, but it was mostly to protect you.

David Well, it didn't really work.

Mona I know. But I'm hoping that nothing else happens to you because of me.

David If we could stop at accessory to murder of four cops and mutilation of the fifth, that'd be nice.

Mona On the other hand, your jacket looks even cooler like that … Bad Boyish.

Her compliments are getting to him. She knows it.

David What are you playing at?

Mona I don't know, but I'm having fun over here, aren't you?

David I am … It's almost as if these lines hadn't been written beforehand.

Mona You must be connected to powerful sources then.

David Probably.

Mona I am too … That's why I'm able to do motivated psychophysical actions.

David Me too.

They gaze at each other silently for a few seconds …

David What's your psychophysical action right here, right now?

Mona I can't tell you. The entire point of this scene is to help actors understand how to rehearse—crossed out—create a scene. *Ergo*, like you say, to help the readers find the psychophysical actions by themselves.

David So you really did read my book?

Mona You know, the whole true, false thing, real or imaginary … To me, all of that's relative.

David (officially charmed) You drive me crazy.

Mona I'm not sure what you mean by that, but know that it's the same for me.

David And what do you mean by that?

Mona Do that experiment of yours with actors. I'll tell you in the next scene, the one that they'll have to work on alone. Which just so happens to be the one where we'll see if you're really a failed boyfriend or not.

David Do I have your word?

Mona (putting her hand to her heart) As a liar.

To be continued!!!

Time to play!

Since I'm a little too biased with this scene, I'll of course let you use your own judgment when it comes to your first reading and your first impressions. Obviously, feel completely free during this process. If you like the scene, that will give us a lot of elements to work with. If you don't like it, that'll give us a lot of elements too.

... ...

For this first step, identify which elements of the scene speak to you and which elements don't speak to you. And most importantly, according to the character that you've chosen to work on.

... ...

As we discussed earlier, this will help you figure out which elements you'll need in order to choose sources, and/or which elements inspire you "spontaneously." Whatever they might be, identify these elements precisely and write them down.

... ...

Even though the idea of this experiment is to work on this scene together, only you can know what resonates within you and what doesn't.

... ...

– CUT –

Breaking down a scene

As we saw earlier, the first step to giving life to what's written in white on the page is answering the W.W.W. questions of the scene. But the W.W.W. exercise itself needs the breakdown of the scene in order to work. This breakdown consists of pinpointing the major beats of the scene, and particularly those of the character that you're going to play. These beats are defined by changes in the objective, in the psychophysical actions, motivations, stakes, and obstacles.

So we're going back to the scene to figure out how it's broken down from David's point of view. In order to do that, we're going to work on two opposite pages that are next to each other, as I often encourage actors to do. The pages on the left will have the scene written down with little dots that will indicate where there's an important break in the structure. The pages on the right will indicate the choices that motivate these breaks and will be indicated by little dots as well. I'll also add comments and examples of the types of questions that you need to ask yourself when breaking down a scene. Lastly, since the subtext of a scene (indicated on the right page) is much more important than the actual lines (indicated on the left page), don't be surprised at how uneven the layout seems.

Time to play together!

The first order of business is to figure out and understand how the scene is structured. But hold on—for now, we'll only work on the major beats in order to identify the main turning points. We'll only focus on detailing our answers to the W.W.W. questions that directly concern the structure of our scene and its psychophysical actions. Still, do the same work for the questions "Where?" and "When?"

Miss M.

Starring

David (You) and Mona (You too!)

Worksheet

INT/NIGHT—RESTAURANT *MIN-MÂN'S PLACE*/DINING ROOM

Once again, police sirens can be heard throughout this entire scene and they sound even closer than in the previous scene.

David is seated at a table. With his "hottie" jacket around his shoulders and his face still covered in a bright green liquid mask, he's playing a Vietnamese electric sitar that was hanging on the wall as decoration. He's playing a Vietnamese-variety sounding melody, which is childish yet touching. He masters the instrument but can't carry a tune in a bucket.

                        DAVID

        Failed actooor, you won't go tooo faaar. That's whyyy you started coachiiing … Oh, failed actor, yeah! Failed actooor …

Then, we see that he's actually singing along with the lyrics of a karaoke video that's pretty corny and tasteless. But it's still pretty touching, despite the very bad actor that looks like a Vietnamese version of David and the just as bad actress who looks like the Vietnamese version of Mona.

                        DAVID

        You could siiing tooo … Unless yooou're a faailed singer … Oh, failed singer, yeah! Faailed singer …

Where am I?

At Min-Mân's Place, a Vietnamese restaurant.

If you're playing David, make sure to specify "At Min-Mân's Place, a Vietnamese restaurant that I go to often."

If you're playing Mona, make sure to specify "At Min-Mân's Place, a Vietnamese restaurant that I know well, considering my relation to Min-Mân and the fact that I worked there."

Then go into the details of the question "Where?" The fact that you know the place really well, no matter which character you're playing, will definitely influence your behavior. To help you believe in it, go into the details of your relationship to the place, but also to …

When is it happening?

At night.

Again, I'll let you go into the details about the question "When?" For instance, for David, this is not just any night. In this case, many elements need a work process around sense memories, poetic or not.

Since the other W.W.W. questions are in relation to the structure, we'll go back to answering them on the opposite page.

So you'd become a varietyyy coach, who would teach a few beautiiies … But who would have no affeeect on yooou … Because you only think ooof Mona! Phoenix! Zoeee, yee hah! Aurora! Angela! And Pamelaaa! Clementine! Samanthaaa! Let's not forgeeet Bào-Châuuu … Or that yooou're … a faaailed boyfriend … Oh, failed boyfriend, yee hah! Oh yeah, failed boyfriend …

Why am I here: what is my objective?

While writing this scene, I voluntarily put in a few "traps," if you will, that can appear in other scripts when you'll work on other roles. Of course, the whole point of putting them in here is to help you avoid falling into them at other times.

At the opening of the scene, there are already two traps that have been set which concern the objective. Can you identify them?

... ...

There's the trap of anticipating and "acting the emotion," which, as we've already brought up, shouldn't actually be acted. In order to not anticipate, we need to define an objective for David that doesn't concern Mona. Everything points to his objective including her, but that's actually not the case—that's why it's a trap. So, according to you, why does David's objective actually not concern her?

... ...

Simply because she isn't there. Keep this in mind, an objective can never be directed towards a person who isn't present. You could counter that with an example where a person, let's call him Johnny, is looking for a gift to surprise, let's say, Jenna. Well, again, I insist and stand by the fact that Johnny's objective can't be directed towards Jenna, because she simply isn't there. In this type of situation, what could Johnny's objective be?

... ...

"I want to find the best gift for Jenna." Despite what it may seem like, the objective is not directed towards Jenna but rather towards Johnny himself. Or, if you prefer, towards the idea of Jenna that he currently has. In order to choose the right gift, Johnny can only be guided by what he thinks of Jenna, what he thinks she's like, what he knows about her tastes, what he projects onto her, what he's guessed about her. But nothing in all of that is directly addressed to her.

To be precise, the only cases when an objective is directed towards someone who isn't physically present, are when we're in direct contact with that person. Do you see what that means?

... ...

Obviously, when we're on the phone, texting, or on a video call with someone. But there are other cases … What are they?

... ...

When we're praying to an entity, a god or some kind of invisible higher force. Or when we're calling upon a spirit.

... ...

Now that we've cleared that up, back to our scene. So, for the time being, David doesn't know that Mona is going to show up. *Ergo*, he has at least two objectives in this scene. We're only going to define the first one for now. In your opinion, what could David's objective be at the beginning of the scene?

... ...

That's where I set up the second trap—acting the emotion. Because at first sight, it might not seem like David has a specific objective at the beginning of the scene. But remember, there's never a moment when a character doesn't have an objective. In order to find the answer, let's try and answer this question: What are we trying to achieve when, while being bluesy, sad, or nostalgic, we start singing and listening to songs that obviously aren't going to help us, but rather plunge us into that state even more?

... ...

Did you find anything? When it comes to me, in those moments, I feel like we're looking to fully experience the emotion in its entirety. As if you're ... almost voluntarily wallowing in your own unhappiness, to the point of aggravating it. So, here's how I'd put David's first objective into words: I want to reach the very bottom of my blues and fully express the melancholy that I feel about Mona. You could legitimately raise questions about that, since in order to be able to reach the depth of an emotion (in this case, the blues) you need to feel it. That's a fact. But even though you do need a source that will make you feel blue, that's not an end in itself. The end in itself being: trying to reach the bottom of it. There's a huge difference between that and acting the emotion. And it's in the fact that even though you need to find a source for the initial state of blues, your relation to it is active: trying to reach the bottom of it, rather than passive, which would be acting the blues.

What's pushing me to want to accomplish my objective: what are my motivations?

Mona's absence itself.

What are the stakes?

If I accomplish my objective, I'll fully experience the "presence of loss" that I feel towards Mona.

If I accomplish my objective, I'll be able to think of myself as a guy who followed all the way through, even though I did end up hitting rock bottom.

If I accomplish my objective, I can more easily get rid of my blues later on.

What are the obstacles standing between me and my objective?

My self-esteem, my pride, my self-love.

What am I doing to beat my obstacles in order to accomplish my objective?

Physical actions:
None. Playing an instrument is a psychophysical action.

A single tear drips down his bright green mask ... when suddenly, he can hear someone clapping.

------------CHANGE OF OBJECTIVE------------

He turns around to see Mona. She also has a bandage on her shoulder and seems to have gotten beat up too. But that doesn't take away any of her unique charm.

Psychophysical actions:

To sing, but that's too vague. The action "to sing" is like "to act": both can potentially contain any number of psychophysical actions. Here, we could use "to make fun of myself," "to soil my self-love," "to darken myself," "to look to hit rock bottom," "to keep my blues intact."

------------CHANGE OF OBJECTIVE------------

This first break is obviously due to Mona's unexpected and unhoped-for arrival.

So, what happens next? In other words, what does our beautiful heroine's arrival change for David?

… … …

Apart from the question "Where?" and the question "When?", absolutely everything.

David's objective, the stakes of his situation, his motivations, his obstacles, his physical actions, and his psychophysical actions. So, once again:

Why am I here: what is my objective?

In order to formulate this new objective, first, we have to define how long this particular objective is present in the scene. Read the scene again and try to answer the question yourself.

… … …

What do you think? In my opinion, I'd say that David tries to accomplish this objective all the way to the end of the scene. But I'd say that it's a double objective. On the one hand, he wants to understand what all of these setbacks were for, what's going on with Mona. On the other hand, he wants Mona, which is no longer a scoop. You might even say that the second objective depends on the first. So, here's how I would formulate this new objective: I want to understand what all of these setbacks are for, what's going on with Mona, AND I want her.

What's pushing me to want to accomplish my objective: what are my motivations?

I'm motivated by these strange coincidences that I've come across during all of my adventures connected to Mona.

I'm motivated by my attraction to her.

What are the stakes?

If I accomplish my objective, all of my doubts about Mona's intentions will be erased.

If I accomplish my objective, after my doubts have disappeared, I'll finally be able to fully live out my relationship with her. Well, that is, if there is a relationship.

If I accomplish my objective, I'll be with the woman that I want to be with.

What are the obstacles standing between me and my objective?

My doubts. Mona's unclear intentions. The fear of rejection.

What am I doing to beat my obstacles in order to accomplish my objective?

Physical actions:
Let's define the moment-to-moment throughout the scene, in order to understand when they start and what provokes them. They'll be indicated by **"PA."** We'll also bring up a few other things along the way.

Psychophysical actions:
Same thing, except that they'll be indicated by **"PPA."**

PPA #1

MONA

(without her accent)

You might be a failed actor, but for the boyfriend part, that has yet to be seen.

PPA #2 and #3

DAVID

Ah, there you are, you ungrateful bitch!

She turns pale as a ghost.

DAVID

Don't make that face. Kidding! And, I admit, I just needed to vent a little.

PPA #4

DAVID

Where did it go?

MONA

What?

DAVID

Your accent.

MONA

I never had an accent.

PPA #1

"To discover her," "Trying to realize that she's really here."

PPA #2 and #3

What are the psychophysical actions here?

... ...

David sort of says them. That's right, "To kid" and "To vent."

PPA #4

You could be tempted to say "To question," but even though that is indeed a psychophysical action, the verb is still a little vague. What could we replace it with?

... ...

"To demand an explanation." Isn't that a little more specific?

PPA #5

DAVID

(suspicious)

Kidding?

MONA

No, that was a fantasy of yours.

PPA #5

In this case, it's the stage directions that give us the answer: "To suspect."

PPA #6

DAVID

That's definitely possible …

PPA #7

… but you still had an accent.

MONA

If that's what makes you happy.

PPA #8

DAVID

Ok, we'll get back to that later.

PPA #9

God damn it, where were you?!

MONA

Your place.

PPA #6

"To recognize."

PPA #7

Let's go back to "suspect."

As you can see, a psychophysical action can be in place for quite a while or only last a second.

Also, a psychophysical action always happens before, during and after the script lines. Even in silence.

PPA #8

"To put aside."

PPA #9

"To demand an explanation."

PPA #10

He stares at her, trying to figure out if she's telling the truth …

MONA

By the way, I read your book.

DAVID

That's impossible, I'm still working on it.

MONA

Of course it's possible, otherwise how could I be saying the lines that are written in there?

PPA #10

Once again, the directions give us the answer: "Analyzing in order to distinguish true from false."

PPA #11 and #12

DAVID

Don't get too excited, I'm still not sure if I'll put this scene in ... it might be more private rather than it is intimate.

MONA

Private? Don't get too excited either, I'm still not sure if it's a sure win yet.

PPA #13

DAVID

For you or for me?

MONA

For us.

PPA #11 and #12

Alright, I'll be honest: "To show off," but also "To test out her reaction."

PPA #13

"Looking to find out."

------------NEW BEATS------------

PA #1 and #2, PPA #14

Silence ... He puts the sitar down and takes off the mask. She's happy to see his face again, even if he's also all bruised up.

                      MONA

What happened to you?

------------NEW BEATS------------

Mona's answer obviously is the marker of an important change. Based on what we know about David, we know how much that "us" meant to him. The script also indicates it clearly, by "Silence …." But it's also indicated by the fact that for the first time since she's gotten here, David does physical actions. The first one is taking off his mask, which is pretty important. With that same idea in mind, you could say that his psychophysical action at that point is "To become closer or more vulnerable." Yet, that doesn't mean that he has to get closer physically.

PA #1 and #2, PPA #14

PA: "To put down the sitar" and "To take off the mask."
PPA: "To get closer and more vulnerable."

PPA #15

DAVID

(pointing at her own bruises)

You're one to talk.

MONA

I slipped on a banana peel. What about you?

PPA #16 and #17

DAVID

I ran into a few guys who really wanted to know where you were.

MONA

I can see that. Do you have it with you?

PPA #15

"To retort."

PPA #16 and #17

"To insinuate" and "to scan": David is insinuating in order to figure out Mona's reaction. So that means that he'll take in her answer, which is: "I can see that." What does that answer say to us?

... ...

That Mona understands what he's talking about. That's important.

PPA #18

DAVID

Of course! I just love walking around with 100 grams of cocaine on ...

MONA

Not that, the phone, my phone.

PPA #19

DAVID

Yeah.

She comes and stands closer to him.

PPA #18

"To turn to sarcasm."

PPA #19

Those three dots aren't there for nothing. What do they mean to us? Why is it there?

... ...

Because of the fact that the phone that she's talking about has played a big part in all of this, ever since the night she "randomly" dropped by. "Randomly" with quote marks because all of the events that followed have shown that her visit was not spontaneous at all, and that she had planned every detail. That point is *specifically* related to the moment that David is living right now. Do you see why?

... ...

Because Mona's arrival is no coincidence either. Which could lead us to think that missy has a secret objective. Which is important to David. All he has to do now is figure out if her objective is similar to his. So, there's an endless stream of subtext here that you have at your disposal. Mix it up with real questions that you can actually ask yourself while you're with your scene partner. With all of these elements in mind, according to you, what is psycho-physical action #19?

... ...

"To scan," the entire time that missy is speaking, all the while trying to get closer to him.

PPA #20

They lock eyes, both a little overwhelmed by this proximity ...

MONA

Hand it over.

He gives her the smartphone and she goes to throw it in one of the fish tanks of the restaurant.

MONA

There! Now no one else can mess with you, since no one can know where you are.

(discreetly, like it's a secret)

It's tapped.

PPA #21

DAVID

Thanks, I got that. By the way, thanks for making me take the risk.

PPA #20

What do we do when we feel that kind of discomfort?

… … …

We "observe," we "look for clues," we "test out the connection."

PPA #21

Once again, "To turn to sarcasm."

MONA

I needed to be able to find you.

DAVID

Well, you have my number. You know, a lot of people do that. They each have a number and they call each other. You should try it, it's pretty practical.

MONA

I really thought that it would be too risky to call you on your phone.

DAVID

You've got a point, as you can see, everything worked out really well. I only got completely wasted by cops who seemed to be fresh out of the nuthouse, then by a 7-foot Bulgarian dude in shorts, then just to be shot in the shoulder which, as icing on the cake, made a hole in my favorite jacket.

MONA

I'm so sorry. Seriously.

PPA #22 and #23

DAVID

… It sure seems like it. Ok, now you've got some explaining to do.

MONA

No prob.

She goes behind the bar to get a bottle of Saigon Export and drinks directly from the bottle.

PPA #22 and #23

Once again, "To scan" then "To seize the opportunity."

PPA #24 and #25

DAVID

What's the deal with the phoenix tattoo on the deaf cop's arm? Well, the deaf cop's ex-arm now, the one who calls you Samantha? While he's listing everything that he has questions about, we see flashes of the things that he's talking about.

DAVID

How interesting, a phoenix with the words "Mori et resurgere," just like the engraving on your gun. Ahh, there's another one, a phoenix, just like the name on your Russian passport, Mona from Romania.

While he's talking to her, he goes to sit down at the bar.

DAVID

Again, the same words as on the origami, how interesting, of a phoenix made by Hemanovitch, who calls you Pamela-like-Pomelo-but-for-a-girl and also Clementine-like-a-little-orange, for you. How interesting, an orange just like the one that strangely rolled over from your bag towards me. How interesting, the Bulgarian origamist has the same flame tattoo that you have on the back of your neck. Again, how interesting, just like Min-Mân, who calls you Bào-Châu, who has your face tattooed onto his chest.

PPA #24 and #25

"To ask for an explanation" and "To turn to sarcasm."

PPA #26

He gets behind the bar to face her, literally and metaphorically and looks like he definitely expects answers.

MONA

I do want to answer you, I'm just not sure if I get the part about the rolling orange.

PPA #27 and #28

DAVID

Forget about the rolling orange. Talk about the other stuff.

MONA

Well, first of all, I don't have a flame tattoo on the back of my neck, or anywhere else for that matter.

PPA #26

Did you find the action verb in the stage directions? "To face." In this case, we could even say "To confront," maybe even "To push up against the wall."

PPA #27 and #28

Once again, "To put aside" and then "To push up against the wall."

PPA #29

Seeing how suspicious he is, she turns around on her bar stool and pushes her jet-black hair away from her neck ... where there isn't, in fact, any tattoo.

PPA #30

Despite how bewildered he is by this discovery ...

PPA #29

"To suspect."

PPA #30

What do we do when we're bewildered?

... ...

We "try to touch base with reality." Here, how does David do that? By "trying to put the pieces back together." Which pieces? On the one hand, the pieces of information that he knows about. For instance, the flame tattoo on the back of Mona's neck. On the other hand, the pieces that he's just discovered—Mona doesn't have any tattoo on the back of her neck.

You could say that in moments like these, we're faced with two pictures that don't go together. Two puzzle pieces that don't fit together the way that they should ... That's what creates subtext and real questions that you should ask yourself during your performance. If this scene in itself is enough, then use it. And if all else fails ... you can try doing complex mental calculations. (Kidding ... Sort of.) The point being that you (David) are racking your brains at that moment in order to "Find an answer." Or, like we said before, "To try and get back in touch with reality."

------------SENSORY TROUBLE------------

PPA #31

David can't stop himself from savoring the fumes of her fig perfume. She turns back around to look at him and sees that he's tripping out a little.

                        MONA

Are you ok?

                        DAVID

Yeah, yeah, I'm fine. It's just that I love your perfume!

                        MONA

Ah, that must be another one of your fantasies, just like the accent and the tattoo—I never wear perfume.

------------**SENSORY TROUBLE**------------

But that attempt to reach reality is interrupted by the fascination that you have with the smell of her fig perfume. Which tools are you going to use in order to portray that?

… … …

A reflex source, of course. You could use what the script already offers, but under the condition that it hits you the way that it hits the character. If that's not the case, then what smell has that same impact on you? Maybe you already know which one it is? Great. But if that's not the case, that's great too—you'll be able to travel through your senses and throughout all of the olfactory propositions of the world.

PPA #31

"To savor."

------------BACK TO "REALITY"------------

PPA #32 and #33

DAVID

(mockingly)

Oh, really? And the one that's in your bag is just for decoration, I suppose?

MONA

That's not my bag. And what's in it doesn't exist. There's really no bag anyway.

DAVID

Is that so? What's this then?

He "brandishes" the bag from beneath the bar counter.

MONA

Uh … my bag.

He nonchalantly sets it on the counter between them.

DAVID

And everything that's in it? Are those fantasies too?

MONA

No. A gun …

------------BACK TO "REALITY"------------

PPA #32 and #33

Mona's lie brings David back to reality. That's because, unlike the flame tattoo, David knows that he'll be able to "make Mona face the truth," therefore to "own up to her lies." *Ergo*, he'll get closer to achieving a part of his objective: "I want to understand what all of these setbacks are for and what's going on with Mona … "

No matter what scene you're working on, always keep track of whether you're getting closer to your objective or not. That aspect is a treasure trove full of subtext, real questions, and the creation of a solid moment-to-moment. That's what we do in life and that's what your characters have to do on stage.

Now, back to psychophysical actions #32 and #33, which are "To make Mona face the truth and own up to her lies." Also, "To mock" for David, who knows that he's finally about to win this battle.

PPA #34

She takes it and with precise and quick gestures, checks if it's loaded.

MONA

… that's loaded, a real fake passport, very real coke and … my perfume.

PPA #34

I voluntarily didn't write in David's reaction in the script when Mona "takes the gun and *with precise and quick gestures*, checks if it's loaded." It's to help you realize that not everything is written in a script, and that the results are not always spoon-fed, if you will. So always stay alert to the possibilities of choices that are at your disposal, without necessarily being written in black and white.

If we base ourselves off of David's reaction when he discovers the gun in Miss M.'s "misplaced" bag, we could say that David doesn't seem to be used to the underworld. So what could his psychophysical reaction be when he watches her "take the gun and *with precise and quick gestures, check if it's loaded*"? … "To notice," "To take in," "To make a mental note of … "

PPA #35 and #36

                    DAVID

What kind of perfume?

                    MONA

              (with a slight smile)

Fig.

                    DAVID

So?! Fantasies, huh?!

She holsters the gun in her belt, squirts some perfume onto her, and her seductive accent reappears.

                    MONA

The two aren't incompatible.

PPA #35 and #36

Back to "making Mona face the truth and own up to her lies" and "To mock."

------------PROXIMITY------------

PPA #37 and #38

They understand each other …

MONA

But even though I'm truly, sincerely flattered that you went through my bag, those are the only answers that you'll ever get, Barroukovitch.

DAVID

Just like in the text that you sent me, right? No questions about your life?

MONA

That's right.

------------PROXIMITY------------

PPA #37 and #38

The answer "The two aren't incompatible," then the direction "They understand each other ..." definitely indicate that they've become closer. So, the psychophysical action is "To get closer." Since David's objective is "I want her," we can even add in the action "To savor the moment."

PPA #39

He gets lost in thought. She observes him.

PPA #40

MONA

You wanna know why I never answered that text that I told you I loved so much?

DAVID

To make me want you even more? You didn't need to.

MONA

Kind of, but it was mostly to protect you.

DAVID

Well, it didn't really work.

MONA

I know. But I'm hoping that nothing else happens to you because of me.

DAVID

If we could stop at accessory to murder of four cops and mutilation of the fifth, that'd be nice.

PPA #39

Since "To think" is too vague, what could we use instead?

... ...

"To try to make a decision."

PPA #40

"To flirt."

MONA

On the other hand, your jacket looks even cooler like that … Bad Boyish.

Her compliments are getting to him. She knows it.

------------MASKS OFF------------

PPA #41 and #42

DAVID

What are you playing at?

MONA

I don't know, but I'm having fun over here, not you?

DAVID

I am … It's almost as if these lines hadn't been written beforehand.

MONA

You must be connected to powerful sources then.

DAVID

Probably.

MONA

I am too … That's why I'm able to do motivated psychophysical actions.

DAVID

Me too.

------------MASKS OFF------------

PPA #41 and #42

Encouraged by the fact that they're getting closer and Miss M.'s pretty positive reactions to his flirting, David can "turn things up a notch" and "take off his mask."

PPA #43

They gaze at each other silently for a few seconds ...

                           DAVID

What's your psychophysical action right here, right now?

                           MONA

I can't tell you. The entire point of this scene is to help actors understand how to rehearse—crossed out—create a scene. *Ergo*, like you say, to help the readers find the psychophysical actions by themselves.

PPA #43

"To strengthen our complicity."

DAVID

So you really did read my book?

MONA

You know, the whole true, false thing, real or imaginary … To me, all of that's relative.

PPA #44

DAVID

(officially charmed)

You drive me crazy.

MONA

I'm not sure what you mean by that, but know that it's the same for me.

PPA #45

DAVID

And what do you mean by that?

MONA

Do that experiment of yours with the actors. I'll tell you in the next scene, the one that they'll have to work on alone. Which just so happens to be the one where we'll see if you're really a failed boyfriend or not.

DAVID

Do I have your word?

PPA #44

"To declare one's love."

PPA #45

"To look for validation."

                        MONA

                (putting her hand to her heart)

   As a liar.

   To be continued!!!

                        — CUT —

I'm voluntarily repeating myself here:

> *Without a source, an action remains mechanical.*
> *Without an action, a source remains lifeless.*

Whether it be physical or psychophysical, every action must be motivated and provoked by a source! Always put that into practice and I can assure you, your acting will be as true as nature. Also, don't forget that some sources are spontaneously offered to you by your scene partners, and what the scene itself makes you feel.

Once the scene has been broken down into parts, don't spend too much time doing what we call "table work." Don't get lost in analysis, which could turn out to be endless and too cerebral. But, speaking of which …

Active analysis and psychophysical structure

As we briefly said in "*Aaaaaaaaand ACTION(S)!!!*", active analysis is a method that Stanislavski developed towards the end of his life. It's explored more in detail in his third book about the Method, called *Creating a Role*, published posthumously.

Basically, this technique consists of pulling the actor away from pure, almost factual analysis as early as possible, because it's much too cerebral. It's commonly known as "table work." However, don't confuse "table work" with breaking down a scene. The latter allows us to understand the structure of a scene. Whereas table work often turns out to be excessive babble, but done as a group. Now, of course it's crucial to truly understand a story and every scene that's part of it. However, the problem with table work is that in general, it turns into a pseudo-psychoanalysis of the characters and of the plot. It's not that there aren't a few good elements that you can get out of it once in a while, it's just I find that they rarely help the actors to *embody* their roles. Every time that I've participated in one of these (rather counterproductive) table works, this is what I always end up thinking to myself: Stop overthinking the scene just because you're afraid to approach it, and try to understand it!

Rightly so, this type of work seemed fruitless to Stanislavski. He always preferred to immerse actors directly into a scene, on stage, with all of the questions that it begs.

So, the actor gets thrown into the given circumstances of the scene, script in hand, even if their senses haven't yet made all of the elements "real." At this point, they probably only know the main beats in the scene, as we saw earlier. That's how they can start working on the embodiment, with the help of this broad skeleton. That's where the crucial difference between this and table work lies: actors explore their numerous choices *in* and *with* their body, actively! That's why we call it "active analysis." It's also worth noting that it's very important to remain flexible with all of your choices (even those that could've been made before the breakdown of a scene).

At the beginning, there's sometimes a hectic mess that can ensue, filled with millions of questions that challenge the actor's choices. Sure, you can answer them mentally, but what you really need to do is *try out* all of your answers. Question them, change them, perfect them, enrich them, before finally validating them. In this way, your choices have been tested throughout the body, as well as the spirit.

By the way, that's why explaining active analysis on paper is quite complicated … The dynamic of writing and reading is not the same as the dynamic of acting—especially when it comes to active analysis. Here's why: while I'm writing these words, I'm only writing one at a time. Just like when you're reading, you're only reading one word at a time. The dynamic of acting and active analysis makes the actor work on different levels at the same time. That's precisely one of its goals: to break down the barrier between the *idea* of acting and actually acting. Sometimes, during this process, an actor can stop and untangle all of the different levels, and only work on one of them. But one of the main benefits of active analysis is that the actor doesn't suddenly go from a cerebral point of view (table work) to the embodiment and all of its facets: physical, sensory, psychological, psychophysical, active, emotional, etc. This function is made for two fundamental, precious reasons:

1) To stop the actor from "playing an idea."
2) To take the pressure off the actor.

To stop the actor from "playing an idea."

When table work is taken too far, it can make the actor "fantasize" about acting. That fantasy is not necessarily bad in itself—in fact, it can even be a very strong source of inspiration. But, if it remains a fantasy for too long, it can become a sort of fixed idea in the actor's mind.

In this case, once they reach the physical, psychophysical and emotional step of exploring their role, actors often get stuck—because they remained in their head and their fantasy for too long. They become stifled by the idea that they've made of their performance, before even having tested it out on stage. And the more mentally anchored it is in them, the harder it will be for them to get rid of it and to achieve a sensitive performance.

Active analysis doesn't create that mental prison at all. It allows actors to feel, with their body and in their spirit, the choices that they've made! Their choices, which are tested out almost immediately, can't remain intangible ideas. They're not stifled by the heaviness of a potential disappointment, after discovering that one of their choices was actually a conceptual error. With active analysis, a potential mistake doesn't have enough time to become "fossilized." Thus, it helps actors to remain relaxed with the choices that they try out during each scene.

To take the pressure off the actor.

Once again, when table work is taken too far, actors inevitably end up feeling some sort of pressure. Will they be up to the standards of all the conceptualized and fantasized choices? The endless discussions about their points of view?

At first, it's almost unnoticeable, but that pressure gets more and more intense each day. Acting promise after acting promise, until it all comes crashing down on actors when they have to start embodying and exploring their choices.

Active analysis offers a flexibility to actors, concerning their choices. They can try something out, before definitively heading in one direction or another. They're free to change and try out their propositions, before they're validated and then become acting promises. Not to mention that I've often noticed that when in action (when making mistakes is still possible), the discussion part is much more inventive.

Time to play!

In order to illustrate the process of active analysis, let's work on an excerpt of *Miss M.* and the breakdown that we did.

INT/NIGHT—RESTAURANT *MIN-MÂN'S PLACE*/DINING ROOM

Once again, police sirens can be heard throughout this entire scene and they sound even closer than in the previous scene.

David is seated at a table. With his "hottie" jacket around his shoulders and his face still covered in a bright green liquid mask, he's playing a Vietnamese electric sitar that was hanging on the wall as decoration. He's playing a Vietnamese-variety sounding melody, which is childish yet touching. He masters the instrument but can't carry a tune in a bucket.

David Failed actooor, you won't go too faaar ... That's whyyy you started coachiiing ... Oh, failed actor, yeah! Failed actooor ...

Then, we see that he's actually singing along with the lyrics of a karaoke video that's pretty corny and tasteless. But it's still pretty touching, despite the very bad actor that looks like a Vietnamese version of David and the just as bad actress who looks like the Vietnamese version of Mona.

David You could siiing tooo … Unless yooou're a faailed singer … Oh, failed singer, yeah! Faailed singer … So you'd become a varietyyy coach … Who would teach a few beautiiies … But who would have no affeeect on yooou … Because you only think ooof Mona! Phoenix! Zoeee, yee hah! Aurora! Angela! Krikri the crackhead from Mars! And Pamelaaa! Clementine! Samanthaaa! Let's not forgeeet Bào-Châuuu … Or that yooou're … a faaailed boyfriend … Oh, failed boyfriend, yee hah! Oh yeah, failed boyfriend …

A single tear drips down his bright green mask … when suddenly, he can hear someone clapping.

He turns around to see Mona. She also has a bandage on her shoulder and seems to have gotten beat up too. But that doesn't take away any of her unique charm.

We brought up a lot of different elements when breaking down this scene. But we have to start somewhere, so let's start out with the fact that Mona's arrival was, at the least, very unexpected, and definitely unhoped-for.

Ok. Even if it's short-lived, get connected to a source that gives you the blues. I'm pretty sure that you have lots of those in stock, right? If you feel like it, listen to a song that makes you feel sad. *Hotel California* by the Eagles, *Lovely* by Billie Eilish or *The Sound of Silence* by Simon and Garfunkel are very good for that.

… … …

Do you feel a little bluesy? Great![3] Now, sit down at a table and bust out your Vietnamese electric sitar. *What do you mean you don't have one?!* Just kidding, that's ok, a frying pan or a racket should do the trick. Don't forget to use something for your face as a relaxation mask. A warm towel should do it. Then start singing whatever comes to mind.

… … …

Keep singing while thinking of someone who you want or wanted and who, *unfortunately*, slipped away from you.

… … …

Don't look for the emotion. Look for its source and light switches: the details about this person that you like the most.

… … …

---

[3] As we said earlier, one of the privileges of being a creator is not having to classify emotions as "good" or "bad." With us, they're all welcome! Not that they're mushed together without distinction between them, but there's no prefabricated label put on them. No avoidance.

Start all over again: get your banjo-frying pan and warm towel on your face, source in mind and start singing your bluesy song.

... ...

Once you start to feel even a little connected, stop singing and imagine someone applauding, then turn around: it's him or her, your source. Look at him/her. We'll go back to the moment when you hear the applause: turn around and "discover the person," "try to realize that they're really there." Those are your **"PPA #1."** Take in the details that you like the most about them.

... ...

We'll go back to the same moment. Did you really take the time to imagine the applause? Before turning around, are you really asking yourself who it could be? Who does David think it could be? The cops, of course.

... ...

Start again at the same place and test out all of the steps.

... ...

That's the moment-to-moment and active analysis is there to create it. But not as a mere fantasy. It's created with the help of all the details that weave it together: your blues source, your lost love source, the arrival of the cops, not to mention the thoughts that go with it. Like, it's all over, you're gonna end your life in jail, the thoughts that go with that: imagining the person that you love the most coming to see you during visiting hours, their face ... The fact that no mother in the world thinks that one day, she'll only ever see her child through armored glass, with authorization, being watched by guards, their intrusive looks and silent criticism that speak loud and clear ...

... ...

Then turn around. Slowly. Touched by all of those sources.

... ...

And then discover that it's not the police, it's the person that you desire the most in the world ... and let yourself get lost in the details that you like the most about him or her. Once again, "discover" and "try to realize that they're really there," which are your **"PPA #1."** Take the time to really do them.

... ...

Remember that Mona also got beat up. Have you ever lived through that? Seeing that someone who you love passionately has been beaten, hit, to the point of having a bloody face? I sure hope not. If you have though, imagine your loved one, face covered in blood, dried in some places, dripping in others, bruises, straight red lines between their teeth.

... ...

Who in the hell could've done that to them? Whose horrid hands? What monstrous mind? What kind of asshole?

... ...

– CUT –

Do you understand the way it works? That's active analysis. We won't keep working on the entire scene and all of the acting elements that it holds, but I encourage you to always follow that same process. And remember, in order for the active analysis to be able to work its magic, don't jump to the results. Search and explore the scene: you have my word as a coach, it'll pay off big-time.

The process of active analysis is the same concept as *"learning by doing."* In that way, it's perfect for actors, because they can't just be content in drawing up blueprints, no matter how beautiful they might be. They need to feel it all in their flesh and bones, *step by step*, moment after moment after moment after moment … until they weave together a completely organic scene. Then, scene after scene, a real live character is born. Plus, when you explore a scene this way, you'll see that its psychophysical structure appears completely naturally!

Psychophysical structure is the combination of all of the psychophysical actions, as well as their embodiment. It is the physical expression and translation of the psychological world that's in us. It becomes a very important guideline for actors, because it's so tangible. It's the layout of what we call the character's conscious and unconscious strategies and it's the physical echo of the soul's movement.

Don't worry if active analysis of a scene seems slow and awkward to you at first: it's because it is. You'll only be able to find the accuracy of a scene if you're willing to take your time and dig deeper. But, in order for that to happen, you *must* allow this—the space for the scene to not immediately work. Remember that this step is still part of the exploration and is not yet part of the show. Accept to go step by step, on tippy toes, to discover the scene, to allow yourself to be surprised by it, to search, which means to sometimes make mistakes. Try and try again. If you allow that and immerse yourself in creating the moment-to-moment of the scene, I can promise that you'll be surprised to see the scene start to become alive, *almost* without you realizing it. And you'll finally become a human being in an imaginary situation rather than an actor on stage. And that's what I meant when I said that, eventually, it feels like magic.

There's another very good reason to do active analysis: in order to be able to pinpoint the moments of a scene when actors will have to work on specific tools, and how they will breathe life into their performance.

In continuation: choices and execution

This sub-chapter is called "In Continuation" because the steps of the process that we're going to bring up here occur naturally with the process of active analysis. Here are the different steps of this process:

1. Identifying the moments that need a tool, which will be worked on outside of the scene.
2. Selecting the tool.
3. Testing out the tool, more or less out of context of the scene.
4. Changing or validating the tool.
5. Incorporating the tool into the context, meaning the scene.

Time to play!

Identifying the moments that need a tool, which will be worked on outside of the scene.

In the excerpt of the scene that we just worked on with active analysis, it's most likely that certain elements need one or more tools. So, you'll select them and work on them a bit out of context.

Go back to that scene and pinpoint the moments where you need to choose and work on a tool, to help broaden your performance.

… … …

Did you find them? For instance, the choice of the source that makes you bluesy could be one of these moments.

Selecting the tool.

Let's imagine that the same thing that happened to Karl, happens to you: your scene partner doesn't have the needed effect on you. Which tool could you use in order to create the relationship written in the script, and to make you vibrate when seeing Miss (or Mr.) Perfect?

… … …

If you can't find it, check out the table of contents, under Chapter 5 "Exploration."

… … …

An imaginary fact about your scene partner could help you, or a substitution. It's up to you, but either way, don't settle for a missing piece in your acting. Add the missing pieces by using the tools of the Method: that's what they're here for.

Testing out the tool, more or less out of context of the scene.

Now, it's time to try out the tool that you've chosen. Refer to the chapter corresponding to the chosen tool and work on it accordingly, more or less out of context.

Let's say that you've chosen an imaginary fact about your scene partner. Try it out at home, alone. How? By "living in a fantasy world," as they say. Even though I'm not a fan of that expression, I'll use it here because it describes a part of the actors' work pretty well: they're fantasizing, they're imagining things. But just like we do in life, these fantasies and imaginary things can only seem real to us if …?

… … …

If you didn't find the answer, then I'm very offended! I'm half-kidding, but the answer to my question is of course: "if we go into the details"!

So, for the needs of this exercise, imagine someone specific who would be your scene partner, but who doesn't move you the way Mona moves David. Unless you choose to really work on the scene in person (which I'd advise you to do), and the partner that you have doesn't affect you that much. Which would be pretty interesting for this exercise.

… … …

Then, start testing out imaginary facts that might influence what you feel towards this person, to resemble what David feels for Mona. I did say "might," so that you don't directly act out the results of your imaginary facts, but that you really try them to see what actual effects that they have on you.

… … …

Remember? An imaginary fact is a type of "magic if" that you project onto someone. It's almost a *pre-judgment*, that can be positive or negative, or something else. Ok. Did you find something?

… … …

Here are a few examples that can help out in the direction of the relationship between the characters. In order to find these examples, I'm imagining (a little painfully, I'll admit) that it's not Mona who's playing her own character, but that it's my neighbor from across the hall. I'm honestly pretty neutral when it comes to her, since she has about as much charisma as a shovel. Well, that being said, my enthusiasm has just gone down from + infinity to about minus 253 000. So I'll have to choose a pretty powerful imaginary fact, to say the least. Umm … I'm having a hard time. Really hard. Uhhh …. Oh! What if she pretended to be bland on purpose to hide something? My enthusiasm immediately just shot up to minus 137 000. So far, so good. So, I'm pushing that direction a little further … what could she be hiding? … I'm thinking that maybe, she's a spy … though that's a little hard for me to believe. Then I think to myself that spies don't only exist in James Bond and that not all of them are picked out of modeling agencies. Now, I'm at minus 103 000. So I have to go into more detail. The way that she says "Hello," as if her subtext was screaming "I don't exist, I'm invisible" brings me to minus 98 000.

Come on, we're almost there! Then I remember how surprised I was when watching a show where an ex-spy from the CIA was being interviewed. I remember how surprised I was to discover how "normal" she looked—minus 76 000. Anyway, the more I explore and the more details I have, I finally get up to minus 11 000. Etc. ... You get the picture.

... ...

Try out your tools, your sources, imaginary facts, and others just the way that you try on clothes. You don't make it fit you or not, but either way, you have to try it on in order to know. The same goes for sources that you might choose for a scene.

... ...

Changing or validating the tool.

It could happen that you find a tool that works great with you, but that while working on it, you realize that it doesn't quite fit the needs of the scene. If that's the case, then obviously, you'll have to change it by going through steps 2 and 3 again, until you find the right tool. Once you've found one that passes all of the tests, you can validate it.

Incorporating the tool into the context, meaning the scene.

Now, it's time to incorporate your tool into the scene. This step needs flexibility because for the first time, the tool is being mixed in with a bunch of different elements. At this point, there's always the risk that you stay connected to the tool, but that you forget to take all of the other elements into account. Keep in mind that the way that you use the tool isn't engraved in stone. It has to be incorporated to serve the scene, to blend in.

—CUT—

Once again, don't expect that everything's going to work together perfectly all at once. If you need to, you can incorporate your tools in a pretty mechanical process at first, so as to help them find their place and infuse with the rest.

Lastly, always be careful to not mistake non-choices for choices. I'll explain. It often happens on stage, just like in life, that we attempt to create an identity. Fair enough, but we often try to justify what we don't do or refuse to do with that, and only that. That's what I call non-choices. At every moment, there are millions of things that we don't do. For example, at the exact moment that I'm writing these words, I'm not washing the dishes, nor am I picking my teeth, nor am I floating around the cosmos, nor this, that, or the other thing ... endlessly. But none of those things define me and that's what makes them non-choices. So, when you're on stage (and, why not, in life in general), define your choices and your character's traits by what you do, and not by what you don't do. For these two reasons:

1) as we just said, what we don't do does not define us.

2) choices are more active than non-choices.

So, for instance, if your character is giving the silent treatment to their girlfriend or boyfriend in a scene, privilege "To ignore" or "To give the cold shoulder" rather than "To not acknowledge."

Loosen up the structure

Every scene is an improvisation.

That opening sentence doesn't mean in any way that a scene shouldn't be profoundly and meticulously worked on. But it means that this type of work doesn't exclude a share of improvisation. As I already said:

Stop systematically making yourself choose between prior work and spontaneity. The two go hand in hand.

Among other techniques, working on active analysis with a scene helps to breathe life into it. However, once actors have established the psychophysical structure and mixed it up with their sources and other tools, usually one of two things can happen: they stiffen the psychophysical structure, or they manage to loosen it up. Obviously, the second option works much better. Actually, it's essential in order to keep your performances inventive, fresh, and alive. One of the main ideas of working on the psychophysical structure of a role is to meticulously prepare *almost* everything, in order to be able to confidently improvise. The fact that you've determined where you're going and how you're going to get there is what gives you the freedom to leave the chosen path, without the fear of getting lost! Without being afraid of taking risks, daring, and inventing *at the exact moment* of the performance. You'll be like cats: capable of being so flexible and adventurous, since they know that they'll always land on their feet.

Acting is writing on sand.

(Lee Strasberg[4])

If, nonetheless, you can't help but stiffen up your psychophysical structure, concentrate more on your scene partners and what they're offering you here and now. Dare to surprise them as well, and try out new things! Not just anything though: always in relation to the given circumstances of the scene, and of the entirety of the story.

Also remember that one of the advantages and goals of the Method is to help actors truly live out a real experience on stage, rather than a bland representation. Stay alert. Listen. Stay fresh. In order to do that, allow yourself to depend on your scene partners—even if they're bad! Pay attention to the slightest details of their performances that change, fill yourself with real questions, get connected to the details of your sources and even look for new ones at the exact moment that *you're performing*. As if it was the first time every time. That's how you'll once again feel refreshed and feel like you're improvising. Let me specify something: Most of the time, we don't improvise with the lines, but rather with the tools that bring life to the subtext. Meaning how you execute your choices of action, the connections to your sources, truly listening to what your scene partners are offering you, etc.

---

[4] Just like living. And that's partially why we encourage actors to create life, rather than representing a lukewarm version of it.

Dialogue

> *Words, words, words with nothing to refer to, analogous to nothing, symbols of themselves.*
> **(Gabriel Veraldi)**

As you've probably noticed by now, I love words—debates, discussions, nattering, chatting. But you've also probably noticed that we haven't yet talked about dialogue and we only get to it later in the book. That's on purpose. Words are not part of an actor's job. Period.

As we've already clarified a few times, the actor creates what the scene needs *in the white* of the page. It's the author's job to create what's in black. The author writes the words and the actor breathes life into it by creating the *subtext*.

Here's a reminder of what it's made of: everything that's not blatantly written in the dialogue. Meaning thoughts, real questions, physical and psychophysical actions, gestures, movements, expressions, beats, and the tones of voice that will *naturally* bring the dialogue to life. By "naturally," we mean that, in the Method, actors are not in any case supposed to work directly on the tone in their voice. Those who work like that sound false, as it's been prefabricated. The tone must naturally come from the sources, which push actors to act psychophysically. It's merely the derived product of the inner world. Yet, so many actors fall into that trap by directly working on their lines, in order to say them in a certain way. You have to do the exact opposite: work on the sources and let them *involuntarily* influence the way that you talk. Just like in life!

Again, here's a reminder that you're "act-ors," not "speak-ors."

The quote by Gabriel Veraldi, cited above, perfectly captures what all actors must keep in mind when approaching any dialogue. Whether it's the work of Shakespeare or an episode of *Friends*, whether it's from a play or a movie, dialogue *does not mean anything* ... not unless we fill it with subtext, interpretation and embodiment. That's where the very essence of acting comes from. It comes from nothing else, much less words!

Time to play!

Get connected to a source of a person that you hate. Go into all of the miserable details of this awful individual. You got one? Now imagine that they're in front of you and you have to say to them "I'm happy to see you." Really do it. But remember to not act out the lines, simply stay connected to all of the horrible things about this person. Ok?

Aaaaand action!

... ...

If you were truly connected to your sources, you'll have noticed that they naturally brought a psychophysical action out of you. So, at the same time, it affected the way that you said the words. Now, while saying the same line, "I'm happy to see you," do the exercise while connecting to someone that you love very much.

... ...

– CUT –

You see? Dialogue means nothing. ABSOLUTELY NOTHING! What I mean by that is that they truly don't contain any inherent meaning. The context and the subtext around it are not only much stronger than the words themselves (always), but that's what gives them their meaning.

The mouth must always be the last piece of your being to speak.

Have you ever gone into a store where just the sales-person's "Hello" either makes you think "God, what a bitch!" or "Wow, they seem so nice!"? Yet, they didn't insult you nor did they recite a poem, all they did was say "Hello." *Non-verbally*, they said way more than just "Hello." It's those silent words, that mute dialogue, which have created your opinion, your reaction and your actions towards them. Stanislavski said this beautiful phrase:

Do not talk to the ears, but to the eyes.

For him, the most important thing is that actors be connected to sources so powerful that they practically "sweat" them. So powerful that they "touch" those listening to them, their scene partners, the entire audience. It's actually astonishing to me that we call what's non-verbal "non-verbal," rather than calling the verbal "non-psychophysical." Because that's really the foundation of all communication between human beings.

How to "learn" dialogue?

You better sit down for this ... because, the best way to learn dialogue is to not learn it. Or, in any case, to not learn your lines by heart but rather "by bones." The first time that I heard Michael Beckett say that during one of his classes, I didn't really get what he was talking about. How on earth could you learn lines "by bones"? It turned out to be fundamental advice.

Once, while working on a scene through active analysis, I was shocked to find that I knew my lines perfectly without even having bothered to learn them. Obviously, that was part of the magic of the active analysis. When working on that process, at first script in hand, actors ask themselves all kinds of questions: what they feel in the present moment, *in* and *with* their body. And little by little, they'll be able to literally incorporate the lines, in an organic way, in complete accordance with the story and the needs of the character. And that's not all! The body incorporates the *needs* of the dialogue, which does end up "coming to it naturally."

However, there is a down side with this technique, when it comes to what we call "classical" works. Because of the fact that the meaning and the architecture of the words are very far from our current language—in this case, it can't just come naturally. Whether it be classical or contemporary, however, there is a "school," even among the Method, that encourages actors to learn their lines by heart before anything else. That process can be useful to actors who pretty much master the Method and have experience behind them. However, it's not always such a good idea with beginner actors. They often have trouble creating an organic connection between what they're saying, what they're doing and their inner world. That's partially due to the fact that *to learn by heart* is actually a psychophysical action in itself! And it can often end up taking over a scene. As a result, it then becomes *to recite lines*.

But if, for whatever reason, you really want to use that approach, make sure to learn your lines in a completely neutral way. So that your inner world will be able to structure the way that you say them, "on its own."

There is a third technique, which kind of meets in the middle. It consists of writing out the actual lines of the scene, by hand or on the computer. It allows the lines to naturally sink in, even if it's not all at once. This process above all can also help you understand the meaning behind the script—therefore, to get a feel for its structure. This can be a very helpful step in breaking down a scene.

Diction and projection

Speak the speech, I pray you, as I pronounced it to you, trippingly on the tongue: but if you mouth it, as many of your players do, I had as lief the town-crier spoke my lines. Nor do not saw the air too much with your hand, thus, but use all gently; for in the very torrent, tempest, and, as I may say, the whirlwind of passion, you must acquire and beget a temperance that may give it smoothness. O, it offends me to the soul to hear a robustious periwig-pated fellow tear a passion to tatters, to very rags, (...) I would have such a fellow whipped (...)

(Hamlet in *Hamlet*
by William Shakespeare)

Who can do the most can do the least! Well, not always actually. Because the "most" is more often than not "the least" in acting, especially when it comes to diction. Of course, an actor needs to have good diction. But he also needs to have "bad" diction.

Here's the thing: in certain countries, like France or England, student actors often spend endless and laborious hours working on diction. But they're rarely told that it's only necessary for certain roles, like when one of the character's specificities is that they have good diction. So the actor doesn't need to have "good" or "bad" diction. He needs to be able to adapt his diction to the physical, social, and cultural conditions of his role.

In short, he doesn't need to speak like an actor, but rather like a specific human being—his character.

So be careful of teachings that insist a lot on working on your voice. And why not work on the look in your eyes? Because that's not natural ... just like working on your voice! However, what would be completely natural is working on your character's inner life, which in turn, will influence the way that you talk.

The same goes for voice projection. Even though it's of course necessary when working in the theater, it shouldn't become an acting tic. Or worse, overacting. Not that there's anything wrong with projecting ... as long as you actually have something to project. Otherwise, you end up projecting emptiness, which means that you project just for the sake of projection. As Shakespeare would say, which pretty much sums it up: much ado about nothing. So always adapt the level of your voice projection to the size of the theater, while making sure to always be connected to sources. Otherwise, it's just blowing hot air.

Now that we've made that clear, obviously, actors still need to be audible and their movements must be visible all the way from the back of the theater. But it must never take away from the truthfulness of the situations, nor from the characters' humanity. It's about finding the right balance. However, 99 percent of the time they're not addressing somebody at the back of the theater, they're addressing somebody who's on stage with them, only a few feet away. So, work on your voice and the sound box that your entire body can become. Work on the expressiveness of your body movement. But do all of that without falling into this nauseating *theatrical* coding that turns your work into the voice and movement of an actor playing a character. When it really should be the character's voice and movement. Besides, that coding is much too often merely a disguise for certain actors' emptiness.

To be honest, I don't have a long list of exercises here to help you train your voice for theater conditions. For this one simple reason though: these two exercises that I'm about to list are more than enough to get the job done, if they're practiced regularly:

1) Take a singing class once in a while

2) ...

Time to play!

Go back to the first exercise in the sub-chapter called "Relaxation" in Chapter 5. Redo the whole exercise, then at the end, add a long "Ooooooommmmm ..." Breathe deeply, then again, say "Oooooommmmm ..." Breathe deeply, then once again "Ooooooommmmm ..." Continue to let out "Ooooooommmmm ...," keep taking deep breaths and pay attention to the vibrations that sound creates in your throat and mouth. Then, while continuing to let out the "Ooooommmmm ...," visualize those vibrations. Be specific, give them a type of movement. Is it circular? Vertical? Horizontal? Random?

Keep saying "Ooooooommmmmm ...," each one with a deep breath, this time adding a color to the vibrations of the sound. Choose a warm, soothing, soft, and powerful color. Purple? Fire orange? Sky pink? With each new "Oooooooooommmmm ...," visualize the vibrations grow, in movement and in color, through your throat and your mouth, going up through your face, then progressively coming down, "Ooooooooommmm ..." after "Ooooooommmm ...," all the way to your feet.

A few days of practicing might go by before you're actually able to feel your whole body literally vibrate and resonate. But if you keep at it, with attention and gentleness, this simple but profound exercise will undoubtedly work. You'll be surprised by how it will deeply benefit your well-being, and by the power and solidity that it can give your voice.

—CUT—

When it comes to the projection of gesture, I can only think of one exercise that's worthwhile.

Time to play!

Choose a partner and get connected to a powerful source in relation to them. Now stand face to face, very close to one another, and express psychophysically (so without words or miming) the effects that your sources have on you.

... ...

Take as much time as you need. Once you're completely connected and that you've both truly physicalized the effects of your sources, put about three feet between you and redo the exercise.

... ...

When you've done that, put another three feet in between you and redo the exercise. Your physicalization will naturally adapt to the distance that's between you.

... ...

Redo the exercise a bunch of times while adding three feet between you each time.

—CUT—

When it comes to gesture projection, the most important point is having good sense about how to adapt it to distances and to the size of the theater. But always make sure you know the difference between good projection and bad coding. In order to sharpen your critical sense as well as your observation skills, go to the theater regularly in order to get accustomed to those differences. Deep down, in plays and in movies, you'll see that what Michel Serrault (a very talented French actor) said, pretty much sums up everything about projection:

You can't do too much, you can only do badly.

In other words, you can be as dramatic as you want, on these conditions:

1) that the drama be founded and vibrating with sources.

2) that it be adequate to the situations and to the characters that you're playing.

Guess which actor, in my opinion, brings that concept to light best? Good old Jack! Watch or re-watch Nicholson in different movies and see how his physicalization is always perfectly adapted to the needs of the story. Without there being any kind of coding whatsoever.

Monologues

Good news: monologues don't exist. End of chapter.

All right, all right, if you really want to know ... Monologues are either dialogues with the "audience," with a higher force (an entity or a god), or a presence that's physically "absent." It could be a dialogue with oneself or with someone who's physically present but only speaks psychophysically, without words. When we finally realize that, the anxiety of not having a scene partner or having a scene partner who isn't speaking verbally will start to slowly disappear. Then, the actor can bring the same energy, the same intensity, the same dynamic and breathe the same amount of life into a monologue as any other scene.

Here, when I say dialogue, I mean interactions. In order to make these interactions alive and dynamic, the actor/character has to address their words to someone and to always interpret the silence of the person/people that they're addressing. Isn't that what we always do in real life? One type of silence could mean approval or consent, another type could mean rejection or disdain. Another silence could mean that the characters' complicity is so deep that no words are needed, etc. Silence is a powerful means of communication and has sometimes the *most* powerful, magnificent, or terrible meaning in a dialogue. It's also a very fruitful source for real questions. So use it by "writing" down everything that it contains.

When it comes to dialogue with the audience, the answer is in the quotation marks. The question that needs to be answered is from the character's point of view: who is the "audience" to them? Are they people that the character knows? Strangers? What are they doing there? Is their presence friendly or worrying? But be careful, in some cases, the audience simply represents the audience. But even works by the Commedia dell'Arte or stand-up require a specific relationship to the audience. So it's up to you to create it, just the way that you would create any other relationship: with precision, in detail, and keeping track of all of their reactions so that you can take them into account in your acting.

When it comes to dialogues with a presence that's physically "absent," it's really about working with the same level of precision and detail in identifying who your character is addressing. It can also be a higher force, an entity, a god, or maybe someone who's passed away or is on the other side of the world, etc. Also, write down the answers that they would give you if they could hear your character's words. That's also what a lot of us do everyday, for better and for worse: to "talk" to someone internally, imagining their answers, thinking up comebacks, etc. Pay close attention to that process the next time that you live through it, so that you see how it can inspire you when working on monologues.

Actors of today and of tomorrow definitely have an advantage compared to their predecessors: answering machines. Don't laugh, I'm being serious! Everyone, at least once, has left a message on someone's answering machine with the same *natural* intensity as if the person was right there with them. That's actually a good starting point in letting yourself fully believe in a presence that's physically "absent."

> *Only, I feel a curious stirring within me, as if undreamed of things were forcing their way up into the light—and I'm helpless against them.*
>
> (Caligula in *Caligula*, by Albert Camus)

When it comes to "dialogues with yourself," this quote from Camus perfectly sums up any monologue's structure (even though it's from a dialogue), as it clearly underlines the character's inner duality.

"Only, I (Caligula #1) feel a curious stirring within me, as if undreamed of things (Caligula #2, meaning his demons) were forcing their way up into the light—and I'm (Caligula #1) helpless against them (his own demons)."

In other words, Caligula #1 is expressing the difficulty of the inevitable battle that he's going to have to fight against … Caligula #2. The actor is no longer having to deal with a monologue and how abstract it can be, but rather a conflict. And not just any conflict, one of the most concrete and exciting conflicts that there can be: an internal difference of opinions, aka duality.

I is another.
(Arthur Rimbaud)

That goes for Caligula, as well as any other monologue under the category of "dialogue with oneself," including, obviously, the most famous of them all: "To be or not to be?" It's no coincidence that it starts out with a question, which is directed to himself. Hamlet, who's torn between doubt and spleen, paces back and forth between he and himself, between the coward and the brave, between his "small" being and his "larger than life" suicidal self. Rimbaud's phrase sums up that whole explanation: "I is another."[5] Then, you have to work on the scene with two different sets of W.W.W. questions. The first defending one of the people within you, then defending the other one just as much.

Here's a more light-hearted example. I have a certain tendency to be prone to chubbiness. So I'm constantly on a diet. As of today, I've been relentlessly working on writing this book for what feels like 123 years, 11 months, 2 days and 17 hours. I'm thinking that I deserve to take a little stroll. On my walk, I come across a bakery and I think to myself that I also deserve a nice chocolate croissant, or maybe seven of them. Then a merciless monologue/inner dialogue ensues between two opposing me(s):

Me #1(aka "The chubby guy")

Ah, a bakery! It must be a sign.

Me #2 (aka "The inner top model")   You're not gonna stuff your face with 25 chocolate croissants again, are you!?!

Me #1   Ugh, give me a break! I've been working like crazy all day!

Me #2   Yeah, sat on your fat ass! You've probably burnt about 4 or 5 calories today.

Me#1   But I'm exhausted …

Me #2   You wouldn't be so exhausted if you weren't so fat.

Me #1   You shut up!

Me #2   Fat pig!

---

[5]Speaking of which, the brilliant title of Claude Arnaud's essay "Who Says I In Us?" sums up everything.

Me #1 Fascist!

Me #2 Porky!

Etc., etc., etc.! Multiple times a week. Well … *But that's not a monologue*, some will protest. Well …

O, such delicacy! O, such pleasure! Soothe, through my solitary mouth, the hardships of my lost soul. But why should it be I, amongst all mortals, why of all paths hath mine been chosen, to stumble upon this cavern of temptation and, of all sins, this malicious invitation? Your name is … bakery! Well, by the grace that Life has granted me, I shall join it with precipitation! I see a sign! A fiasco, you loathsome toad! I see a sign! Before my own weakness, I am a giant with feet of clay. O, croissants and other baked goods! Why must you torture me so?! For once, can't only joys be bestowed upon me, without the price to pay? But 'tis life and I accept thee: as the gourmand, the epicurean, indulging pleasures before God.

So there you have it. But these types of passages are rarer than dialogues with people who aren't speaking verbally, but rather psychophysically and emotionally. As we've just seen here, as well as in the sub-chapter called "Dialogue," those are the most important aspects to take into account. The silence of those who you're talking to is systematically a message that you need to take in. Head back to sub-chapter called "Listening" in Chapter 5, when I talked about how you shouldn't only listen with your ears, but with your entire body. Basically, with our entire body, we listen to those of others. So if someone else is present, even if they don't speak verbally, it's still a dialogue.

So, every time that you have to work on a monologue, remember that it's actually a dialogue. Then, clearly define whether the character is having this dialogue with the audience, with a presence that's physically "absent," with themselves, or with one or more people who are only speaking psychophysically. In that last case, use what your scene partners offer you. For the other cases, let's try out this next exercise.

Time to play!

Choose a monologue where the character is addressing a presence that's physically "absent," "themselves," or one or more people who aren't speaking verbally.

… … …

In the first case, clearly define what this physically absent "presence" is. Define what it means to you, what do you want from it, etc.

… … …

Also, while addressing your listener(s), define whether you're at peace with yourself or if you're torn between two points of view. In the latter, use the example that we gave earlier, with the answering machine. That kind of experience can help you realize that you are capable of speaking to someone as if they were there, when they aren't. That comes from the fact that you know who that person is in detail, and what you want from them. Essentially, you know the answers to your W.W.W. questions well. The same goes for the type of monologue where the character is at peace and isn't torn between two opinions while addressing their listener. If they are, then that takes us to the type of monologue when the character is also "dialoguing with themselves."

... ...

Now, go back to the monologue that I wrote or choose another of the same type, meaning when the character is dialoguing with himself/herself.

Start by underlining the sentences belonging to character #1 and the sentences belonging to character #2 (with different colors, to differentiate the two). Then, instead of numbers, name them as adjectives. Or you could give them nicknames that describe their role in the monologue. For instance, I named the two me's "The chubby guy" and "The inner top model." Create two W.W.W. sets of questions for each of them. Even though the tangible circumstances, like the questions "Where?" and "When?" will most likely be the same in both exercises, that won't be the case for anything else: the objectives, the motivations, the stakes, the obstacles, the physical and psychophysical actions.

Then take the leap. At first, don't work too hard on your sources, just embody little by little the dialogue of one of the parts. Then the other. Do you see how they answer to each other?

The rest of the work is exactly the same as every other scene: active analysis, psychophysical structure, exploration and research, deepening sources, execution, and making the scene more flexible.

... ...

—CUT—

Breathing life into the statue

There's actually only one true obstacle to approaching works of art that we call "classical": the very fact that we call them that. Or perhaps it's more the loads of nonsense that often comes with that label.

Besides the works that are commonly called "classical" by all (such as plays by Racine, Shakespeare, Musset, etc.), that label should also be meant for contemporary works of art that speak of the biggest human passions. It's just that they often don't make a big deal about the context surrounding the plot. For instance, the question "Where?" has a more emphasized importance than in most realistic stories. The same goes for the relationship between the characters and the material aspects that surround them—the furniture, the objects, etc. The characters also have physical actions in the play, but much less than in more realistic stories. And when they do, it's very rarely trivial. The characters do of course live in a reality that is important and necessary to represent on stage. But that reality still remains a little abstract and is sometimes very much above strictly material aspects of life. It's not that none of these characters polish their shoes or wipe their nose, it's just that we never see them do that kind of action. They almost never participate in the trivial agitation of the world.

To better illustrate what I mean, here are a few examples of contemporary pieces that should, in my opinion, be considered classical: *Caligula* by Camus, *No Exit* by Sartre or *DNA* by Dennis Kelly. In this case, the pieces that I call "classical" are those in which the characters have very logical and realistic motivations, yet remain very disconnected to the material world around them.

Back to the loads of nonsense that often comes with the label "classical." For most actors and most spectators actually, the word "classical" spurs two beliefs, both false and terribly detrimental to any good understanding and interpretation of these kinds of pieces.

The first belief is the preconception that they're dusty, if you will, and almost pompous. The second belief (which can be a consequence of the first) is that they must be approached with solemn respect, almost smarmy. Actors who have to work on a classic are then set up by a double trap, making them stuck in their interpretation, and feeling too tight in their role, which has become rigid. Basically, they've missed the whole point. The belief that classical pieces are dusty mainly comes from three elements:

1) Lack of knowledge about them.
2) A sort of pretentious stupidity concerning "modernity."
3) The incomprehension that the reader/actor can experience sometimes.

The belief that classical plays are dusty partially comes from a lack of knowledge about them.

The only way to mend a lack of knowledge in respect of classical plays is to know them. That might seem ridiculously obvious, but it's the truth. Reading and rereading classics, studying them with the most detailed observation is the only way to *really* know them. I'm talking about the necessary knowledge for actors who will have to interpret, embody and live the role that they're reading. Not just the simple knowledge of the reader who's content in just reading the play—which is already great! But the task of breathing life into it is quite another thing.

If they put their heart into classics, at first just by reading them and then working on them, actors break the distance that's between them and the play. They're also able to build an intimate relationship with the *grandiose* roles that are depicted, not to mention a certain fondness for how extravagant they are. That way, they develop a much-needed profound, and sensitive knowledge. Believe me, classics are insane, inspiring, and make for an excellent tool for learning and sharpening your acting!

After having plunged into the depths of the classics, actors start to be immune to the two other reasons that we mentioned earlier.

The belief that classical plays are dusty partially comes from a sort of pretentious stupidity concerning "modernity."

There's a very common mistake, which has been repeated over and over again throughout history: thinking that the generations that came before us were less "developed" than those who are alive right now. Thinking that the one who gets the last word is right.

Sure, materialistically speaking, our development is undeniable. Technologically, we're much more developed than the Neanderthal men were. But it doesn't work the same at all when it comes to human experience. Everything that we have is universal: emotions, desires, passions, relationships to the world, to ourselves, to others, and to what's above and beyond us. It's been the same old song! Again and always! For centuries and centuries.

Thank God and Amen to the fact that human experience is wonderfully timeless. And actors must reach that timelessness, whether they're working on a classical piece or not. That doesn't mean that the given circumstances of the role (their profession, their social background, the time period) don't have their importance. But fundamentally, whether the piece be contemporary or classical, all of that is of secondary importance. The most important order of business has always been, is and always will be the embodiment of the human soul. So when you hear classical, think more about the passion that these pieces ignite, making them fundamental—they're classics of humanity. What I feel for Mona isn't any more passionate than what a man could feel for a woman 5,000 years ago or 5,000 years from now. Here's how one of our predecessors perfectly summed it up:

> *Nothing of what we live has not already been lived through before us.*
> *(Marc Aurèle[6])*

The belief that classical plays are dusty partially comes from the incomprehension that the reader/actor can experience sometimes.

Most of the time, the incomprehension that the reader/actor can sometimes experience when taking on a classic comes from the two elements that we just talked about. Once actors have been relieved of those two weights, there's still one lethal enemy that they have to get rid of: thinking that classical plays must be approached with this sort of solemn

---

[6]When it comes to timelessness, of course. Not on the level of the latest smartphone, which in the near future, will seem just as obsolete as a CD player or a VCR.

and smarmy so-called respect. False! So, so false! Why, you ask? Because, as we said earlier, actors must embody the extravagance and the share of grandiose that classical roles contain. In order to get to that, they must go through these two steps, which at first, might seem contradictory to you:

a) Bringing the extravagance to *their* level.

b) Pulling themselves up to *their* grandeur.

Actors must first bring the extravagance to *their* level.

This first step has a lot in common with the phase that we talked about earlier: the sensitive knowledge that actors must have concerning their role. The majestic extravagance of classical roles can be intimidating, especially to actors who are just starting out. That's perfectly legitimate. It's because they're pushed into a dimension where the trivial practically doesn't exist: in the heart of all passions. We're pushed into a kind of ethereal reality where no one goes to the supermarket, nor gets caught in traffic. Washing the dishes doesn't exist, nor does losing your phone, nor does flushing the toilet, because in this world, no one has to do a number two. Well, I have something to tell you. It might not seem that important, and even quite vulgar, but it can be useful to be aware that Hamlet poos, Antigone has her period every month and Macbeth's anxiety gives him bad breath.

Of course, realizing these small truths is not enough to be able to embody Hamlet, Antigone, Macbeth, and others. But they give the characters humanity and flesh and create a doorway to access that, to make them real and approachable. So look for the details that will help you perceive a "larger than life" character as accessible and tangible. Is he afraid of heights? Does she have a masochistic side? What's his favorite dish? Does she do well with alcohol? Does he smell good? Is he clean, organized, greedy? Etc.

You have to go through the same process for the secondary characters that surround yours. Make them real people with specific traits, not abstract characters that just came from a book written by some guy, who we're told to respect without understanding him first.

In order to embody the extravagance and the share of grandiose that classical roles contain, actors must pull themselves up to *their* grandeur.

Once you've found the entryway to classical characters, now you have to face the size of their passions. In order to be able to do that, actors have to call upon the most grandiose thing that they have in them: their own passions. That's partially why the state of mind that we talked about in "Playing the Game" is so necessary to make these passions exist.

Time to play!

In order to awaken these passions, ask yourself these next questions. We already mentioned some of them in sub-chapter called "Reflex sources" in Chapter 5. And for a good reason—they concern the deepest parts of our being.

What are you prepared to die for, to kill for? Truly. What cause would you give everything for? Who would you sacrifice everything for? Don't bluff. What is vital to you? Really and truly? What is unbearable to you? Truly unbearable? Literally? What would push you to take up arms? For which country, which idea, which type of love?

— CUT —

If no answer comes to mind, if you remain feeling cold and far away from it all, then sorry, the only lifeless statue here is you. However, if you start feeling the deepest angels and demons buried down inside of you start to shake, then you're on the right path to embodying the extravagant passions of classical roles. Amen to that!

To sum up, actors have to demystify the extravagance of classical roles, then find deep inside them the grandeur that their inherent theatricality requires. Also, in classical plays, one of the recurring terms that describe these characters is the adjective "theatrical." From Hamlet who's hesitating to kill himself and talking to a skull, to Antigone who's ready to die for a proper burial of her brother's remains, there are many examples of classical characters who are "theatrical." In these cases, the word "theatrical" isn't meant in a superficial or old-fashioned, conventional way. Actors must embrace true, extravagant, expressive theatricality. But not as actors—as human beings, again and always. As the role that they're embodying.

There's an exercise for actors that consists of paraphrasing the classical lines with their own words. While the concept is interesting, it's really not fruitful at all actually. Here are three reasons why:

1) Paraphrasing the classical lines means that actors will be solely focused on the words, so their concentration won't have any room left for the actual scene, the subtext, or their scene partners.

2) Our "everyday language," with its taboos, censorship, etc., could never hold a candle to the classics.

3) The uncensored flavor of classics could rev up the actors' share of extravagance! As long as they agree to play the game, even just a little, and awaken an inspiration inside them that they didn't even know they had.

A word on tragedy

Tragedy is a sport.
(Louis Jouvet[7])

What Jouvet meant by that is that it's absolutely necessary to give body to classics in general, but especially to tragedy. More than any other style of writing, tragedy lays so many traps for actors, and can turn the stage into a black slope during an avalanche. Monologues that seem impossible to embody, a kind of seemingly imposed stillness, practically nonexistent objects or physical actions … the list goes on. And yet, actors must give it all their body! Don't let yourself drown in the words, don't stay rigid in some sort of one-dimensional space, which would lead to being fake. In order to be able to do that, always look for the character's physical aspect, their attitude and movement. And more than ever, look for and create the actions and psychophysical structure. The more the play seems "still," the more actors have to pay attention to its physical dimension.

Sure, some science-fiction and superhero-themed movies took Jouvet's saying a tad too literally. But still, let us recognize that the best of them are true modern tragedies, with other-worldly heroes. That's the way that they should be approached.

---

[7]An amazing French actor of the twentieth century. A brilliant character actor, even though he didn't use that part of his talent often enough. Speaking of which, you should see *Les Bas-Fonds*, which is *The Shallows* in English, by Jean Renoir. You'll find a very moving performance in there by Jean Gabin. A movie inspired by a play of the same name by Maxime Gorki.

A word on contemporary roles

As we saw earlier, obviously, the last thing that we're here to do is to make classics appear trivial. However, when taking on more contemporary roles, remember that one of your goals is to bring the sublime out of their sometimes trivial appearance.

As realistic actors discover a play or a script, they have to constantly remind themselves that the grandeur of the story also resides in the reader's outlook—in this case, them. Whether it's openly grandiose like the classics or rather in disguise at first, like most worthy contemporary pieces, any self-respecting story contains its own portion of transcendence and timelessness. Once again, it's up to actors to breathe life into it.

If it's truly worthy of interest, the more a story appears trivial, the more actors need to pay attention to its grandiose dimension. That's one of the biggest challenges of taking on, for instance, the works of Anton Chekhov.

When approaching a character, at first, it will be about figuring out what kind of realism the story is made of. Even though *Hamlet* is considered a realistic piece, William Shakespeare doesn't show the same process as, for instance, John Cassavetes in *Opening Night*. Myrtle Gordon, the main character, runs into the same kind of trouble as Hamlet—both have seen and become obsessed with a ghost. The difference is that Hamlet's ghost appears on horseback on a foggy night, whereas Myrtle's ghost appears in a reflection on a window. Whether they be more dramatic or slier, both ghosts' visits have a major impact on Myrtle and Hamlet.

Basically, these two realistic pieces are highly poetic, but the poetry that is inherent to each is not the same type. Just as you don't have to be intimidated by the magnificence of classics, don't neglect the poetry of the "contemporaries," even when it's just a tad off the beaten track.

Laaadies and gentlemeeeen!!!

Miss M.

Starring

David (You!) and Mona (You too!)

INT/NIGHT—RESTAURANT *MIN-MÂN'S PLACE*/DINING ROOM

As we hear the police sirens get even closer than in the previous scene …

… a very long line of coke is snorted up through a straw … by Mona.

Mona (a little tipsy)   Wow! *Sniff.* I forgot how good it was.

She drinks another shot of Saigon Export at the bar, then sets down her bottle among the many other empty ones that now crowd the counter top. She hands her straw to David, who's facing her from behind the bar.

David   No thanks.

Mona   Really? But I thought you worked in the movies.

David   What about you? The Colombian import–export trade?

She doesn't answer. He keeps organizing the little bundles of cocaine on the counter top in a specific design.

David   I can't imagine that all of this is only for your own personal use.

Mona   Remember what we said: no questions about my life.

David   That was a supposition, not a question.

Mona   No, it's not for my own personal use.

David   So, I would deduce from that …

Mona   Listen: no questions, no suppositions and no deductions about my life, ok?

David   Do I have a choice?

Mona   Nope. And look …

She stands up from her bar stool and takes out a copy of *Stanislavski and The Method for the 21st Century Actor* from beneath the bar. She "skims" through it.

Mona   That's it, here we go:

(reading)

"David starts demanding answers," blah blah blah, then: "He finds out next to nothing." You see? But this is where it gets interesting: "but once again falls hard for this irresistible, charming Beauty. Who, by the way, can't seem to ignore this excellent Method coach's legendary charisma and humility either." Well, you might've overdone the whole self-degrading humor thing, this time.

David   You think?

Mona   I don't know, whatever.

("skimming" through the book)

Blah blah blah, blah blah blah, then: "When it seems like they're about to finally have their first kiss" yeah yeah yeah, and then we get to: "Seeing how many charming qualities that he has, she promises him that after this exercise, they'd see if he was really a failed boyfriend or not …" whatever.

She closes the book and stares at David, with that confident look that people get when they've just executed an unquestionable demonstration.

David   So what?

Mona   So what?! Wouldn't you rather know *that* rather than talk about things that we said we wouldn't talk about!?!

He suddenly stops organizing the cocaine bundles.

David No, no, no! WE didn't say shit, YOU said all that! And *I* think that I have the right to know a few things because *I* got my ass beat and *I* have four cops' murders on my conscience, because of you.

Mona I got my ass beat because of you too.

David Is that so? I thought that you slipped on a banana peel.

Mona And I was chased down by a few girls who don't seem to support our relationship.

David (even though he's flattered) What relationship?! The one where you decide everything and I just have to shut up or the one where I'm as important to you as your dog?

Mona I can't fucking believe you! I'm not the one writing these damn lines, just make me say whatever you want.

That idea certainly seems to appeal to him.

David Are you sure?

Mona Yeah, go ahead, make me say what you want.

David Are you really sure?!

Mona (calmly) Yes.

David Cool! … Ok! Uuuuuuhhh, blapblap tikitup.

Mona Blapblap tikitup.

David Woah, this is crazy!

Mona "Woah, this is crazy!"

David No, not that.

Mona "No, not that."

David Stop! Cut, stop. Wait, we'll use a signal when I say something that you have to say, ok?

She remains stone-still.

David Ok?

Same thing.

David Helloooo, I'm talking to you.

(realizing)

Oh right, the signal is:

(snaps his fingers)

After a sentence that I've written for you, ok?

(snap)

Mona "Oh right, the signal is (snap) after a sentence that I've written for you, ok?"

David No, that's not what I meant! Well, I mean … ok, fine. So … David!

(snap)

Mona David!

David I'm … No wait … I … I have something to tell you.

(snap)

Mona I have something to tell you.

David It really moves me that you're writing this book for me.

(snap)

Mona It really moves me that you're writing this book for me.

David Perfect! Ok, now: You're much more important to me than Lassie.

(snap)

Mona You're much more important to me than Lassie.

David You … No. I'm sorry that I compared you to a dog. (snap)

Mona You … No. I'm sorry that I compared you to a dog.

David Uh, sorry, but this game really isn't fun anymore.

She remains stone-still.

David Please, stop. Come back. I … this just makes me feel weird. I miss you.

Mona Are you sure?

David Positive.

Mona You do realize that I'm not actually here?

David (not too sure of himself) Of course.

For the first time, we can see that David is actually alone in the restaurant.

Mona And that I never actually randomly dropped by your office.

David I made it all up.

Feeling a little guilty and sad, he avoids facing this moment by going back to organizing the little cocaine bundles.

Mona All of it. Because you're a little weird, right?

David Yeah … yeah, I'm … make that a lot weird.

Mona And I never talked to you about any Lassie.

David I know. I made everything up.

Mona By the way, Lassie isn't even a real dog, you know?

David I know. I'm the one who made it all up. Lassie doesn't exist.

Mona No.

She looks at him a long while, shamelessly scanning him …

Mona You know, even though I'm not here, I can still do whatever you want.

David I know, but I don't want you to do what I want, I want you to do what you want, and to be honest, all the while hoping that it goes with what I want, without having to tell you.

Mona You wanna try?

David Let's try.

He places the last bundle of cocaine. He's managed to write the word "Illusion" on the counter top with all of the little bundles. She gently takes one of the bundles, pokes it with her scorpion ring, which lets the powder fall out. She uses it to write a question mark next to the word: "Illusion?"

Mona I just adored your text, you know …

David (amused) Yeah.

From this moment on, every one of her gestures and movements is calm, steady, just like a ritual. All the while looking at David, she stands up, gets behind the bar and fiddles with something on a shelf. He's intrigued.

Mona You want me to prove to you how much I adored your text?

Even her voice has become softer and deeper, ageless, from the beginning of time.

David I don't need you to. But if you'd like to, yes.

Mona Then look and see, hear and listen.

She puts on music. We can recognize the sidereal melody that David was listening to when she came to see him: *The Fire Rain* by Padij Namarapa Swandipak.

Mona Every reality is immediate.

He nods and his eyes follow her as she practically floats to the restaurant entrance … She stops to look outside the glass door.

Mona Every boundary is mental.

She presses a button. The steel blinds start to come down, perfectly to the rhythm of the sitar, slowly making the outside world disappear …

Mona We walk, along a string of water, along a string of fire.

He watches her cross the dining room as if she was, in fact, walking on a string … without any fear of falling, as if the possibility didn't even exist.

Mona Just like particles of dust … of … star dust.

She stops to activate a light dimmer. The restaurant lights slowly turn down, as the steel blinds completely close. Only a few neon signs stay shining, red, blue and orange, as well as the aquariums, lit up in the big, dark room.

Mona Only the present moment exists. Infinity.

She stops in front of a big aquarium and looks at David. He ends up only a few feet away from her, though we didn't see him move. She's still speaking in a soft voice, coming from the beginning of time. He answers her in the same type of voice.

Mona Does this go with what you wanted me to do?

David That and way better … Am I in my room right now, dreaming?

Mona No. You are here and now. With me.

David Did I swallow down about a pound of magic mushrooms without realizing it?

Mona Yes. In the Pho soup.

They smile at each other with a brand-new, much deeper complicity and serenity …

Mona Sit down.

He sits down on a chair, only a few feet away from her. She slowly gets closer to him, then, standing in front of him, looks him deep in the eyes and smiles strangely …

Mona If the doors of perception were cleansed, everything would appear to man as it is …

David and Mona   … Infinite.

They smile at each other, profoundly connected to one another.

David I think that I've found the perfect name for you … "Her."

Her That's Me.

At that, she slowly turns around to have her back to him, but is still looking at him out of the corner of her eye. She slowly moves the hair away from the back of her neck, to show him what she has tattooed there:

Beyond ideas of Right and Wrong, there is a field; I will meet you there.

Very slow fade to black ...

THE END

and

THE BEGINNING

Well ... it seems that at *this point*, we might be about to slip into the private zone. And what is private should stay that way. Anyway, I think you have plenty of fish to fry—so find a scene partner to help you embody the scene that you've just read. But remember to always heed our five safety rules! Which include no alcohol or drug consumption, no feeling yourself and, no, you can't, *ever*, feel up your scene partner.

8 Playing With Your Instinct

Anxious,[1] *inexperienced writers obey rules. Rebellious, unschooled writers break rules. Artists master the form.*

(Robert McKee)

Playing by instinct is an amazing idea … yet, it's completely false. For this one, simple reason—*it's absolutely impossible*. Here's the thing: actors don't play the scene that *they* want, whenever they want. They play a *specific* scene at a *specific* time, whether it be in a movie or at the theater. Like every human beings, they have many types of instincts, survival instinct, fighting instinct, playful instinct, etc. So how could they call on the "right" instinct, which would allow them to play the needed scene, every night, *at the exact same time?* It's about as doable as bungee-jumping upwards or playing a trumpet underwater. Period.

The "acting by instinct" theory is mostly thrown around when it comes to movie actors. But the exact same thing goes on with theater actors. In the movies, you have to act the same scene over and over again or in parts. Sometimes different bits are filmed days apart, in complete disorder and, unfortunately, while being totally dependent on weather, technical and financial conditions. So actors would have to be able to program their instincts. In order to do that, they would need a method. And, in that case, they would no longer be playing "by instinct."

It's noteworthy that a lot of actors who claim to play by instinct really aren't that bright and totally stink when it comes to character acting. They just sort of float around the surface of their character. And because they refuse to go deeper, the rare flashes of instinctive inspiration that they get just enclose them even more into their own identity, rather than answer their character's needs. After many years of research, I've never heard a great, truly experienced actor talk about playing by instinct. That's probably because they're perfectly aware of the amount of work that is needed for their performances.

And, as ironic as it might seem, the Method and mostly the work done on sources, are there precisely to learn how to choose, program, and unleash your instinct. But not just any one of them, at just any moment. It's in order to unleash the particular, specific instinct needed for the scene, for a particular moment.

Time to play!

Give yourself a specific acting appointment, let's say next Thursday at 7:07 p.m. sharp. Imagine that the character that you're playing gets a phone call from a total stranger that he or she immediately falls in love with, just by the sound of this person's voice. Don't prepare

---

[1] In our case, the same goes for actors.

anything. Don't choose any source. Play with your instinct! And enjoy the disaster that ensues.

... ...

Then repeat the exercise, but this time, choose a specific source, whether it be experienced or imaginary. Pinpoint the details that make you fall in love with that stranger and connect to them the moment that you need them.

... ...

Of course, it's not 100 percent guaranteed that you get it perfect on the first try. But all you need is a little bit of rehearsal and the magic will set in.

... ...

– CUT –

Of course, it can happen that a scene partner, a scene in itself or a role inspires you so much that you get it instantly and accurately. But that kind of situation happens very rarely throughout a career. So be ready to confront all acting challenges that cross your path, chock full of sources.

The only moment that you could say that instinct plays a major role is during first readings and when you get your first impressions. But only when the story that you're reading deeply inspires you. At that moment, sources can instinctively come to you. But when actors have to call upon them again to play a scene at another specific moment, we can no longer call that "playing by instinct."

Fifty percent machine, 50 percent animal

Even though instincts are a key part of acting, playing by instinct doesn't mean anything, for the reasons that we just talked about. Or at least not what we commonly mean by that. We could at least replace it by saying "playing by knowing how to unleash your instincts." But then again, you might as well just say playing with a Method.

Maybe like a few of you out there, I never learned how to play the piano. I still don't know how to play. And yet, probably like a few of you out there, I've often fantasized about being able to impress a whole audience by nonchalantly sitting down at a piano in a bar and just magically playing a whole piece by Chopin, instinctively. It doesn't work.

Yeah, I know, Jimi Hendrix never took guitar lessons ... but he didn't just wake up one morning and suddenly know how to play with those masterpieces of his. He *gave himself* guitar lessons. But how could he do that if he didn't know how to play at first? He spent hours and hours and weeks and months and years studying his guitarist idols, then exploring and discovering, by himself, how to play the guitar. Basically, he created his own Method.

A self-respecting actor who truly loves his art cannot remain satisfied in merely embodying self-portraits.

(Michael Chekhov)

What Hendrix did for the guitar is obviously possible for actors when it comes to their art. Some of them actually never took classes, like for instance, Aaron Paul, and were still very good. But they still can't say that they've never trained, sharpened and bettered themselves. Among those rare people, it's even rarer to find those who know how to character act. Best case scenario, they excel in roles that strongly resemble who they already are as people. That's already pretty great! But deep down, they'll still be pretty far from the essence of being an actor, which means being able to embody not only all human emotions, but also diverse and very different kinds of human beings. Therefore, they're sort of half of an actor—they only know how to embody who they already are or what comes pretty close to it. They confuse instinct with the limits that they've set for themselves and the usual bubble that they remain closed in. A random pair of glasses or a mustache isn't enough to create a character. Now, these people aren't necessarily completely inaccurate or void of charm. But their limited accuracy becomes repetitive and after many (maybe successful) self-portraits, their charm inevitably becomes bland.

However, this topic does legitimately beg this question: are actors at the mercy of directors who only look to hire people that are as close as possible to their characters? Or is it because these actors don't know how to create characters in the first place, so they're only offered parts that resemble them? Well, I'd say that most of the time, it's an endless abyss full of colossal laziness, lack of knowledge, *plus* the fear of taking risks. And as it's often the case, when that wretched cocktail is topped off with some pretentiousness, it becomes literally nauseating.

As already mentioned, Stanislavski happily recognized that good actors have always been around. His initiative came from learning from them. As we talked about earlier, the Italian theater actress whom he so deeply admired, Eleonora Duse (aka the Duse), was one of them. When he approached her to ask if he could study her technique, she said that she didn't have one. Stanislavski still insisted on seeing how she worked. She eventually accepted his request, all the while still saying that he wouldn't find anything. He then specified that he'd like to watch her go through all the steps of approaching a role, from her first reading to her last public performance.

So they agreed upon an appointment. The Duse was going to start reading for her next role, Lady Macbeth. She invited Stanislavski to her house and asked him to be as discreet as possible, so as not to disturb her reading. He sat in the living-room where he could see her sit down at her balcony, book in hand. She didn't start reading right away though. First, she spent a few long minutes just gazing at the sky … Then after a while, she got out her book and started reading the first page. Quite a few minutes went by, but the Duse did not turn the page. She just sat there, almost as still as stone. Stanislavski stayed where he was too, as he had promised to not interrupt her. He just stayed there, watching her for many more long minutes … He tried to check on her from a distance, thinking that she must've fallen asleep. No, she was in fact gazing at the sky again, before once again going back to her reading. And on and on it went, for many hours, during which the Duse had only read a few pages. And the same ritual went on until she had finished reading the play! When he felt that the moment was right, Stanislavski asked her what the purpose of this type of reading was. That's when the Duse explained to him how she was simply searching for what motivated Lady Macbeth to want what she wanted, to act how she acted, to say what she said, and how all of that resonated with herself. That's how Stanislavski understood that the Duse was looking for, you guessed it, sources within herself, that would be in accordance with the story of the play. And, more specifically, with her character's behavior. Despite what she stated and believed, she most definitely had a very specific, rigorous and inspiring Method, which allowed her to give such great performances. The other steps of her work process confirmed it. She didn't have a name for any of her tools, and yet used them all the time. The same went with defining each scene's W.W.W. questions, sources, substitutions, the search for similarities with her own life, etc.

Stanislavski kept having the same experience while studying other actors. Despite what they genuinely believed and claimed, none of those who were known for giving inspiring performances spoke of acting "by instinct" or "naturally." They all based themselves off of a detail-oriented and profound work process, which consisted of exploring their characters' souls. And once they understood how those elements could resonate in their own, they would be able to fully identify with their characters and embody them with conviction.

As an acting coach, I've often been asked to define what is, in my opinion, a good actor. One answer can't sum it all up (which is partially why I'm writing this book), but this reflects my overall opinion pretty well: a good actor is 50 percent a machine and 50 percent an animal. The Method is knowing how to identify, name, and provoke the physical, psychological, and emotional levers, which will release "the beast" in you.

The method is "the machine" which revs up "the animal."

9   The "Good" and The "Bad" Ego

Ah, here's another false, yet commonly accepted truth: actors shouldn't have an ego. However, there is a "good" ego and a "bad" ego. And by "good" and "bad," I'm not trying to spread any judgmental morals, but I'm rather trying to define "good" as useful and "bad" as toxic.

We first need to get rid of the bad ego and in order to do that, we need to define what that is. Do you want to become an international superstar? There's no harm in that! No one blames a politician for wanting to become president, rather than the assistant to the vice mayor of a desert island. Anyway, if that is the case, ask yourself this one question: do you want to become a world-famous superstar, or a world-famous superstar who's *also* a good actor? If the only thing that you want is to be a world-famous superstar, then you can get rid of this book right now, because it won't help you at all. Nor will any other book about acting for that matter.

So, if you want to become a good actor and, possibly, become a world-famous star, then it's important that you know how to keep perspective.

Time to play!

Make a few appointments with yourself. No, for once, I'm not kidding! Real appointments, that you write down on your schedule and that you attend.

… … …

During these appointments, truly ask yourself what, deep down, really motivates you to pursue an acting career … Is it your ego? Or your passion for acting?

—CUT—

Like I said, the two aren't incompatible. And I don't see any problem with wanting to be a superstar … as long as that motivation doesn't take over your ambition of becoming a good actor. And when that happens, that's where the bad ego comes in. Why? Because it wreaks havoc in the acting game, which is already complex enough.

Let me explain. As we've talked about, actors are constantly working on themselves. While doing that, they need to create an inner space within themselves in order to develop their concentration, find their sources, and explore them, etc. It's very meticulous work, which very much resembles meditation. Listening and silence are needed; you also need a method and to allow yourself to take risks. But none of that is possible if the ego systematically associates the actor's work with a "successful" career. Because the two have nothing to do with each other! I'd like to encourage everyone to go get this tattooed, preferably on the forehead in huge letters:

SOCIAL SUCCESS
HAS NOTHING TO DO
WITH MERIT

As we've seen some of the time, the two can be compatible. But as we've seen *nearly 100 percent of the time*, they are absolutely not codependent on one another! When the ego comes and literally scrambles the actor's work or any other creative process, that's when it becomes toxic.

Everything is pretty much summed up in the W.W.W. exercise itself: its main function is to help actors stay occupied with the needs of the scene, rather than stay preoccupied with themselves. Really, the creative acting process is the last place where you should be worrying about your career's success. Because if you're worried about your success, you're also obviously worried about possible failure. That's where the fiasco starts—when the line between your performances and their social recognition becomes blurry and lets in a very sticky doubt. And that doubt goes hand in hand with the misplaced and formatted ego, along with all of its curses, which are poisonous to acting, as well as your mental and physical health. A very common and deep confusion can get instilled in you, which doesn't help your performances, your career, or any other aspect of your life. I mean, when you send your résumé to an agent or a casting director, you probably don't decide to practice an emotional memory or to look for the psychophysical action that's appropriate. No, you're just sending your résumé. Well, whether you're in class or on set/stage, the same goes for your acting process: just work on your acting. Now, here's what I define as the "good" ego. The good ego is the one that allows you to challenge yourself artistically. It's the one that makes you want to discover yourself in order to better surpass and transcend yourself, in order to reach your maximum potential. It also helps you make daring choices in your performances and gives you the means to embody them. The good ego is the one that makes you ask yourself the right questions about your roles and gets you to be active in your relationship to acting. Basically, it's the one that keeps your desire alive by making you challenge yourself, which allows you to have more fun.

I feel a profound affection and respect for actors who are often chosen for supporting roles. They are, in fact, the ones who support the whole movie. They keep the whole thing together by helping the audience to truly believe, which is necessary for any realistic piece. They seem to care little or not at all about the importance of their part, the number of scenes that they have or the amount of screen-time that they get. They perform with the same dedication as if they had the main role. In some cases, that's actually how they came to get the parts of main characters. They're honest craftsmen, dedicated to their art. Passionate and inspiring. What I admire is their good ego helping them to believe that their role is the most important one in the whole movie, despite what it might seem like. Which means that it deserves every ounce of their artistic dedication and creativity. They embody the nobility of acting and perfectly represent this quote by Stanislavski: "There are no small parts, only small actors."[1]

So don't throw away your ego. But make sure to identify all of its facets—we'll talk about one of them more in depth at the end of the next part. Do some sorting through, let go of the parts that are crushing your acting, and make use of the ones that boost it.

---

[1] Let me specify that in great works of art, no parts are small. But in bad works of "art," even the big roles are small.

10 Two Essential Flaws

"A good actor can't be shy."

What blatant idiocy! That statement is as far away from the truth as a bowl of hot sand is from a glass of fresh, cold water. It's one of the most terrible stereotypes spread about actors. As far as I know, there is only one other statement which is as spurious as that one: artists, so for instance, actors, cannot doubt themselves. Let me say this loud and clear: the greatest actors are the ones that doubt themselves and have two "flaws" that are so *essential* that they become qualities, *must-haves*. These must-haves are to be preserved and even cultivated: they are shyness and modesty.

But how are they able to go on stage, if they're so shy and modest? Well, by simply being able to overcome their shyness and modesty. At first glance, that answer probably seems flat and childish to you. But it does hold an important truth: the key is in overcoming and *not* in erasing their shyness and modesty. And that key is mostly where the humanity, the strength, and the beauty of the actor's self-exhibition lie. And take a guess at how they manage to overcome their shyness and modesty.

… By using, more or less consciously, the Method.

But why would anyone look to preserve and even cultivate feelings that were just going to be overcome anyway? Well, just as courage needs fear in order to exist, harmony needs chaos, music needs silence, the Yin needs the Yang, etc. The actors' performances become strong and gentle at the same time, mostly thanks to them having been able to overcome their shyness and modesty. Let's go back to the things that I just listed:

1) It's by overcoming, *not* erasing shyness and modesty that we see the actor's humanity.

Speak the speech, I pray you, as I pronounced it to you, trippingly on the tongue: but if you mouth it, as many of your players do, I had as lief the town-crier spoke my lines. Nor do not saw the air too much with your hand, thus, but use all gently; for in the very torrent, tempest, and, as I may say, the whirlwind of passion, you must acquire and beget a temperance that may give it smoothness. O, it offends me to the soul to hear a robustious periwig-pated fellow tear a passion to tatters, to very rags, (...) I would have such a fellow whipped (...)

(Hamlet in *Hamlet* by William Shakespeare[1])

And because of the nonsensical belief that actors mustn't be shy or modest, a lot of them throw themselves into an awful attitude that ruins their acting: pretending that nothing

---

[1] Yes, I know I already used this quote in the sub-chapter called "Diction and projection," but in my opinion, it has everything to do with this subject too. Especially the way that it's demonstrated in this breath-taking *mise en abyme*, where the main character, Hamlet, is speaking to other characters/actors.

scares them, that they're ready to go in deep, to give everything they've got, as they say. And you want to know why that attitude is terrible for their acting? Because except if you're playing a fridge or a corner of a room, every character has a more or less hidden, more or less obvious part of them that is shy and modest. That's partially what makes them human. How can you embody a character if your first goal is to annihilate who he or she is? If you define actors as the opposite of what they have to express? At best, you get a circus animal who's randomly gesticulating and yelling for nothing. At worst, you get a bragging, aggressive ham, whose eyes remain empty. I can't tell you how many times I've had to put up with the pitiful show of actors who were ready to "give everything they've got," more often than not on movie sets. It's actually quite sad to see, because they claim to be ready to "give everything," and yet don't have any glimmer left in their eyes, their soul having been washed out, with nothing left to give.

Maybe that's what Brando meant when he said that every actor and actress needs to find their share of femininity. For an actor, wanting to fear nothing is, really, blatantly fearing everything. With this type of actor, "going in deep" means not understanding that you can't go in deep while staying on the surface. In order to *truly* go in deep, you need to reach the deepest parts of human beings. And among everything else, you'll find shyness and modesty. That's where a big part of humanity comes from in great performances. Those are the ones that keep us glued to our seats with tears in our eyes, after witnessing this hero who, deep down, is like all of us: fragile, vulnerable, humane. Deep down, beneath the mask, they're no different from you and me.

2) It's by overcoming, *not* erasing shyness and modesty that we see the actor's strength.

Whether it be thunder, electrical, or atomic energy, all of these elements are born from resistance, friction, or the existence of a counterpoint. The same thing usually happens between an acting performance and the actor's shyness and modesty. The very existence of them in the actor already creates a possibility of internal tension. And it's that conflict that helps actors to overcome it and at the same time, gives strength to their performances. If we take one of the many examples that Mother Nature has to offer, let's remember that tsunamis and earthquakes are born from a resistance, which at its peak, ends up collapsing in a powerful explosion.

Speaking of natural explosions (this one being just as tragic but a little less detrimental to the whole world), think of the last time that you were overwhelmed, by seeing someone that you love cry. Are you connected yet? Ok, good. Now, tell me the *exact* moment that you were moved the most. There are many possibilities, the moment just before they started crying, the moment where they were resisting the most, the peak of the friction between their emotion and the desire to push it away. The strong impact that it had on you also comes from shyness and modesty. Don't worry too much about tears, but when they do come, don't cry with pride, like an actor would. Cry like a human being, with embarrassment.

3) It's by overcoming, *not* erasing shyness and modesty that we see the beauty of the actor's self-exhibition.

Let's not pretend to go out of our way in apologies—actors, in a way, are self-exhibitionists. Whether it's more or less consciously, more or less admitted to, they're still exhibitionists. And exhibition, whether it be in this case or another, remains uninteresting unless there's a grain of shyness somewhere. Truly worthy exhibition is only possible if it has transcended an enemy force, a convention, a forbiddance. If it's so exposed that we don't even see it anymore, it becomes invisible. Senseless. Bleak.

If all of that speaks to you, then don't fight off those two essential "flaws." Don't think that shyness and modesty are the enemies to your performances, it's just the opposite! Don't hate them, don't erase them. Transcend them. Play with them. They're really valuable allies.

All great actors are very sensual.

The self-exhibitionism that we've just talked about reminds me of one of the facets of the good ego. As we said in the beginning, the first and foremost goal of the W.W.W. exercise is to occupy the actors' attention *with the situation*, rather than with themselves and the presence of the audience. That being said, after a few years of practicing, a slight change can happen with a small, but precious percentage of their attention. They can start directing that percentage of attention toward themselves. When actors start studying, any attention that they direct toward themselves is so immense and "toxic" that it'll stop them from concentrating on the situation and will make them only focus on their appearance. Once they've mastered their performances, the attention that they direct toward themselves can only better their performances. Then, with enough experience, actors can partially see themselves and their own exhibition through the eyes of the audience. Have you ever seen in the eyes of someone that you like that your seduction was working? Then you must also realize that your own consciousness of the situation didn't take anything away from your seduction, but rather doubled it … as well as its effect on the person that you want to seduce. That's the exact kind of virtuous circle that sets in once actors have mastered their W.W.W. questions and can watch themselves being watched, all the while mastering the whole thing. That's one of the keys of acting that Jack Nicholson excels in and partially what makes his aura so unique.

It's time for you to create your own.

11 To Conclude

Maybe I should've told you this earlier. But if you got this far, then you'll very much understand what I'm about to say: acting doesn't really interest me that much. Well, to be exact, it doesn't interest me as an end in itself. The same goes for the theater, the movies and any other art, no matter how thrilling it might be. Art is worth nothing if it is merely an end in itself, if it is the finality. Its point is not to self-contemplate in vain, in a never-ending, narcissistic abyss. Its point is to hold up a poetic mirror—sometimes distorting, sometimes embellishing—that reflects our own lives, our bodies, our souls.

I find it interesting that actors, in particular, have the choice between two extreme opposite attitudes: the vile and the sublime. The first one consists of imprisoning oneself in a pitiful exhibition of a lukewarm version of oneself. The second one consists of opening up to understanding others and offering to embody human passions in their flesh. Without that share of sublime, the art of acting isn't worth anything in my eyes, nor will it pass the test of time. It's merely empty chattering that pollutes and adds to human misery, rather than choosing to surpass that, in order to reach humanity's beauty, freedom, and grace.

I hope that this book will help you reach that, a little or a lot.

And since you've gotten this far, thank you for having "played the game"! Keep going in that direction, remain the researchers that you are, don't make anything rigid, and always remember that:

Man's maturity is to have regained the seriousness that he had as a child at play.

So ...

Time to play!

Index

acting 1–3, 5, 7–9, 10–11, 14, 16, 20, 22, 29–30, 34–5, 44–5, 49, 55–6, 60, 62, 72, 75–6, 81–2, 85–7, 89–90, 97, 99, 100, 103–4, 107–9, 116, 119, 121, 125–7, 130–2, 139, 140, 146, 160–1, 163, 169, 172, 174, 176, 178, 181, 184–6, 265–7, 271, 274–5, 277, 280, 285, 297, 299, 300–3, 305–7, 309
active analysis 171, 193, 266–7, 269, 270–1, 274, 276, 283
acting class 3–5, 10, 69, 70, 140
acting coach 1, 3, 8, 10, 22, 62, 97, 150–1, 166, 172, 189, 300
active listening 32, 72, 77, 79, 82, 125
actor(s) 1–17, 19, 20–5, 28, 30, 32–3, 35–7, 41, 43–7, 49, 50, 59–64, 68–73, 75–7, 79, 81, 84, 86, 89, 92–4, 97, 101–8, 116, 119, 121–4, 126, 130–2, 134–5, 137, 139–43, 151, 153–5, 161, 164, 170–2, 174, 176, 184–6, 189–93, 198, 200, 260, 262, 266–7, 270–6, 280, 284–9, 297–303, 305–7, 309
Actors Studio 13, 15
Adler, Stella 12, 15–16, 75, 108

Beckett, Michael 2, 276
Berghof, Herbert 3, 5, 12
Brando, Marlon 8, 10–11, 15, 41, 94, 103, 154, 190, 306

Cassavetes, John 1, 6, 11, 14, 189–90, 289
character(s) 1, 3, 5, 9, 15, 31–3, 42, 46–7, 50–1, 55–6, 61–3, 70, 77, 79–80, 82, 84, 86, 88–91, 94, 100, 118, 126–7, 140, 152, 154, 156, 164, 174, 184–7, 190–2, 199–200, 204, 208, 245, 247, 266, 270, 272–3, 276–84, 286–7, 289, 297, 299, 300, 302, 305–6
Chekhov, Michael 11, 15, 299
cinema 5, 9, 13–15, 22, 33, 41, 143
concentration 36, 42, 72–5, 137, 155–6, 287, 301
creativity 14, 20, 24, 189, 302

Dean, James 8, 11
De Niro, Robert 11, 150–1
dialogue(s) 45, 47, 91, 275–6, 280–3
director(s) 13–15, 28, 62, 117, 122, 160, 171, 174, 189, 192, 299, 302
drama 9, 23, 31, 62, 279
dramaturgy 31–2, 34–5, 69

ego 31, 33, 41, 301–3, 307
emotional memory 16, 77, 107, 130–1, 139, 140–2, 144, 147, 152, 156, 168, 302
exercise(s) 2–3, 8, 15, 17, 27, 29, 38, 47, 49–50, 52, 56, 59–62, 64–5, 68, 70, 72, 75–9, 81–2, 84, 86, 90, 93–4, 100–2, 106, 108, 110, 114–15, 119, 122–4, 126, 131, 135, 139, 141, 147, 153, 158, 162, 168, 170, 177, 180, 200, 272, 275, 278–9, 282–3, 287, 290, 298, 302
exploration 7, 11, 28, 30, 59, 84, 164, 189–90, 270–1, 283
external source(s) 75, 105, 176, 179, 180

Falk, Peter 11, 14
feelings 7, 14, 37–9, 40, 50, 55, 63–4, 66, 68, 70, 78, 80, 83, 89–90, 96, 101, 112, 127, 139, 140–1, 144–6, 155, 158, 160–1, 164, 171, 173, 267, 284, 287, 292, 295, 305
focus 8, 43, 46, 88, 142, 144, 177, 200, 307

Gazzara, Ben 11, 14, 189, 190

Hagen, Uta 4, 12, 14
Hamlet 25, 32, 82, 89, 174, 277, 281, 286–7, 289, 305
HB Studio 2, 4, 116
Hoffman, Dustin 11, 174

imaginary fact(s) 124–7, 156, 272–3
imagination 16, 27, 30, 47, 50, 55–6, 77, 80, 84, 90, 100–1, 105–9, 110–11, 113–17,

119–20, 122–4, 129–30, 133, 139, 147, 153, 158, 168
improvisation 19, 190, 274
internal source(s) 105, 180
intimacy 105–7, 140, 161

Kazan, Elia 13, 15

Lewis, Robert 11, 13, 15–16, 75, 108, 151, 189

magic if 121–4, 168, 272
McKee, Robert 2, 297
Meisner, Sanford 15–16, 75, 77–9
Method Acting Center 34, 42
monologue(s) 3, 174, 280–3, 288
motivation(s) 14, 28, 33–4, 41–3, 45, 50, 53, 55, 84, 100, 155–6, 186, 200, 210, 212, 214, 283–4

Nicholson, Jack 10–12, 41, 94, 139, 151, 190, 279, 307

objective(s) 30–1, 33–4, 45, 79, 80, 179, 186–7, 208, 283
obstacle(s) 28, 34–5, 41–6, 50, 53, 55, 84, 100, 156, 186, 187, 200, 210, 212, 214, 283

Pacino, Al 11, 150–1, 176
physical action(s) 35, 44, 53–4, 61, 172–4, 176–9, 180–1, 184, 210, 212, 214, 226, 284, 288
play(s) 3, 14, 23, 174, 191–2, 279, 284–5, 287
poetic sense memory 135, 137, 153
psychophysical action(s) 35, 44–5, 54, 115, 171–2, 176–9, 180–1, 184–7, 198, 200, 210, 212, 214, 216, 220, 226, 230, 247, 253, 258, 260, 270, 275–6, 283, 302

reflex source(s) 63, 158–9, 160, 168, 245, 286
relaxation 63–5, 68–9, 70, 81, 103, 182, 191, 268, 278
role(s) 266, 277, 285–7, 289, 299, 302

scene partner(s) 3, 11, 70, 76, 79, 82, 86, 88, 94, 126–7, 129, 152, 156, 168, 174, 230, 265, 271–2, 274, 276, 280, 282, 287, 295, 298
sense memory 16, 30, 77, 89, 132–3, 135–7, 139, 141, 152–3, 168, 184
Sergava, Katharina 11, 15, 116
Shakespeare, William 1, 6, 14, 82, 175, 275, 277, 284, 289
source(s) 11, 33, 41–2, 44, 49, 50, 63, 68–9, 73, 75–6, 85–6, 88–9, 92–4, 99, 100–9, 110–16, 120, 123–4, 126, 129, 130, 133, 136, 139–45, 152, 154, 158, 160–1
stage fright 36, 61–4, 72, 161
stake(s) 23, 28, 34–5, 41–3, 45, 47, 50, 53, 55, 62, 69, 79, 84, 93, 100–1, 200, 210, 212, 214, 283
Strasberg, Lee 8, 15–16, 64, 77, 82, 108, 139, 143, 146, 151
Streep, Meryl 10–11, 190
substitution(s) 33, 108, 153–6, 168, 300
subtext 32–3, 40, 43, 50–1, 77–8, 200, 230, 243, 247, 272, 274–5, 287

visualization 8, 65–7, 70, 109

Where? When? Why? 27, 29, 30, 35, 37, 39, 50, 52, 100, 134, 204, 208, 212, 277, 284

yoga 64–5